THE BLACK EXPERIENCE IN AMERICA

FROM CIVIL RIGHTS TO THE PRESENT

AFRICAN AMERICAN HISTORY AND CULTURE

THE BLACK EXPERIENCE IN AMERICA

FROM CIVIL RIGHTS TO THE PRESENT

EDITED BY JEFF WALLENFELDT, MANAGER, GEOGRAPHY AND HISTORY

Britannica®
Educational Publishing

IN ASSOCIATION WITH

ROSEN
EDUCATIONAL SERVICES

Published in 2011 by Britannica Educational Publishing
(a trademark of Encyclopædia Britannica, Inc.)
in association with Rosen Educational Services, LLC
29 East 21st Street, New York, NY 10010.

Distributed exclusively by Rosen Educational Services.
For a listing of additional Britannica Educational Publishing titles, call toll free (800) 237-9932.

First Edition

Britannica Educational Publishing
Michael I. Levy: Executive Editor
J.E. Luebering: Senior Manager
Marilyn L. Barton: Senior Coordinator, Production Control
Steven Bosco: Director, Editorial Technologies
Lisa S. Braucher: Senior Producer and Data Editor
Yvette Charboneau: Senior Copy Editor
Kathy Nakamura: Manager, Media Acquisition
Jeff Wallenfeldt: Manager, Geography and History

Rosen Educational Services
Hope Lourie Killcoyne: Senior Editor and Project Manager
Nelson Sá: Art Director
Cindy Reiman: Photography Manager
Matthew Cauli: Designer, Cover Design
Introduction by Eve Creary

Library of Congress Cataloging-in-Publication Data

The Black experience in America: from civil rights to the present / edited by Jeff
Wallenfeldt.—1st ed.
    p. cm.—(African American history and culture)
"In association with Britannica Educational Publishing, Rosen Educational Services."
Includes bibliographical references and index.
ISBN 978-1-61530-146-1 (library binding)
1. African Americans—History—1964- 2. African Americans—Civil rights—History.
3. United States—Race relations—History. I. Wallenfeldt, Jeffrey H.
E185.615.B541523 2011
323.1196'073—dc22

                                                   2010014639

Manufactured in the United States of America

On the cover: Oprah Winfrey, one of the richest and most influential women in the United
States (pictured here at the 2002 Emmy Awards), gives smiling testament to the great
heights that have been reached by black Americans—heights civil rights leader Martin
Luther King, Jr., could have indeed only dreamed of when delivering his stirring and pro-
phetic "I Have a Dream" speech on Aug. 28, 1963, at the Mall in Washington, D.C., capping
the March on Washington. *Kevin Winter/Getty Images (Winfrey); AFP/Getty Images (King)*

On pages 17, 30, 54, 74, 106, 125, 153: U.S. Pres. Barack Obama delivers his first State of
the Union address, Jan. 27, 2010, as Vice President Joe Biden listens. *Mandel Ngan/AFP/
Getty Images*

CONTENTS

18

36

37

59

68

78

CHAPTER 5: GOSPEL, BLUES, R&B, AND DOO-WOP 106

84

108

113

126

137

161

INTRODUCTION

As World War II drew to a close the door of equality for African Americans was slowly being pried open. An executive order by Pres. Franklin D. Roosevelt in 1941 had banned discrimination in federal agencies and all unions and companies engaged in war-related work, though only after A. Philip Randolph, president of the Brotherhood of Sleeping Car Porters, and other African American leaders had threatened a march on Washington. Randolph was also behind the threat of mass civil disobedience that prompted Pres. Harry S. Truman to issue the executive order in 1948 that desegregated the military. The notable accomplishments of triumphant African American soldiers in World War II, as well as the sense of equality they had enjoyed while off-duty in Europe, led many to protest the varying degrees of racism, discrimination, and disenfranchisement they encountered upon their return to the United States. The nature of the prejudice African Americans experienced, however, depended on whether they faced the blatant segregation of the Jim Crow South or the more subtle discrimination of the North.

Since the arrival of the first slave ships in colonial America, freedom and equality have been the goal of African Americans, who, as a people, refused to accept institutionalized segregation and the unfulfilled promise of constitutionally guaranteed rights. The brutal struggle for abolition grew into the long battle for civil rights that crested in the 1950s and '60s. In the process, setbacks and solidarity, injury and intestinal fortitude, upheaval and uplift ultimately led to tremendous political, social, and economic advancement and extraordinary accomplishment in arts and culture by African Americans. Readers of this volume will learn how events and individuals, both past and present, contributed the rich and diverse threads of African American history and culture that have been woven into the fabric of the American story and how a dream deferred has increasingly been delivered.

One of the first mid-20th century signposts on African Americans' deliberate and persistent march toward civil rights was the sit-in at a Chicago coffee shop in 1942 staged by an organization that would become the Congress of Racial Equality (CORE). Founder James Farmer, a student of Mohandas Gandhi's nonviolent approach to political and social progress, was instrumental in organizing demonstrations that would ultimately eradicate public segregation in northern cities. Small, spontaneous acts of protest, such as Rosa Parks's refusal to give up her seat on a bus in 1955, gave rise to larger organized actions, such as the

In the early 1960s, nonviolent responses to segregated lunch counters included sit-ins and picketing. In this 1960 photo, African Americans associated with CORE (Congress of Racial Equality) and the NAACP (National Association for the Advancement of Colored People) picket the lunch counter of the chain store Grants in Norfolk, Va. Howard Sochurek/Time & Life Pictures/Getty Images

Montgomery Bus Boycott, orchestrated by the young Rev. Martin Luther King, Jr. King, another disciple of nonviolent civil disobedience, helped found the Southern Christian Leadership Conference (SCLC) in 1957 to coordinate future protests and civil rights actions.

Earlier decisions by the Supreme Court had already reversed previous rulings that permitted segregation and racial discrimination. During the 1940s and 1950s, the legal arm of the National Association for the Advancement of Colored People (NAACP), in particular future Supreme Court justice Thurgood Marshall, argued that separate meant inherent inequality in education. The Court's landmark 1954 decision in *Brown v. Board of Education of Topeka* rendered segregation in public schools unconstitutional. While this ruling legally ended de jure segregation in schools, it would take much longer to affect de facto segregation. Not until the 1971 Supreme Court decision to uphold *Swann v. Charlotte-Mecklenburg Board of Education* did the use of busing more effectively integrate public schools.

In the 1940s and '50s, the walls of segregation were being breached in other realms as well. Baseball icon Jackie Robinson broke the colour barrier in the major leagues when he began playing for the Brooklyn Dodgers in 1947. Robinson—who four years earlier, as second lieutenant in the Army, had faced court-martial for refusing orders to sit in the back of a military bus—endured racist

taunting and death threats with equanimity. He opened the door for an unending parade of great African American players such as Willie Mays, Hank Aaron, Rickie Henderson, and Bobby Bonds.

As the National Basketball Association (NBA) began to integrate in the 1950s, the Harlem Globetrotters increasingly embraced showmanship and comedy after spending decades as the standard bearers for black basketball. Early African American NBA stars such as Elgin Baylor, Wilt Chamberlain, and Bill Russell went on to blaze the trail that by the 1970s and '80s led to African American domination of the professional game. African American participation in football had followed a different arc. In their early stages, both collegiate and professional football were integrated to the extent that teams often had one or two black players. By World War II, however, the professional National Football League reverted to an "all-white" status. With the rising tide of the civil rights movement of the 1950s and '60s, however, black participation in both the college and the pro game increased rapidly.

African Americans were a major presence in boxing for much of the 20th century, especially after Joe Louis had captured the world heavyweight championship in the 1930s. Muhammad Ali not only dominated but politicized boxing during his reign as heavyweight champion in the 1960s and '70s through his refusal, as a conscientious objector to the Vietnam War, to join the Army. Before the spiritual and political awakening that led him to Nation of Islam and to adoption of his Muslim name, however, Ali had grown up in the 1950s in segregated Louisville, Ky., as Cassius Clay.

In the late 1950s sit-ins aimed at desegregating public facilities were conducted in more than a dozen American cities, but it was the sustained sit-in at a lunch counter in Greensboro, N.C., in 1960, that sparked a wave of similar actions throughout the South. Forcing compliance with Supreme Court rulings that prohibited desegregation of interstate transportation was the goal of the Freedom Rides. In 1961, following the example of an interracial group of activists that had ridden together on a bus through the upper South in 1946, another group of Freedom Riders repeated the action in the Deep South, ultimately prompting the administration of Pres. John F. Kennedy to order the Interstate Commerce Commission to enforce even stricter guidelines banning segregation in interstate travel.

In the 1950s African American literature reached ever wider audiences, especially as it continued on the path of urban realism explored by Richard Wright, James Baldwin, and Ralph Ellison. In 1950 poet Gwendolyn Brooks became the first African American to receive the Pulitzer Prize. In the theatre, *A Raisin in The Sun*, playwright Lorraine Hansberry's 1959 gritty portrayal of a family's struggle with the economic and social reality of integration, earned her a New York Drama Critics' Circle Award and the distinction of being the first African American woman to have her work produced on Broadway. Hansberry's declaration that "all art is ultimately social" presaged the movement by African American writers, poets, and artists toward works that were more explicit in their social engagement. By the mid-1960s, with black nationalism on the rise, young African American writers such as Ed Bullins and Nikki Giovanni moved beyond social commentary and set as their purpose the promotion of self-determination, solidarity, and nationhood among African Americans.

By the end of World War II, the revolutionary bebop style had taken hold and created a schism in the jazz world, reshaping the music harmonically, melodically, and rhythmically. Jazz fans split dramatically into three groups: those who remained loyal to the ever-popular swing; those who gravitated toward the emerging new breed of vocalists that included Nat King Cole, Sarah Vaughan, Ella Fitzgerald, and Billy Eckstine; and those who made the leap to bebop, whence extraordinary musicians such as Dizzy Gillespie, Charlie Parker, Thelonious Monk, Miles Davis, John Coltrane, Sonny Rollins, and Charles Mingus took jazz in exciting but complex new directions. That way ultimately laid the rules-breaking free jazz, pioneered in the late 1950s by Ornette Coleman

While Coleman and the free jazzmen were liberated musically, the struggle for social, political, and economic equality was reaching a crescendo. In the wake of the massive March on Washington in 1963, Pres. Lyndon B. Johnson signed the landmark 1964 Civil Rights Act into law. The Twenty-Fourth Amendment, which abolished poll taxes for federal elections, was also ratified in 1964, and in 1965 the Voting Rights Act removed the longstanding barriers that had prevented African Americans from exercising their constitutional right to vote. Change, however, was neither welcomed by segregationist defenders of the status quo nor implemented fast enough for some of those who sought it. Violent reaction took the form of police repression, vigilante terror, murder, and bombings; and urban upheaval encompassed rioting, arson, and looting. Within the civil rights movement, frustration led to fracture. Only a few short years after King had received the Nobel Peace Prize, Stokely Carmichael, leader of the Student Nonviolent Coordinating Committee (SNCC), altered the direction of the civil rights movement for many with a new phrase, "black power." The Black Panther Party, originally organized as a protective unit against police brutality, took a turn toward Marxist revolutionary tactics.

Dramatists and writers such as LeRoi Jones joined the new black aesthetic movement, which espoused separatism as it promoted the relevance of African history and culture; Jones changed his name to Amiri Baraka in 1968 to signal his commitment to the movement. Other writers, such as Margaret Walker and Ernest J. Gaines, used somewhat more personal voices to broaden the concept of "blackness" in literature. African American women, in particular, experienced a renaissance, both in visibility as artists as well as in self-perception. Leading the way was novelist Toni Morrison, whose eponymous female protagonist in *Sula* (1973) and Aunt Pilate in *Song of Solomon* (1977) mirrored the dual liberation of African American women through the civil rights and women's movements.

Keeping pace with the evolving concept of black consciousness, black music also underwent a radical makeover, with the rhythm and blues of an earlier era taking an ever more impassioned and often political tack as soul music in the 1960s and '70s. Recording for talismanic labels such as Atlantic Records and Stax/Volt, vocal powerhouses James Brown, Aretha Franklin, Otis Redding, and Wilson Pickett set the standard. African American entrepreneur Berry Gordy, Jr., and his highly successful Motown imprint brought soul a wider crossover audience with an array of immensely talented and polished performers that included Smokey Robinson and the Miracles, Martha and the Vandellas, the Supremes, the Temptations, the Four Tops, and Stevie Wonder. Among the African American artists who most prominently took on the issues of the day were Curtis Mayfield, the prime mover of Chicago soul, who urged civil rights activists to "Keep on Pushing" (1964), and Motown's Marvin Gaye, who questioned American involvement in the Vietnam War as well as political unrest at home in his powerful

What's Going On? (1971). Later, the pride of soul music was absorbed into the pulsating rhythms of 1970s funk, the stomping ground for artists such as Sly and the Family Stone, Parliament-Funkadelic, and Kool and the Gang.

As a direct benefit of the Voting Rights Act and the subsequent voter registration drives, African Americans were elected to public office in ever increasing numbers, at both local and national levels. In the mayoral elections in the 1970s, '80s, and '90s, African Americans took office in major cities such as Los Angeles, Detroit, and New York, as well as former bastions of segregation such as Birmingham, Atlanta, and New Orleans. On the national level, too, African American men and women became federal officials and office holders in increasing numbers.

Accolades and recognition continued to accrue for African American writers. Charles Gordone became the first black playwright to win a Pulitzer Prize, for his 1969 play *No Place to Be Somebody*. The first Pulitzer for fiction awarded to an African American woman went to Alice Walker in 1983 for her popular novel *The Color Purple,* which was later adapted for film and stage. In 1988 Toni Morrison claimed a Pulitzer for *Beloved.* In 1993 she became the first African American writer to receive the Nobel Prize for Literature. Dramatist August Wilson looked backward to record the changing nature and commonalities of African American life in his historical cycle of plays, winning Tony and Pulitzer prizes for his accomplishments.

Born on the streets of the South Bronx in New York City in the late 1970s, hip-hop and rap had become the dominant form of African American musical expression by the 1980s and grew in popularity through the rest of the century and into the next. Along the way, rappers began to differentiate themselves into the "old" and "new" school. By the 1990s gangsta rap, which presented a violent, often graphic portrayal of inner city life, had become hip-hop's most notable genre. But as the 20th century flowed into the 21st, hip-hop had diversified further to encompass just about any subject matter or approach imaginable.

The African American journey to equality has been long and arduous, and it has been different from that experienced by any other American ethic group by virtue of its grounding in slavery. It is a story of deep tragedy and tremendous triumph. Undeniably some disadvantages still exist for African Americans in terms of educational, economic, and social opportunity, which are a result of lingering racism, but the election of an African American, Barack Obama, to the highest office in the land points to the great distance African Americans and America have come.

CHAPTER 1

OVERVIEW: WORLD WAR II TO THE PRESENT

This study of recent African American history starts with a survey of the period that begins with World War II and continues into the early 21st century. Its primary purpose is to introduce the people, events, organizations, and concepts that will be the focus of more detailed treatment in the ensuing chapters, but it is also intended as a summary that provides sufficient background to allow readers to jump into the rest of the book at any point.

WORLD WAR II

The industrial boom that began with the outbreak of World War II in Europe in 1939 ended the Great Depression. However, unemployed whites were generally the first to be given jobs. Discrimination against African Americans in hiring impelled A. Philip Randolph, head of the Brotherhood of Sleeping Car Porters, to threaten a mass protest march on Washington. To forestall the march, scheduled for June 25, 1941, Pres. Franklin D. Roosevelt issued Executive Order 8802 banning "discrimination in the employment of workers in defense industries or government" and establishing a Fair Employment Practices Committee (FEPC) to investigate violations. Although discrimination remained widespread, during the war, African

This World War II war bonds poster features a member of the Tuskegee Airmen, the first African American flying unit in the U.S. military. Hulton Archive/Getty Images

Americans secured more jobs at better wages in a greater range of occupations than ever before.

In World War II as in World War I, there was a mass migration of blacks from the rural South; collectively, these population shifts were known as the Great Migration. Some 1.5 million African Americans left the South during the 1940s, mainly for the industrial cities of the North. Once again, serious housing shortages and job competition led to increased tension between blacks and whites. Race riots broke out; the worst occurred in Detroit in June 1943.

During the war, which the United States had entered in December 1941, a large proportion of African American soldiers overseas were in service units, and combat troops remained segregated. In the course of the war, however, the army introduced integrated officer training, and Benjamin O. Davis, Sr., became its first African American brigadier general. In 1949, four years after the end of World War II, the armed services finally adopted a policy of full integration. During the Korean War of the early 1950s, blacks for the first time fought side by side with whites in fully integrated units.

THE CIVIL RIGHTS MOVEMENT

At the end of World War II, African Americans were poised to make far-reaching demands to end racism. They were unwilling to give up the minimal gains that had been made during the war.

The campaign for African American rights—usually referred to as the civil rights movement or the freedom movement—went forward in the 1940s and '50s in persistent and deliberate steps. In the courts the National Association for the Advancement of Colored People (NAACP) successfully attacked restrictive covenants in housing, segregation in interstate transportation, and discrimination in public recreational facilities. In 1954 the U.S. Supreme Court issued one of its most significant rulings. In the case of *Brown* v. *Board of Education of Topeka* (Kan.), the court overturned the "separate but equal" ruling of the *Plessy* v. *Ferguson* case and outlawed segregation in the country's public school systems. White citizens' councils in the South fought back with legal maneuvers, economic pressure, and even violence. Rioting by white mobs temporarily closed Central High School in Little Rock, Ark., when nine black students were admitted to it in 1957, prompting Pres. Dwight D. Eisenhower to dispatch federal troops to protect the students.

Direct nonviolent action by African Americans achieved its first major success in the Montgomery, Ala., bus boycott of 1955–56, led by the Rev. Martin Luther King, Jr. This protest was prompted by the quiet but defiant act of an African American woman, Rosa Parks, who refused to give up her seat on a segregated bus to a white passenger on Dec. 1, 1955. Resistance to African American demands

A group of white segregationists gather at the Little Rock, Ark., state capitol to protest the admission of the nine African American students to Little Rock Central High School, Aug. 20, 1959. Library of Congress Prints and Photographs Division

for the desegregation of Montgomery's buses was finally overcome when the Supreme Court ruled in November 1956 that the segregation of public transportation facilities was unconstitutional. To coordinate further civil rights action, the Southern Christian Leadership Conference (SCLC) was established in 1957 under King's guidance.

Within 15 years after the Supreme Court outlawed all-white primary elections in 1944, the registered black electorate in the South increased more than fivefold, reaching 1,250,000 in 1958. The Civil Rights Act of 1957, the first federal civil rights legislation to be passed since 1875, authorized the federal government to take legal measures to prevent a citizen from being denied voting rights.

Beginning in February 1960 in Greensboro, N.C., student sit-ins forced the desegregation of lunch counters in drug and variety stores throughout the South. In April 1960 leaders of the sit-in movement organized the Student Nonviolent Coordinating Committee

(SNCC). In the spring of 1961, to defy segregation on interstate buses, Freedom Rides in Alabama and Mississippi were organized by the Congress of Racial Equality (CORE) under its national director, James Farmer.

The NAACP, SCLC, SNCC, and CORE cooperated on a number of local projects, such as the drive to register black voters in Mississippi, launched in 1961. In April 1964 they worked together to help found the Mississippi Freedom Democratic Party (MFDP), which later that year challenged the seating of an all-white Mississippi delegation at the Democratic National Convention in Atlantic City, N.J.

Activist African Americans adopted "Freedom Now" as their slogan to recognize the Emancipation Proclamation centennial in 1963 (indeed, a short-lived all-black Freedom Now Party was formed in Michigan and ran candidates in the general election of 1964). National attention in the spring of 1963 was focused on Birmingham, Ala., where King was leading a civil rights drive. The Birmingham authorities used dogs and fire hoses to quell civil rights demonstrators, and there were mass arrests. In September 1963 four African American girls were killed by a bomb thrown into a Birmingham church.

Civil rights activities in 1963 culminated in a March on Washington organized by Randolph and civil rights activist Bayard Rustin. From the Lincoln Memorial, King addressed the throng of some 250,000 demonstrators gathered on the Mall. The march helped secure the passage of the Civil Rights Act of 1964, which forbade discrimination in voting, public accommodations, and employment and permitted the attorney general of the United States to deny federal funds to local agencies that practiced discrimination. Efforts to increase African American voter participation were also helped by the ratification in 1964 of the Twenty-fourth Amendment to the Constitution, which banned the poll tax.

The difficulties in registering African American voters in the South were dramatized in 1965 by events in Selma, Ala. Civil rights demonstrators there were attacked by police who used tear gas, whips, and clubs. Thousands of demonstrators were arrested. As a result, however, their cause won national sympathy and support. Led by King and by John Lewis of SNCC, some 40,000 protesters from all over the country marched from Selma to Montgomery, the Alabama state capital. Shortly thereafter Congress passed the Voting Rights Act of 1965, which eliminated all discriminatory qualifying tests for voter registrants and provided for the appointment of federal registrars.

URBAN UPHEAVAL

During the 1960s the country's predominantly African American inner cities were swept by outbreaks of violence, the basic causes of which were long-standing grievances—police insensitivity and brutality, inadequate educational and recreational facilities, high unemployment, poor housing, and high prices. Yet the outbreaks were mostly unplanned. Unlike the "race riots" of earlier decades, when whites menaced African Americans, the outbreaks of the 1960s involved the looting and burning of mostly white-owned property in black neighbourhoods by African Americans. The fighting that took place was mainly between African American youths and the police. Hundreds of lives were lost, and tens of millions of dollars' worth of property was destroyed. The most serious disturbances occurred in the Watts area of Los Angeles, Calif., in July 1965 and in Newark, N.J., and Detroit, Mich., in July 1967.

During the 1960s, militant black nationalist and Marxist-oriented African American organizations were created, among them the Revolutionary Action Movement, the Deacons for Defense, and the Black Panther Party. Under such leaders as Stokely Carmichael and H. Rap Brown, SNCC adopted increasingly radical policies. Some of the militant black leaders were arrested, and others, such as Eldridge Cleaver, fled the country. This loss of leadership seriously weakened some of the organizations.

"Black power" became popular in the late 1960s. The slogan was first used by Carmichael in June 1966 during a civil rights march in Mississippi. However, the concept of black power predated the slogan. Essentially, it refers to all the attempts by African Americans to maximize their political and economic power.

Among the outstanding modern advocates of black power was Malcolm X, who rose to national prominence in the early 1960s as a minister in the Nation of Islam, or Black Muslim movement. Malcolm X broke with the leader of the Black Muslims, Elijah Muhammad, and founded the Organization of Afro-American Unity before he was assassinated in February 1965.

Soul Food

The term soul food *was first used in print in 1964 during the rise of "black pride," when many aspects of African American culture—including soul music—were celebrated for their contribution to the American way of life. The term celebrated the ingenuity and skill of cooks who were able to form a distinctive cuisine despite limited means.*

Although the name was applied much later, soul food originated in the home cooking of the rural South, using locally raised or gathered foods and other inexpensive ingredients. Following their emancipation from slavery in the 1860s, African American cooks expanded on the coarse diet that had been provided them by slave owners but still made do with little. Most of the foods they prepared were common to all the rural poor of the South—light- and dark-skinned alike— but these foods and food-preparation techniques were carried north by African Americans during the Great Migration and thus became identified with African American culture. African

Americans were often employed as cooks in white households and in restaurants, and they incorporated the influence of their employers' favoured dishes into their home cooking.

Although there were regional variants, such as the Creole influence from Louisiana, many of the same foods were eaten throughout the South. Corn (maize) was raised as a staple, to be ground into cornmeal for cornbread and its local variants hoecakes, baked on a griddle, and hush puppies, usually fried with fish. Corn also provided hominy grits, to be eaten as a breakfast food or a side dish. Biscuits were a popular form of bread. Rice was an important staple, especially in the Carolinas and in Louisiana. Molasses and a syrup made from sorghum provided sweetening.

Chickens and pigs could be raised on small-scale farms without special fodder, and pork, fresh or smoked, appeared in many dishes. The inclusion of smoked pork, often in the form of fatback or bacon, is a common thread in soul food dishes, as is the use of lard as shortening or for frying. All parts of the pig were used; sometimes only the bony or less desirable cuts were available for purchase. Pig's tails, feet, ribs, ears, jowls, hocks, liver, and chitlins (chitterlings; i.e., intestines) became part of the soul food repertoire. Barbecuing—the slow cooking of meat over a wood fire—became a specialty, with regional variations in sauces and seasonings. Opossums, raccoons, rabbits, squirrels, and deer were hunted, and fish, frogs, crayfish, turtles, shellfish, and crabs were collected from fresh waters, salt waters, and marshes. Freshwater catfish was especially identified with soul food.

Vegetables of African origin, such as okra and sweet potatoes, were widely grown, as were melons, greens (including mustard and collards), turnips, cabbage, and beans. Lima beans, crowder peas, black-eyed peas, butter beans, and green beans were used fresh or dried. Spicy vinegar-based pepper sauce remains a widely used condiment. Other popular dishes are fried chicken, short ribs of beef, macaroni and cheese, and potato salad. Desserts include pies and layer cakes, cobblers, and puddings, often incorporating pecans, peaches, and berries.

From the 1940s, soul food restaurants appeared in every large American city with a sizeable black population and began to attract a diverse clientele. More recently, health-conscious contemporary cooks have sought to limit the use of animal fat and salt, especially in light of the prevalence of high blood pressure and diabetes in the African American population.

The black power movement was stimulated by the growing pride of black Americans in their African heritage. This pride was strikingly symbolized by the Afro hairstyle and the African garments worn by many young blacks. Black pride was also manifested in student demands for black studies programs, black teachers, and dedicated facilities and in an upsurge in African American culture and creativity.

The new slogan—updated from Harlem Renaissance poet Langston Hughes—was "Black is beautiful."

The Vietnam War, in which African American soldiers participated in disproportionately high numbers, tended to divide the black leadership and divert white liberals from the civil rights movement. Some NAACP and National Urban League leaders minimized the war's impact on the

KWANZAA

Celebrated from December 26 to January 1, the Kwanzaa holiday was adapted from an African harvest festival called Kwanza (which means "first fruits" in the Swahili language). It was created in 1966 by Maulana Karenga, a professor of black studies at California State University in Long Beach, who added an additional "a" to the end of the name to distinguish it from the African festival. Although Kwanzaa is primarily an African American holiday, it has also come to be celebrated outside the United States, particularly in Caribbean and other countries where there are large numbers of descendants of Africans. It was conceived as a nonpolitical and nonreligious holiday for the affirmation of African family and social values. The holiday is not considered to be a substitute for Christmas.

Each of the days of the celebration is dedicated to one of the seven principles of Kwanzaa: unity (umoja), self-determination (kujichagulia), collective responsibility (ujima), cooperative economics (ujamaa), purpose (nia), creativity (kuumba), and faith (imani). There also are seven symbols of the holiday: fruits, vegetables, and nuts; straw place mats; a candleholder; ears of corn (maize); gifts; a communal cup signifying unity; and seven candles in the African colours of red, green, and black. On each day the family comes together to light one of the candles in the kinara, or candleholder, and to discuss the principle for the day. At the end of the celebration, on December 31, families join in a community feast called the karamu. Some participants wear traditional African clothing during the celebration.

African American home front. A tougher view—that U.S. participation had become a "racist" intrusion in a nonwhite country's affairs—was shared by other African American leaders, including King. He organized the Poor People's Campaign, a protest march on Washington, D.C., before he was assassinated in Memphis, Tenn., in April 1968. Anger and frustration over his assassination set off more disturbances in the inner cities. (James Earl Ray, a white small-time crook, was tried and convicted of the murder.)

A NEW DIRECTION

The civil rights movement underwent a marked shift in emphasis after 1970.

Legislative goals had largely been achieved. And even more significant than some of the civil rights laws was Pres. Lyndon B. Johnson's Great Society program. Established as a War on Poverty, it greatly expanded welfare programs. One goal of the Great Society was to help realize some of the intentions of civil rights legislation. This could only be done by opening up opportunities for African Americans in schooling, housing, and the labour force. Thus, a new emphasis emerged wherein affirmative action programs tried to remedy the effects of historical discrimination by assuring present opportunities. Sometimes quota systems were used in school admission and job hiring, a policy that was denounced by some nonblacks as reverse discrimination. Affirmative action programs helped African Americans achieve notable gains in education and allowed black families to rise into the middle and upper-middle class.

Nevertheless, many African Americans continued to face difficult social and economic challenges, especially in the inner cities. A reminder of the lingering tensions in some impoverished city neighbourhoods came in 1992, when four white police officers were acquitted in the beating of Rodney King, an African American motorist, in Los Angeles. Hours after the acquittal, the city erupted in riots in which more than 50 people were killed. Smaller riots broke out in other U.S. cities.

POLITICAL PROGRESS

The voter registration drives that intensified during the 1960s began to show results by the end of the decade. In 1960 only about 28 percent of the African American voting-age population in the South was registered, and there were perhaps 100 African American elected officials. By 1969, with the number of registrants more than doubled, up to 1,185 African Americans had been elected to state and local offices.

Some of the electoral gains were spectacular. The first black chief executive of a major city was an appointee—Walter E. Washington, who became the commissioner of Washington, D.C., in 1967. But in other cities African Americans were elected mayor—Carl Stokes in Cleveland,

Ohio, and Richard Hatcher in Gary, Ind., in 1967; Kenneth Gibson in Newark in 1969; Tom Bradley in Los Angeles, Coleman A. Young in Detroit, and Maynard Jackson in Atlanta in 1973; Ernest N. Morial in New Orleans in 1977; Richard Arrington in Birmingham in 1979; Wilson Goode in Philadelphia and Harold Washington in Chicago in 1983; Kurt L. Schmoke in Baltimore in 1987. Also in 1987, Carrie Saxon Perry of Hartford, Conn., became the first black woman to be elected mayor of a large city. An African American became mayor of the largest city in the United States in 1989 when David Dinkins won the general election after a stunning primary defeat of New York City's incumbent mayor. Bradley's attempt, in California, to become the country's first elected black governor failed in 1982, but seven years later L. Douglas Wilder of Virginia reached that milestone.

African American politicians made gains on the national level as well. The first black senator since the Reconstruction period was Edward W. Brooke of Massachusetts, who served from 1967 to 1979. In 1992 Illinois voters elected Carol Moseley Braun to be the first African American woman in the U.S. Senate. The first African American named to the Supreme Court was Thurgood Marshall, in 1967. When Marshall retired in 1991, he was succeeded by another black associate justice, Clarence Thomas.

The first African American member of a presidential cabinet was Robert C. Weaver, secretary of Housing and Urban Development (HUD; 1966). Another secretary of HUD, Patricia Roberts Harris, was the first black woman in the cabinet (1977). Andrew Young was named ambassador to the United Nations in 1977. In 1989 Colin Powell, a four-star general in the army, was chosen to be chairman of the Joint Chiefs of Staff—the country's highest military post. In 2001 Powell also became the first African American secretary of state. In 2005 he was succeeded as secretary of state by Condoleezza Rice, the first black woman to hold the post.

African Americans reached the pinnacle of U.S. politics when Barack Obama was elected president in 2008. The son of a black father from Kenya and a white mother from Kansas, Obama was a first-term U.S. senator from Illinois when the Democrats selected him as their presidential candidate. His ascent to the presidency was lauded as a great leap forward for race relations in the United States.

OTHER CONTRIBUTIONS TO AMERICAN LIFE

Ralph Ellison's novel of alienation and the blues, *Invisible Man*, won the National Book Award for 1953. Like its nameless, faceless narrator, many African Americans in the 1940s searched for identity in a white-dominated society. Their concerns were ignored or neglected. Their accomplishments, except as entertainers, went unrecognized. They were excluded from restaurants, theaters, hotels, and clubs.

In protesting the abuse of human rights, King's leadership and the black power movement brought high visibility to African Americans. In the era of the Invisible Man, left-wing causes had exploited African Americans as anonymous symbols of oppression, but in the 1960s the media made celebrities of activists such as Black Panther supporter Angela Davis and SNCC's Julian Bond, who, at age 28, in 1968 was put forward for the Democratic Party's vice presidential nomination. In the forefront of the civil rights marches were author James Baldwin, gospel singer Mahalia Jackson, folksingers Harry Belafonte and Odetta, and comedian Dick Gregory.

TELEVISION AND FILM

Nat King Cole was the first African American entertainer with a network television series (1956–57), but, despite the singer's great talent, his variety show had trouble attracting sponsors. In the decades following Cole's death, many situation comedies were marketed with predominantly African American casts, and the large acting ensembles in dramatic series were often integrated. Redd Foxx and Demond Wilson starred in the popular series *Sanford and Son* (1972–77). One of the most acclaimed weekly shows ever produced was *The Cosby Show* (1984–92), starring comedian Bill Cosby. (Cosby's first acting assignment, in the espionage series *I Spy* [1965–68], made him the first black actor to perform in a starring dramatic role on network television. His portrayal of a black secret agent won him three Emmy Awards and helped to

THE COSBY SHOW

The most popular family comedy of the 1980s, The Cosby Show *was the keystone of Thursday-night television for eight seasons (1984–92) on the National Broadcasting Company (NBC) network; the show was credited with reviving the sitcom genre and raising the network's ratings.*

Inspired by a Bill Cosby stand-up comedy segment about child rearing, NBC producers Marcy Carsey and Tom Werner created an instant hit with this domestic comedy series. The show was filmed in front of a studio audience and focused on the daily happenings and familial interactions of the upper-middle-class Huxtable family in their brownstone home in Brooklyn. Cosby stars as obstetrician and paterfamilias Cliff, whose wife, Clair (played by Phylicia Rashad), balances an equally successful legal career. Together they counsel, admonish, and frequently outmaneuver their five children: at the beginning of the show, they are 20-something Sondra (Sabrina Le Beauf), teenagers Denise (Lisa Bonet) and Theo (Malcolm-Jamal Warner), preteen Vanessa (Tempestt Bledsoe), and young Rudy (Keshia Knight Pulliam). Grandparents Anna and Russell Huxtable (Clarice Taylor and Earle Hyman) frequently appear, and the irresistible Olivia (Raven Symone, who later starred in the Disney Channel's That's So Raven, *2003–07) is eventually introduced as Cliff and Clair's five-year-old step-grandchild.*

The show's most revered yet hotly debated aspect was its attempt to combat stereotypes about African American families. Because of the Huxtables' high-income professions, strong nuclear family, and mixed-race peer group, TV Guide *deemed them "the most atypical black family in television history." But* The Cosby Show *not only reinvented the African American television family (frequently featuring prominent black artists, jazz musicians, and actors in the process); it also established a successful formula for family-centred comedy in general. Moreover, Cosby was one of the first stand-up comedians to become a sitcom star.*

The Cosby Show *was one of only two American shows to top the Nielsen ratings for five consecutive seasons. It received the People's Choice Award for favourite comedy program every year of its run except 1991, as well as three Golden Globes, six of the 29 Emmy Awards for which it was nominated, and more than 40 other awards. It produced a spin-off program,* A Different World *(1987–93), set in a historically black college and initially focusing on Bonet's Denise character.*

advance the status of African Americans on television.) Keenen Ivory Wayans, star of the long-running satirical sketch comedy show *In Living Color*, won an Emmy Award for his work in 1990. *The Bernie Mac Show*, a sitcom starring comedian Bernie Mac, won a Peabody Award in 2001.

One of television's most-watched dramatic telecasts was *Roots*, an eight-part miniseries first shown in 1977. A sequel, the seven-part *Roots: The Next Generations*, appeared in 1979. Based on author Alex Haley's real-life quest to trace his African ancestry, the shows made other African Americans more aware of their rich cultural heritage.

Achievements by African Americans in the field of broadcast journalism included those of Ed Bradley, who became one of the interviewers for the television newsmagazine *60 Minutes* in 1981, and Bryant Gumbel, who became cohost of *The Today Show* in 1982. A former anchor on a local news desk, Oprah Winfrey started a popular daytime talk show in the 1980s that became a cultural phenomenon. She established her own television and film production companies, and her media entertainment empire made her one of the richest and most influential women in the United States.

"Blaxploitation" films such as *Superfly* drew huge audiences in the 1970s, but they did not deal with the everyday experiences of most African Americans. From the 1950s, Academy Award winner Sidney Poitier appeared in more-genuine dramatic roles. By the 1980s other actors were cast in parts that had not been written specifically as "black roles"—for example, Louis Gossett, Jr., in *An Officer and a Gentleman* (1983 Academy Award). "Buddy pictures" paired white actors with African American stars such as Eddie Murphy, Danny Glover, Gregory Hines (who was also a dazzling tap dancer), and Richard Pryor. In 2002 Halle Berry became the first African American woman to win an Academy Award for best actress, for her performance in *Monster's Ball* (2001). African Americans Morgan Freeman, Denzel Washington, and Will Smith were among the most popular and acclaimed actors of the early 21st century. A completely original talent, director-writer-actor Spike Lee had total control over his productions, which examined contemporary African American life. Other prominent black directors were John Singleton (*Boyz N the Hood*, 1991) and Matty Rich (*Straight Out of Brooklyn*, 1990).

LITERATURE

The poet Gwendolyn Brooks was the first African American to win a Pulitzer Prize, for *Annie Allen* in 1950. In 1970 Charles Gordone became the first African American playwright to win the Pulitzer, with his depiction of a black hustler-poet in *No Place to Be Somebody*. *The Color Purple*, a best-selling novel by Alice Walker, won a Pulitzer in 1983. Toni Morrison's novel *Beloved* took the Pulitzer for fiction in 1988, and in 1993 Morrison became the first African American to win the Nobel Prize for literature. The most-accomplished African American dramatist in the second half of the 20th century was August Wilson, a two-time Pulitzer Prize winner. Between 1984 and 2005 Wilson chronicled black American life in a series of 10 plays, one set in each decade of the 20th century.

MUSIC

Almost all of America's popular music—including jazz, blues, rock, soul, and hip-hop—has its origins in black culture. Thomas A. Dorsey was the father of gospel music, and Harry T. Burleigh arranged spirituals for the concert stage. Marian Anderson was the first African American to sing at the Metropolitan Opera House, in 1955. Other African American opera stars include Leontyne Price, La Julia Rhea, Grace Bumbry, Shirley Verrett, Jessye Norman, and Kathleen Battle. Arthur Mitchell, Alvin Ailey, and Bill T. Jones led outstanding dance troupes. Trumpeter Wynton Marsalis emerged as one of the great trumpeters of the late 20th century, winning Grammy Awards for both jazz and classical works. His brother, Branford, became music director for television's popular *Tonight Show* in 1992. Top-selling popular recording artists of the late 20th and early 21st centuries included Michael Jackson, Janet Jackson, Prince, Whitney Houston, Mary J. Blige, Beyoncé, Alicia Keys, and Usher. The hip-hop movement, which originated among African Americans in the South Bronx section of New York City in the late 1970s, produced many waves of rap superstars.

SPORTS

The whites-only barrier was broken in major league baseball by Jackie Robinson in 1947. Today African American athletes dominate most of the professional team sports. Many of the outstanding players in the history of basketball have been African Americans, not least Kareem Abdul-Jabbar, Wilt Chamberlain, Bill Russell, Magic Johnson, Michael Jordan, Shaquille O'Neal, Kobe Bryant, and LeBron James. In football, Walter Payton, Jim Brown, Jerry Rice, Jim Marshall, and Emmitt Smith, among many others, have set records. Hank Aaron held baseball's career home run record from 1974 until

2007, when he was surpassed by another African American, Barry Bonds. Rickey Henderson broke baseball's stolen-base record in 1991 and set a record for the most career runs scored in 2001. Since Joe Louis became the heavyweight boxing champion in the 1930s, African Americans have been among the world's top heavyweight fighters, though the tradition of black champions dates back to Jack Johnson, whose prowess and prominence in the first decades of the 20th century prompted the search for a "Great White Hope" to challenge him. Moreover, for a time in the 1960s and '70s African American world heavyweight champion Muhammad Ali was arguably the most recognizable person in the world. Arthur Ashe, Althea Gibson, and Venus and Serena Williams have all been at the top of the game of tennis. Since Jesse Owens won four Olympic gold medals in 1936, African Americans have excelled in athletics (track and field). In 1960 Wilma Rudolph became the first American woman to win three track gold medals in a single Olympics. Florence Griffith Joyner and Jackie Joyner-Kersee were prominent medal winners at the 1988 Olympics in Seoul. Carl Lewis, Butch Reynolds, Edwin Moses, Bob Beamon, Michael Johnson, and Gail Devers set high-profile track records. In 1997 Tiger Woods, the son of an African American father and a Thai mother, became the first golfer of either African American or Asian descent to win the prestigious Masters Tournament and remained the game's dominant force into the 21st century.

CHAPTER 2

THE CIVIL RIGHTS MOVEMENT AND FREEDOM STRUGGLE

In February 2010, Pres. Barack Obama and first lady Michelle Obama hosted "In Performance at the White House: A Celebration of Music from the Civil Rights Movement," a concert featuring songs from the civil rights movement as well as readings from civil rights speeches and writings. That Obama was the first African American to hold the country's highest office lent special significance to the evening. The event was held in honour of Black History Month, during which the study of the civil rights movement and freedom struggle are central.

THE MOVEMENT

The civil rights movement that came to prominence during the mid-1950s in the United States had its roots in the centuries-long efforts to abolish slavery. Through nonviolent protest the civil rights movement of the 1950s and '60s broke the pattern of public facilities being segregated by "race" in the South and achieved the most important breakthrough in equal-rights legislation for African Americans since the Reconstruction period (1865–77). By the mid-1960s some saw their struggle as a freedom movement not just seeking civil rights reform but instead confronting the enduring economic, political, and cultural consequences of past racial oppression.

ABOLITIONISM TO JIM CROW

American history has been marked by persistent and determined efforts to expand the scope and inclusiveness of civil rights. Although equal rights for all were affirmed in the founding documents of the United States, that affirmation did not include many of the new country's inhabitants, who were denied essential rights. African slaves and indentured servants did not have the unalienable right to "life, liberty, and the pursuit of happiness" that British colonists asserted to justify their Declaration of Independence. Nor were they included among the "People of the United States" who established the Constitution in order to "promote the general Welfare, and secure the Blessings of Liberty to ourselves and our Posterity." Instead, the Constitution protected slavery by allowing the importation of slaves until 1808 and providing for the return of slaves who had escaped to other states.

As the United States expanded its boundaries, Native American peoples resisted conquest and absorption. Individual states, which determined most of the rights of American citizens, generally limited voting rights to white property-owning males, and other rights—such as the right to own land or serve on juries—were often denied on the basis of racial or gender distinctions. A small proportion of African Americans lived outside the slave system, but those so-called "free blacks" endured racial discrimination and enforced segregation.

Although some slaves violently rebelled against their enslavement, African Americans and other subordinated groups mainly used nonviolent means—protests, legal challenges, pleas and petitions addressed to government officials, as well as sustained and massive civil rights movements—to achieve gradual improvements in their status.

During the first half of the 19th century, movements to extend voting rights to non-property-owning white male labourers resulted in the elimination of most property qualifications for voting, but this expansion of suffrage was accompanied by brutal suppression of American Indians and increasing restrictions on free blacks. Slave owners in the South reacted to the 1831 Nat Turner slave revolt in Virginia by passing laws to discourage antislavery activism and prevent the teaching of slaves to read and write. Despite this repression a growing number of African Americans freed themselves from slavery by escaping or negotiating agreements to purchase their freedom through wage labour. By the 1830s free black communities in the Northern states had become sufficiently large and organized to hold regular national conventions, where black leaders gathered to discuss alternative strategies of racial advancement. In 1833 a small minority of whites joined with black antislavery activists to form the American Anti-Slavery Society under the leadership of William Lloyd Garrison.

Frederick Douglass became the most famous of the ex-slaves who joined the abolition movement. His autobiography—one of many slave narratives—and his stirring orations heightened public awareness of the horrors of slavery. Although black leaders became increasingly militant in their attacks against slavery and other forms of racial oppression, their efforts to secure equal rights received a major setback in 1857, when the U.S. Supreme Court rejected African American citizenship claims. The Dred Scott decision stated that the country's founders had viewed blacks as so inferior that they had "no rights which the white man was bound to respect." This ruling—by declaring unconstitutional the Missouri Compromise (1820), through which Congress had limited the expansion of slavery into western territories—ironically strengthened the antislavery movement, because it angered many whites who did not own slaves. The inability of the country's political leaders to resolve that dispute fueled the successful presidential campaign of Abraham Lincoln, the candidate of the antislavery Republican Party. Lincoln's victory in turn prompted the Southern slave states to secede and form the Confederate States of America in 1860–61.

Although Lincoln did not initially seek to abolish slavery, his determination to punish the rebellious states and his increasing reliance on black soldiers in the Union army prompted him to issue the Emancipation Proclamation (1863) to deprive the Confederacy of its slave property. After the American Civil War ended, Republican leaders cemented the Union victory by gaining the ratification of constitutional amendments to abolish slavery (Thirteenth Amendment) and to protect the legal equality of ex-slaves (Fourteenth Amendment) and the voting rights of male ex-slaves (Fifteenth Amendment). Despite those constitutional guarantees of rights, almost a century of civil rights agitation and litigation would be required to bring about consistent federal enforcement of those rights in the former Confederate states. Moreover, after federal military forces were removed from the South at the end of Reconstruction, white leaders in the region enacted new laws to strengthen the "Jim Crow" system of racial segregation and discrimination. In its *Plessy* v. *Ferguson* decision (1896), the Supreme Court ruled that "separate but equal" facilities for African Americans did not violate the Fourteenth Amendment, ignoring evidence that the facilities for blacks were inferior to those intended for whites.

The Southern system of white supremacy was accompanied by the expansion of European and American imperial control over nonwhite people in Africa and Asia, as well as in island countries of the Pacific and Caribbean regions. Like African Americans, most nonwhite people throughout the world were colonized or economically exploited and denied basic rights, such as the right to vote. With few exceptions, women of all races everywhere were also denied suffrage rights.

DU BOIS TO BROWN

During the early decades of the 20th century, movements to resist such racial and gender discrimination gained strength in many countries. While a Pan-African movement emerged in response to European imperialism, African Americans developed various strategies to challenge racial discrimination in the United States. Educator Booker T. Washington emphasized economic development without openly challenging the Jim Crow system; Harvard University-educated scholar W.E.B. Du Bois became a leading advocate for civil rights and Pan-African unity among African descendants elsewhere in the world. In 1909 Du Bois and other African American leaders joined with white proponents of racial equality to form the NAACP, which became the country's most enduring civil rights organization. Under the leadership of Du Bois, James Weldon Johnson, Walter White, Thurgood Marshall, and others, the NAACP publicized racial injustices and initiated lawsuits to secure equal treatment for African Americans in education, employment, housing, and public accommodations.

The NAACP faced competition from various groups offering alternative strategies for racial advancement. In 1941 labour leader A. Philip Randolph's threat to stage a march on Washington prodded Pres. Franklin D. Roosevelt to issue an executive order against employment discrimination in the wartime defense industries. The interracial CORE also undertook small-scale civil disobedience to combat segregation in Northern cities.

In the aftermath of World War II, African American civil rights efforts were hampered by ideological splits. Du Bois and prominent African American entertainer Paul Robeson were among the leftist leaders advocating mass civil rights protests while opposing the Cold War foreign and domestic policies of Pres. Harry S. Truman, but Truman prevailed in the 1948 presidential election with critical backing from NAACP leaders and most African Americans able to vote. Marshall and other NAACP leaders gained additional black support when the Supreme Court ruled public school segregation unconstitutional in 1954 in the NAACP-sponsored case of *Brown* v. *Board of Education of Topeka*.

Yet, even as the NAACP consolidated its national dominance in the civil rights field, local black activists acted on their own to protest racial segregation and discrimination. For example, in 1951 a student walkout at a Virginia high school led by Barbara Johns, age 16, was one of the local efforts that culminated in the Brown decision. When the Supreme Court did not set a time limit for states to desegregate their school systems and instead merely called for desegregation "with all deliberate speed," the stage was set for years of conflicts over public school desegregation and other discriminatory practices.

PAUL ROBESON

The son of a former slave turned preacher, Paul Robeson attended Rutgers University in New Brunswick, N.J., where he was an All-America football player. Upon graduating from Rutgers at the head of his class, he rejected a career as a professional athlete and instead entered Columbia University. He obtained a law degree in 1923, but, because of the lack of opportunity for blacks in the legal profession, he drifted to the stage, making a London debut in 1922. He joined the Provincetown Players, a New York theatre group that included playwright Eugene O'Neill, and appeared in O'Neill's play All God's Chillun Got Wings *in 1924. His subsequent appearance in the title role of O'Neill's* The Emperor Jones *caused a sensation in New York City (1924) and London (1925). He also starred in the film version of the play (1933). In addition to his other talents, Robeson had a superb bass-baritone singing voice. In 1925 he gave his first vocal recital of African American spirituals in Greenwich Village, New York City, and he became world famous as Joe in the musical play* Show Boat *with his version of "Ol' Man River." His characterization of the title role in* Othello *in London (1930) won high praise, as did the Broadway production (1943), which set an all-time record run for a Shakespearean play on Broadway.*

Growing political awareness impelled Robeson to visit the Soviet Union in 1934, and from that year he became increasingly identified with strong left-wing commitments, while continuing his success in concerts, recordings, and theatre. In 1950 the U.S. State Department withdrew his passport because he refused to sign an affidavit disclaiming membership in the Communist Party. In the following years he was virtually ostracized for his political views, although in 1958 the Supreme Court overturned the affidavit ruling. Robeson then left the United States to live in Europe and travel in countries of the Soviet bloc, but he returned to the United States in 1963 because of ill health.

Robeson appeared in a number of films, including Sanders of the River *(1935),* Show Boat *(1936),* Song of Freedom *(1936), and* The Proud Valley *(1940). His autobiography,* Here I Stand, *was published in 1958.*

MONTGOMERY BUS BOYCOTT TO THE VOTING RIGHTS ACT

In December 1955 NAACP activist Rosa Parks's impromptu refusal to give up her seat to a white man on a bus in Montgomery, Ala., sparked a sustained bus boycott that inspired mass protests elsewhere to speed the pace of civil rights reform. After boycott supporters chose Baptist minister Martin Luther King, Jr., to head the newly established Montgomery Improvement Association (MIA), King soon became the country's most influential advocate of the concepts of nonviolent resistance forged by Mohandas Karamchand Gandhi. Despite the bombing of King's house and other acts of intimidation by segregationists, MIA leaders were able to sustain the boycott until November 1956, when the NAACP won a Supreme Court order to desegregate the bus system. In 1957 King and his supporters founded the SCLC to provide an institutional framework supporting local protest movements.

Four black college students in Greensboro, N.C., sparked a new phase of the Southern civil rights movement on Feb. 1, 1960, when they staged a sit-in at a drugstore lunch counter reserved for whites. In the wake of the Greensboro sit-in, thousands of students in at least 60 communities, mostly in the upper, urbanized South, joined the sit-in campaign during the winter and spring of 1960. Despite efforts by the NAACP, SCLC, and CORE to impose some control over the sit-in movement, the student protesters formed their own group, the SNCC, to coordinate the new movement. SNCC gradually acquired a staff of full-time organizers, many of whom were former student protesters, and launched a number of local projects designed to achieve desegregation and voting rights. Although SNCC's nonviolent tactics were influenced by King, SNCC organizers typically stressed the need to develop self-reliant local leaders to sustain grassroots movements.

The Freedom Rides of 1961 signaled the beginning of a period when civil rights protest activity grew in scale and intensity. CORE sponsored the first group of bus riders who sought to desegregate Southern bus terminals. After attacks by white mobs in Alabama turned back the initial protesters, student activists from Nashville and other centers of sit-in activities continued the rides into Jackson, Miss., where they were promptly arrested for disobeying racial segregation rules. Despite U.S. Attorney General Robert F. Kennedy's plea for a "cooling-off" period, the Freedom Rides demonstrated that militant but nonviolent young activists could confront Southern segregation at its strongest points and pressure the federal government to intervene to protect the constitutional rights of African Americans. The Freedom Rides encouraged similar protests elsewhere against segregated transportation facilities and stimulated local campaigns in many Southern communities that had been untouched by the student sit-ins.

SCLC leaders worked with Birmingham, Ala., minister Fred Shuttlesworth to launch a major campaign featuring confrontations between nonviolent demonstrators and the often brutal law-enforcement personnel directed by Birmingham's police commissioner, Eugene T. ("Bull") Connor. Televised confrontations between nonviolent protesters and vicious policemen with clubs, fire hoses, and police dogs attracted Northern support and resulted in federal intervention to bring about a settlement that included civil rights concessions. King's "Letter from Birmingham Jail" of April 16, 1963, defended civil disobedience and

The Rev. Martin Luther King, Jr., on the telephone following his encounter with an anti-Freedom Riders mob, Montgomery, Ala,, May 26, 1961. Express Newspapers/Hulton Archive/Getty Images

warned that frustrated African Americans might turn to black nationalism, a development that he predicted would lead inevitably to a frightening racial nightmare. International news coverage of the Birmingham clashes prompted Pres. John F. Kennedy to introduce legislation that eventually became the Civil Rights Act of 1964.

Similar mass protests in dozens of other cities made white Americans more aware of the antiquated Jim Crow system, though black militancy also prompted a white "backlash." These mass protests culminated on Aug. 28, 1963, in the March on Washington for Jobs and Freedom, which attracted over 200,000 participants. King used his concluding "I Have a Dream" speech at the march as an opportunity to link black civil rights aspirations with traditional American political values. He insisted that the Declaration of Independence and the Constitution comprised "a promissory note" guaranteeing

Civil rights supporters carrying placards at the March on Washington, D.C., Aug. 28, 1963. Library of Congress, Washington, D.C.; Warren K. Leffler (digital file: cph ppmsca 03128)

all Americans "the unalienable rights of life, liberty, and the pursuit of happiness."

While media attention concentrated on the urban demonstrations in Birmingham, the voter-registration campaign in rural Mississippi and Alabama, spearheaded by SNCC and groups under the auspices of the Council of Federated Organizations (COFO), stimulated the emergence of resilient indigenous leadership and the MFDP. COFO director Robert Moses spearheaded a summer project in 1964 that brought together voting rights organizers and hundreds of Northern white volunteers. While the murders of three civil rights workers focused national attention on Mississippi, the MFDP, led by Fannie Lou Hamer, failed in its attempt to unseat the regular all-white delegation at the 1964 National Democratic Convention. During the following year, however, mass protests in the Alabama cities of Selma and Montgomery led Pres. Lyndon B. Johnson to introduce legislation that became the Voting Rights Act of 1965.

From Black Power to the Assassination of Martin Luther King

The Selma-to-Montgomery march in March 1965 would be the last sustained Southern protest campaign that was able to secure widespread support among whites outside the region. The passage of voting rights legislation, the upsurge in Northern urban racial violence, and white resentment of black militancy lessened the effectiveness and popularity of nonviolent protests as a means of advancing African American interests. In addition, the growing militancy of black activists inspired by the recently assassinated black nationalist Malcolm X spawned an increasing determination among African Americans to achieve political power and cultural autonomy by building black-controlled institutions.

When he accepted the 1964 Nobel Peace Prize, King connected the African American struggle to the anticolonial struggles that had overcome European domination elsewhere in the world. In 1966 King launched a new campaign in Chicago against Northern slum conditions and segregation, but he soon faced a major challenge from "black power" proponents, such as SNCC chairman Stokely Carmichael. This ideological conflict came to a head in June 1966 during a voting rights march through

Mississippi, following the wounding of James Meredith, who had desegregated the University of Mississippi in 1962. Carmichael's use of the "black power" slogan encapsulated the emerging notion of a freedom struggle seeking political, economic, and cultural objectives beyond narrowly defined civil rights reforms. By the late 1960s not only the NAACP and SCLC but even SNCC and CORE faced challenges from new militant organizations, such as the Black Panther Party, whose leaders argued that civil rights reforms were insufficient because they did not fully address the problems of poor and powerless blacks. They also dismissed nonviolent principles, often quoting Malcolm X's imperative: "by any means necessary." Questioning American citizenship and identity as goals for African Americans, black power proponents called instead for a global struggle for black national "self-determination" rather than merely for civil rights.

Although King criticized calls for black separatism and armed self-defense, he supported anticolonial movements and agreed that African Americans should seek compensatory government actions to redress historical injustices and to end poverty. He criticized U.S. military intervention in the Vietnam War, which he characterized as a civil war, insisting that war was immoral and that the American government had wrongly opposed nationalist movements in Asia, Africa, and Latin America. In December

1967 he announced a Poor People's Campaign that intended to bring thousands of protesters to Washington, D.C., to lobby for an end to poverty.

After King's assassination in April 1968, the Poor People's Campaign floundered, and the Black Panther Party and other black militant groups encountered intense government repression from local police and the Federal Bureau of Investigation's Counterintelligence Program (COINTELPRO). In 1968 the National Advisory Commission on Civil Disorders (also known as the Kerner Commission) concluded that the country, despite civil rights reforms, was moving "toward two societies, one black, one white—separate and unequal." By the time of the Commission's report, claims that black gains had resulted in "reverse discrimination" against whites were effectively used against significant new civil rights initiatives during the 1970s and 1980s.

INTO THE 21ST CENTURY

As was the case for formerly colonized people in countries that achieved independence during the period after World War II, the acquisition of citizenship rights by African Americans brought fewer gains for those who were poor than for those who possessed educational and class advantages. American civil rights legislation of the 1960s became the basis for affirmative action—programs that increased opportunities for many black students and workers as well as for women, disabled people, and other victims of discrimination. Increased participation in the American electoral system lessened black reliance on extralegal tactics. Some former civil rights activists, such as John Lewis, Andrew Young, and Jesse Jackson, launched careers in electoral politics. Black elected officials, including mayors, began to exert greater influence than either black power proponents or advocates of nonviolent civil rights protests. In 1969, believing that by speaking with a single voice they would have greater influence, 13 African American members of the U.S. House of Representatives formed the Congressional Black Caucus "to promote the public welfare through legislation designed to meet the needs of millions of neglected citizens." By the early 21st century that caucus numbered more than 40 members and could count among its achievements legislative initiatives involving minority business development, expansion of educational opportunities, and opposition to South Africa's former apartheid system.

However, civil rights issues continued to stimulate protests, particularly when previous gains appeared to be threatened. Overall, the 20th-century struggle for civil rights produced an enduring transformation of the legal status of African Americans and other victims of discrimination. It also increased the responsibility of the government to enforce civil rights laws and the provisions of the Civil War-era constitutional amendments. Civil rights reforms did not, however, alter other determinants of the subordinate status of African Americans who remained in racially segregated communities where housing, public schools, and health care services are inferior. Like freedom struggles in Africa, the African American freedom struggle eliminated slavery and legally mandated forms of racial oppression, but the descendants of former slaves and colonized people generally remained in subordinate positions within the global capitalist economic order.

Still, in the early 21st century the ascent to the U.S. presidency of an African American, Barack Obama, seemed to reflect a transformation of American society with ramifications for the civil rights movement. Jesse Jackson in his own landmark campaigns for the Democratic presidential nomination in 1984 and 1988 had reached beyond the effort to mobilize African American voters and attempted to fashion a "Rainbow Coalition" of "red, yellow, brown, black, and white" Americans. Obama—whose father was a black Kenyan and mother was a white American—presented a life story grounded in a search for a satisfactory racial identity. Ultimately, Obama's approach to the world and, arguably, his appeal to many voters were transracial, grounded in a sophisticated understanding of the complex nature of racial identity that was no longer merely dichotomous (no longer simply a matter of black or white). Given the deeply rooted racial conflicts of the American past, however, it is unlikely that Obama's election signaled the start of a postracial era without divisive racial issues and controversies.

ACTIVISM, ACTION, AND ACTS

This section takes a close look at the organizations that were at the forefront of the civil rights movement and freedom struggle, including the strategies and tactics employed in the pursuit of justice and equality. It also considers the legal decisions and legislation that came about as a result of the civil rights struggle as well as some of the concepts and issues that are central to this aspect of African American history.

AFFIRMATIVE ACTION

Affirmative action, the active effort to improve employment or educational opportunities for members of minority groups and for women, began as a government remedy to the effects of long-standing discrimination against such groups. It has consisted of policies, programs, and procedures that give preferences to minorities and women in job hiring, admission to institutions of higher education, the awarding of government contracts, and other social benefits. The typical criteria for affirmative action are race, disability, gender, ethnic origin, and age.

Affirmative action was initiated by the administration of Pres. Lyndon B.

Johnson in order to improve opportunities for African Americans while civil rights legislation was dismantling the legal basis for discrimination. The federal government began to institute affirmative action policies under the landmark Civil Rights Act of 1964 and an executive order in 1965. Businesses receiving federal funds were prohibited from using aptitude tests and other criteria that tended to discriminate against African Americans. Affirmative action programs were monitored by the Office of Federal Contract Compliance and the Equal Employment Opportunity Commission (EEOC). Subsequently, affirmative action was broadened to cover women and Native Americans, Hispanics, and other minorities and was extended to colleges and universities and state and federal agencies.

By the late 1970s the use of racial quotas and minority set-asides led to court challenges of affirmative action as a form of "reverse discrimination." The first major challenge was *Regents of the University of California v. Bakke* (1978), in which the U.S. Supreme Court ruled (5–4)

West facade of the U.S. Supreme Court building. Franz Jantzen/Supreme Court of the United States

that quotas may not be used to reserve places for minority applicants if white applicants are denied a chance to compete for those places. Although the court outlawed quota programs, it allowed colleges to use race as a factor in making college admissions decisions. Two years later a fragmented court upheld a 1977 federal law requiring that 10 percent of funds for public works be allotted to qualified minority contractors.

The Supreme Court began to impose significant restrictions on race-based affirmative action in 1989. In several decisions that year, the court gave greater weight to claims of reverse discrimination, outlawed the use of minority set-asides in cases where prior racial discrimination could not be proved, and placed limits on the use of racial preferences by states that were stricter than those it applied to the federal government. In *Adarand Constructors* v. *Pena* (1995), the court ruled that federal affirmative action programs were unconstitutional unless they fulfilled a "compelling governmental interest."

Opposition to affirmative action in California culminated in the passage in 1996 of the California Civil Rights Initiative (Proposition 209), which prohibited all government agencies and institutions from giving preferential treatment to individuals based on their race or sex. The Supreme Court effectively upheld the constitutionality of Proposition 209 in November 1997 by refusing to hear a challenge to its enforcement. Legislation similar to Proposition 209 was subsequently proposed in other states and was passed in Washington in 1998. The Supreme Court also upheld a lower-court ruling that struck down as unconstitutional the University of Texas's affirmative action program, arguing in *Hopwood* v. *University of Texas Law School* (1996) that there was no compelling state interest to warrant using race as a factor in admissions decisions. Afterward there were further legislative and electoral challenges to affirmative action in many parts of the country. In 2003, in two landmark rulings involving admissions to the University of Michigan and its law school, the U.S. Supreme Court reaffirmed the constitutionality of affirmative action, though it ruled that race could not be the preeminent factor in such decisions as it struck down the university's undergraduate admissions policy that awarded points to students on the basis of race.

Bakke Decision

The Bakke decision was handed down by the U.S. Supreme Court on July 28, 1978. The ruling in the case, formally known as *Regents of the University of California* v. *Bakke*, declared affirmative action constitutional but invalidated the use of racial quotas. The medical school at the University of California, Davis, as part of the university's affirmative action program, had reserved 16 percent of its admission places for minority applicants. Allan Bakke, a white California man who had twice unsuccessfully applied for admission to the medical school, filed suit against the university. Citing evidence that his grades and test scores surpassed those of many minority students who had been accepted for admission, Bakke charged that he had suffered unfair "reverse discrimination" on the basis of race, which he argued was contrary to the Civil Rights Act of 1964 and the equal protection clause of the U.S. Constitution's Fourteenth Amendment. The Supreme Court, in a highly fractured ruling (six separate opinions were issued), agreed that the university's use of strict racial quotas was unconstitutional and ordered that the medical school admit Bakke, but it also contended that race could be used as one criterion in the admissions decisions of institutions of higher education.

BLACK NATIONALISM

The black nationalist movement of the 1960s and early '70s, which sought to acquire economic power for African Americans and infuse them with a sense of community and group feeling, can be traced back to Marcus Garvey's Universal Negro Improvement Association of the 1920s. Many adherents to black nationalism assumed the eventual creation of a separate black nation by African Americans. As an alternative to being assimilated by the predominantly white American nation, black nationalists sought to maintain and promote their separate identity as a people of African ancestry. With such slogans as "black power" and "black is beautiful," they also sought to inculcate a sense of pride among blacks.

BLACK PANTHER PARTY

The original purpose of the Black Panther Party—founded as the Black Panther Party For Self-defense in 1966 in Oakland, Calif., by Huey Newton and Bobby Seale—was to patrol black ghettos to protect residents from acts of police brutality. The Panthers eventually developed into a Marxist revolutionary group that called for the arming of all blacks, the exemption of blacks from the draft and from all sanctions of so-called white America, the release of all blacks from jail, and the payment of compensation to blacks for centuries of exploitation by white Americans. At its peak in the late 1960s, Panther membership exceeded 2,000 and the organization operated chapters in several major cities.

Conflicts between Black Panthers and police in the late 1960s and early '70s led to shoot-outs in California, New York, and Chicago, one of which resulted in Newton's going to prison for the murder of a patrolman. While some members of the party were guilty of criminal acts, the group was subjected to police harassment that sometimes took the form of violent attacks, prompting congressional investigations of police activities in dealing with the Panthers. By the mid-1970s, having lost many members and having fallen out of favour with many American black leaders, who objected to the party's methods, the Panthers turned from violence to concentrate on conventional politics and on providing social services in black neighbourhoods. The party was effectively disbanded by the early 1980s.

BROWN V. BOARD OF EDUCATION OF TOPEKA

On May 17, 1954, in its decision on the *Brown* v. *Board of Education of Topeka* case, the U.S. Supreme Court ruled unanimously that racial segregation in public schools violated the Fourteenth Amendment to the Constitution, which declares that no state may deny equal protection of the laws to any person within its jurisdiction. The decision declared that separate educational facilities were inherently unequal. Based on a series of Supreme Court cases argued between 1938 and 1950, *Brown* v. *Board of Education of Topeka* completed the reversal of *Plessy* v. *Ferguson* (1896), which had permitted "separate but equal" public facilities. Strictly speaking, the 1954 decision was limited to the public schools, but it implied that segregation was not permissible in other public facilities.

CIVIL RIGHTS ACT

Intended to end discrimination based on race, colour, religion, or national origin, the Civil Rights Act of 1964 often has been called the most important U.S. law on civil rights since Reconstruction. Title I of the act guarantees equal voting rights by removing registration requirements and procedures biased against minorities and the underprivileged. Title II prohibits segregation or discrimination in places of public accommodation involved in interstate commerce. Title VII bans discrimination by trade unions, schools, or employers involved in interstate commerce or doing business with the federal government. The latter section also applies to discrimination on the basis of sex and established a government agency, the EEOC, to enforce these provisions. The act also calls for the desegregation of public schools (Title IV), broadens the duties of the Civil Rights Commission (Title V), and assures nondiscrimination in the distribution of funds under federally assisted programs (Title VI).

The Civil Rights Act was a highly controversial issue in the United States as soon as it was proposed by Pres. John F. Kennedy in 1963. Although Kennedy was unable to secure passage of the bill in Congress, a stronger version was eventually passed with the urging of his successor, Pres. Lyndon B. Johnson, who signed the bill into law on July 2, 1964, following one of the longest debates in Senate history. White groups opposed to integration with blacks responded to the act with a significant backlash that took the form of protests, increased support for prosegregation candidates for public office, and some racial violence. The constitutionality of the act was immediately challenged and was upheld by the Supreme Court in the test case *Heart of Atlanta Motel* v. *U.S.* (1964). The act gave federal law enforcement agencies the power to prevent racial discrimination in employment, voting, and the use of public facilities.

Congress of Racial Equality (CORE)

An interracial organization dedicated to improving race relations and ending discriminatory policies through direct-action projects, CORE was established by James Farmer in 1942. Farmer had been working as the race-relations secretary for the American branch of the pacifist group Fellowship of Reconciliation

A march held in memory of the four girls killed in the bombing of the 16th Street Baptist Church in Birmingham, Ala.; the march was sponsored by the Congress of Racial Equality (CORE) and held in Washington, D.C., in 1963. Thomas J. O'Halloran—U.S. News and World Report Magazine Photograph Collection/Library of Congress, Washington, D.C. (digital file number. ppmsca-04298 -6A)

(FOR) but resigned over a dispute in policy; he founded CORE as a vehicle for the nonviolent approach to combating racial prejudice that was inspired by Indian leader Mahatma Gandhi.

CORE's activities began with a sit-in at a coffee shop in Chicago in 1942 for the purpose of protesting segregation in public settings. The event was one of the first such demonstrations in the United States and identified CORE as an influential force in the subsequent desegregation of public facilities in Northern cities. In 1946 the U.S. Supreme Court banned segregation in interstate bus travel. A year later CORE and FOR tested the ruling by staging the Journey of Reconciliation, on which an interracial group of activists rode together on a bus through the upper South, though fearful of journeying to the Deep South.

In the late 1950s CORE turned its attention to the Deep South, challenging public segregation and launching voter registration drives for African Americans. It became one of the leading organizations of the civil rights movement in the early 1960s by organizing activist campaigns that tested segregation laws in the South. From this era, the Freedom Rides of 1961 and the Freedom Summer project of 1964 endure as CORE's most memorable contribution to the civil rights struggle. The group's efforts became all the more dramatic when its nonviolent demonstrations were met by vicious responses from whites. CORE volunteers were assaulted, teargassed, and jailed, and some demonstrators were killed. Farmer himself survived a Ku Klux Klan murder plot and once escaped Louisiana state troopers by hiding inside a coffin housed in a hearse. His leadership contributed to the passage of the Civil Rights Act of 1964 and the Voting Rights Act of 1965.

By the beginning of the 21st century, CORE's program emphases included worker training and equal employment opportunity, crime victim assistance, and community-oriented crisis intervention. The organization maintains its headquarters in New York City.

Freedom Rides

Following the example of CORE and FOR's Journey of Reconciliation and responding to the Supreme Court's *Boynton* v. *Virginia* decision of 1960—which extended the court's 1946 ruling on interstate bus travel to include bus terminals, restrooms, and other facilities associated with interstate travel—a group of seven African Americans and six whites left Washington, D.C., on May 4, 1961, on a Freedom Ride in two buses bound for New Orleans, La. Convinced that segregationists in the South would violently protest this exercise of their constitutional right, the Freedom Riders hoped to provoke the federal government into enforcing the Boynton decision. When they stopped along the way, white riders used facilities designated for blacks and vice versa.

The Freedom Riders encountered violence in South Carolina, but in Alabama the reaction was much more severe. On May 14, upon stopping outside of Anniston to change a slashed tire, one bus was firebombed and the Freedom Riders were beaten. Arriving in Birmingham, the second bus was similarly attacked and the passengers beaten. In both cases law enforcement was suspiciously late in responding, and there were suspicions of collusion in that late response. Although the original Riders were unable to find a bus line to carry them farther, a second group of 10, originating in Nashville and partly organized by the Student Nonviolent Coordinating Committee (SNCC), renewed the effort. Undeterred by being arrested in Birmingham and transported back to Tennessee, the new Freedom Riders returned to Birmingham and, at the behest of U.S. Attorney General Robert F. Kennedy, secured a bus and protection from the State Highway Patrol as they traveled to Montgomery, where, when local police failed to protect them, they were again beaten.

Thereafter National Guard support was provided when 27 Freedom Riders continued on to Jackson, Miss., only to be arrested and jailed. On May 29 Kennedy ordered the Interstate Commerce Commission to enforce even stricter guidelines banning segregation in interstate travel. Still, Freedom Riders continued to travel by public transportation in the South until the dictate took effect in September.

Racial Segregation

The institution of racial segregation against which the civil rights struggle was waged in the United States was grounded in the practice of restricting people to certain circumscribed areas of residence or to separate institutions (e.g., schools, churches) and facilities (parks, playgrounds, restaurants, restrooms) on the basis of race or alleged race. Racial segregation provides a means of maintaining the economic advantages and superior social status of the politically dominant group, and in recent times it has been employed primarily by white populations to maintain their ascendancy over other groups by means of legal and social colour bars. Historically, however, various conquerors—among them Asian Mongols, African Bantu, and American Aztecs—have practiced discrimination involving the segregation of subject races.

Racial segregation has appeared in all parts of the world where there are multiracial communities, except where racial amalgamation has occurred on a large scale, as in Hawaii and Brazil. In such countries there has been occasional social discrimination but not legal segregation. In the Southern states of the United States, on the other hand, legal segregation in public facilities was current from the late 19th century into the 1950s. Elsewhere, racial segregation was practiced with the greatest rigour in South Africa, where, under the apartheid system, it was an official government policy from 1950 until the early 1990s.

SIT-IN

The sit-in was employed as a major tactic of nonviolent civil disobedience during the civil rights struggle, in which its first prominent use came at a Greensboro, N.C., lunch counter in 1960. In staging a sit-in, demonstrators enter a business or a public place and remain seated until forcibly evicted or until their grievances are answered. Attempts to terminate the essentially passive sit-in often appear brutal, thus arousing sympathy for the demonstrators among moderates and noninvolved individuals. Following Mahatma Gandhi's teaching, Indians employed the sit-in to great advantage during their struggle for independence from the British. Taking their cue from civil rights demonstrators, American student activists also adopted the tactic later in the 1960s in protests against the Vietnam War.

A tactic similar to the sit-in, the sit-down, has been used by unions to occupy plants of companies that were being struck. The sit-down was first used on a large scale in the United States during the United Automobile Workers' strike against the General Motors Corporation in 1937.

SOUTHERN CHRISTIAN LEADERSHIP CONFERENCE (SCLC)

Established by the Rev. Martin Luther King, Jr., and his followers in 1957 to coordinate and assist local organizations working for the full equality of African Americans in all aspects of American life, the SCLC occupies a prominent place in African American history. The organization operated primarily in the South and some border states, conducting leadership-training programs, citizen-education projects, and voter-registration drives. The SCLC played a major part in the civil rights march on Washington, D.C., in 1963 and in notable antidiscrimination and voter-registration efforts in Albany, Ga., and Birmingham and Selma, Ala., in the early 1960s—campaigns that spurred passage of the federal Civil Rights Act of 1964 and the Voting Rights Act of 1965.

After King was assassinated in April 1968, his place as president was taken by the Rev. Ralph David Abernathy. The SCLC maintained its philosophy of nonviolent social change, but, having lost its founder, it soon ceased to mount giant demonstrations and confined itself to smaller campaigns, predominantly in the South. The organization was further weakened by several schisms, including the departure in 1971 of the Rev. Jesse L. Jackson and his followers who had staffed Operation Breadbasket in

Chicago, which was directed toward economic goals.

The SCLC nonetheless sustained its mission by organizing voter drives and cultivating African American political candidates. It also lobbied for the designation of Martin Luther King, Jr.'s, birthday as a national holiday. The SCLC has published the *SCLC Magazine* since 1971.

STUDENT NONVIOLENT COORDINATING COMMITTEE (SNCC)

Another organization that played a pivotal role in the civil rights movement and freedom struggle was SNCC. Begun as an interracial group advocating nonviolence, SNCC (pronounced "snick") was founded in early 1960 in Raleigh, N.C., to capitalize on the success of a surge of sit-ins in Southern college towns. This form of nonviolent protest brought SNCC to national attention, throwing a harsh public light on white racism in the South. In the years following, SNCC strengthened its efforts in community organization and supported Freedom Rides in 1961, along with the March on Washington in 1963, and agitated for the Civil Rights Act (1964). In 1966 SNCC officially threw its support behind the broader protest of the Vietnam War.

As SNCC became more active politically, its members faced increased violence. In response, the SNCC migrated from a philosophy of nonviolence to one of greater militancy after the mid-1960s, as an advocate of the burgeoning "black power" movement, a facet of late 20th-century black nationalism. The shift was personified by Stokely Carmichael, who replaced John Lewis as SNCC chairman in 1966–67. While many early SNCC members were white, the newfound emphasis on African American identity led to greater racial separatism, which unnerved portions of the white community. More-radical elements of SNCC, such as Carmichael's successor H. Rap Brown, gravitated toward new groups, such as the Black Panther Party. SNCC was disbanded by the early 1970s.

Other notable figures in SNCC included Ella Baker, Julian Bond, Rubye Robinson, and Fannie Lou Hamer.

TUSKEGEE SYPHILIS STUDY

Although it was not a segregationist act in the strictest sense of that term, the highly unethical Tuskegee syphilis study was arguably among the most odious transgressions against African Americans committed in the name of the U.S. government.

Officially named the Tuskegee Study of Untreated Syphilis in the Negro Male American, this medical research project, which was conducted by the U.S. Public Health Service (PHS) from 1932 to 1972, examined the natural course of untreated syphilis in African American men. The research was intended to test whether syphilis caused cardiovascular damage more often than neurological damage and to determine if the natural course of syphilis in black men was significantly different from that in whites. The original study was scheduled to last only six to nine months. In order to recruit participants for its study, the PHS enlisted the support of the prestigious Tuskegee Institute (now Tuskegee University), located in Macon county, Ala. A group of 399 infected patients and 201 uninfected control patients were recruited for the program. The subjects were all impoverished sharecroppers from Macon county. Many of them were the sons and grandsons of slaves. Most had never been seen by a doctor. When announcements were made in churches and in the cotton fields about a way to receive free medical care, the men showed up in droves, unaware of the high price that would be paid over the next four decades.

The subjects were not told that they had syphilis or that the disease could be transmitted through sexual intercourse. Instead, they were told that they suffered from "bad blood," a local term used to refer to a range of ills. Treatment was initially part of the study, and some patients were administered arsenic, bismuth, and mercury. But after the original study failed to produce any useful data, it was decided to follow the subjects until their deaths, and all treatment was halted. In the mid-1940s, when penicillin became the standard cure for syphilis, the Tuskegee subjects were not given the drug. Even as some men went blind and insane from advanced (tertiary) syphilis, the government doctors withheld treatment (in direct violation of government legislation that mandated the treatment of venereal disease), remaining committed to observing their subjects through to the study's predetermined "end point"—autopsy. To ensure that the families would agree to this final procedure, the government offered them burial insurance—at most, $50—to cover the cost of a casket and grave. It is estimated that more than 100 of the subjects died of tertiary syphilis.

The research project was finally stopped after Peter Buxtun, a former venereal disease investigator with the PHS, shared the truth about the study's unethical methods with a reporter from the Associated Press. On July 25, 1972, news accounts sparked a public outcry that ultimately brought the notorious experimentation to an end. Congressional hearings were conducted, which led in 1974 to passage of the National Research Act, requiring institutional review boards to approve all studies involving human subjects. Fred Gray, a civil-rights attorney, filed a class-action lawsuit on behalf of the men that resulted in a $10 million out-of-court settlement for the victims, their families, and their heirs. The study engendered among many African Americans a legacy of deep mistrust that hampered efforts to promote health and prevent disease in this population group. In 1997 Pres. Bill Clinton issued a formal apology for the study.

PRESIDENTIAL APOLOGY FOR THE STUDY AT TUSKEGEE

On May 16, 1997, in the East Room of the White House, Pres. Bill Clinton issued a formal apology for the Tuskegee Study of Untreated Syphilis in the Negro Male, the "longest nontherapeutic experiment on human beings" in the history of medicine and public health. During the White House ceremony, the president directed his words to Carter Howard, Frederick Moss, Charlie Pollard, Herman Shaw, Fred Simmons, Sam Doner, Ernest Hendon, and George Key, the study's sole survivors, all of whom were more than 85 years of age and the first five of whom were present for the occasion:

[They] are a living link to a time not so very long ago that many Americans would prefer not to remember but we dare not forget. It was a time when our nation failed to live up to its ideals, when our nation broke the trust . . . that is the very foundation of our democracy. The United States government did something that was wrong, deeply, profoundly, morally wrong. To the survivors, to the wives and family members, the children and the grandchildren, I say what you know: No power on Earth can give you back the lives lost, the pain suffered, the years of internal torment and anguish. What was done cannot be undone. But we can end the silence. We can stop turning our heads away. We can look at you in the eye and finally say on behalf of the American people, what the United States government did was shameful, and I am sorry.

The president placed the burden of responsibility for the abuse on the medical research establishment when he stated, "The people who ran the study at Tuskegee diminished the stature of man by abandoning the most basic ethical precepts. They forgot their pledge to heal and repair." The government, Clinton announced, was providing a $200,000 grant to help establish a center for bioethics in research and health care at Tuskegee University as part of a lasting "memorial" to the study's victims. Shaw, age 94 at the time of the apology, expressed gratitude to Clinton "for doing your best to right this wrong tragedy and to resolve that Americans should never again allow such an event to occur."

SWANN V. CHARLOTTE-MECKLENBURG BOARD OF EDUCATION

Despite the Supreme Court's ruling in 1954 in *Brown* v. *Board of Education of Topeka* that racial segregation in public schools was unconstitutional, many schools remained as segregated in the late 1960s as they were at the time of the *Brown* decision—largely because of racially segregated housing patterns and resistance by local leaders. In Charlotte, N.C., for example, in the mid-1960s less than 5 percent of African American children attended integrated schools. Indeed, busing was used by white officials to maintain segregation.

The NAACP, on behalf of Vera and Darius Swann, the parents of a six-year-old child, sued the Charlotte-Mecklenburg school district to allow their son to attend Seversville Elementary School, the school closest to their home and then one of Charlotte's few integrated schools. James McMillan, the federal district judge in the case, ruled in favour of the Swanns and oversaw the implementation of a busing strategy that integrated the district's schools. McMillan's decision was appealed to the U.S. Supreme Court, which, on April 20, 1971, in its decision in the *Swann* v. *Charlotte-Mecklenburg Board of Education* case unanimously upheld the constitutionality of busing programs that aimed to speed up the racial integration of public schools in the United States. The busing strategy was adopted elsewhere in the United States and played an instrumental role in integrating U.S. public schools.

In later decades, court-ordered busing plans were criticized not only by whites but also by African Americans, who often charged that busing harmed African American students by requiring them to endure long commutes to and from school. Busing continued in most major cities until the late 1990s.

VOTING RIGHTS ACT

Enacted on Aug. 6, 1965, the Voting Rights Act aimed to overcome legal barriers at the state and local levels that prevented African Americans from exercising their right to vote under the Fifteenth Amendment (1870) to the Constitution of the United States. The act significantly widened the franchise and is considered among the most far-reaching pieces of civil rights legislation in U.S. history.

Shortly following the American Civil War, the Fifteenth Amendment was ratified, guaranteeing that the right to vote would not be denied "on account of race, color, or previous condition of servitude." Soon afterward the U.S. Congress enacted legislation that made it a federal crime to interfere with an individual's right to vote and that otherwise protected the rights promised to former slaves under both the Fourteenth (1868) and Fifteenth amendments. In some states of the former Confederacy, African Americans became a majority or near majority of the eligible voting population, and African American candidates ran and were elected to office at all levels of government.

Nevertheless, there was strong opposition to the extension of the franchise to African Americans. Following the end of Reconstruction in 1877, the Supreme Court of the United States limited voting protections under federal legislation, and intimidation and fraud were employed by white leaders to reduce voter registration and turnout among African Americans. As whites came to dominate state legislatures once again, legislation was used to strictly circumscribe the right of African Americans to vote. Poll taxes, literacy tests, grandfather clauses, whites-only primaries, and other measures disproportionately disqualified African Americans from voting. The result was that by the early 20th century nearly all African Americans were disfranchised. In the first half of the 20th century, several such measures were declared unconstitutional by the U.S. Supreme Court. In 1915, for example, grandfather clauses were invalidated, and in 1944 whites-only primaries were struck down. Nevertheless, by the early 1960s voter registration rates among African Americans were negligible in much of the Deep South and well below those of whites elsewhere.

In the 1950s and early '60s the U.S. Congress enacted laws to protect the right of African Americans to vote, but such legislation was only partially successful. In 1964 the Civil Rights Act was passed and the Twenty-fourth Amendment, abolishing poll taxes for voting for federal offices, was ratified, and the following year Pres. Lyndon B. Johnson called for the implementation of comprehensive federal legislation to protect voting rights. The resulting act, the Voting Rights Act, suspended literacy tests, provided for federal oversight of voter registration in areas that had previously used tests to determine voter eligibility (these areas were covered under Section 5 of the legislation),

and directed the attorney general of the United States to challenge the use of poll taxes for state and local elections. An expansion of the law in the 1970s also protected voting rights for non-English-speaking U.S. citizens. Section 5 was extended for 5 years in 1970, 7 years in 1975, and 25 years in both 1982 and 2006.

The Voting Rights Act resulted in a marked decrease in the voter registration disparity between whites and blacks. In the mid-1960s, for example, the overall proportion of white to black registration in the South ranged from about 2 to 1 to 3 to 1 (and about 10 to 1 in Mississippi); by the late 1980s racial variations in voter registration had largely disappeared. As the number of African American voters increased, so did the number of African American elected officials. In the mid-1960s there were about 70 African American elected officials in the South, but by the turn of the 21st century there were some 5,000, and the number of African American members of the U.S. Congress had increased from 6 to about 40. In what was widely perceived to be a test case, *Northwest Austin Municipal Utility District Number One* v. *Holder, et al.* (2009), the Supreme Court declined to rule on the constitutionality of the federal-oversight provision of the Voting Rights Act.

CHAPTER 3

AFRICAN AMERICAN LITERATURE SINCE WORLD WAR II

It can be difficult to draw a clear distinction between African American literature before World War II and postwar African American literature. A number of the writers who were the crucial voices of the late 1930s and early 1940s were still making important contributions in the late 1940s, the 1950s, and beyond. This consideration of postwar literature begins in earnest in the 1950s.

JAMES BALDWIN

In 1953 Baldwin's first novel, *Go Tell It on the Mountain*, testified anew to the sophisticated formal experimentation and piercing examination of African American consciousness of which the writers coming of age in the 1950s were capable. The story of religious conversion experienced by 14-year-old John Grimes of Harlem, *Go Tell It on the Mountain* places in creative tension its hero's spiritual awakening and his determination to gain his independence from his oppressive stepfather. The result is a novel of unprecedented honesty in its revelation of generational and gender conflicts between its central characters, who constitute an African American family haunted by self-hatred, guilt, the psychological scars of racism, unsanctioned sexual desire, and a hunger for deliverance. Two years after *Go Tell It on the Mountain*, Baldwin

James Baldwin, arriving back at Kennedy International Airport, New York City, following a European tour with his play The Amen Corner, *Nov. 9, 1965.* Hulton Archive/Getty Images

collected his essays in *Notes of a Native Son*, a mix of autobiography and political commentary on race in America that identified Baldwin as the new conscience of the nation on racial matters. Subsequent volumes of essays, *Nobody Knows My Name* (1961) and *The Fire Next Time* (1963), underlined Baldwin's fame as the most incisive and passionate essayist ever produced by black America. His novels of the 1950s and '60s—particularly *Giovanni's Room* (1956), the first African American novel to treat homosexuality openly, and *Another Country* (1962), a best-seller that examined bisexuality, interracial sex, and the many prejudices that enforced hierarchies of difference in American society—confirmed Baldwin's leadership among those black American writers at mid century who wanted to move fiction toward a renewed search for personal meaning and redemption while challenging the white American consensus that viewed triumph in World War II as a vindication of the American way on the racial home front.

AFRICAN AMERICAN THEATRE

During the decade following World War II, professional African American dramatists—such as William Blackwell Branch, author of *In Splendid Error* (produced 1954); Alice Childress, creator of the Obie Award–winning *Trouble in Mind* (produced 1955); and Loften Mitchell, best known for *A Land Beyond the River* (produced 1957)—found greater access to the white American theatre than any previous generation of black playwrights had known. Baldwin began a dramatic career in 1955 with *The Amen Corner*, which focuses on a female preacher in a Harlem storefront church. Hughes continued his stage presence with his musical comedy *Simply Heavenly* in 1957.

But no one in African American theatre could have predicted the huge critical and popular success that came to Chicagoan Lorraine Hansberry after her first play, *A Raisin in the Sun*, opened at the Ethel Barrymore Theatre on Broadway in March 1959. A searching portrayal of

EBONY

Ebony, *the first black-oriented magazine in the United States to attain national circulation, was founded in 1945 by John H. Johnson of Chicago, whose first publishing venture was the pocket-size* Negro Digest *(1942). Johnson envisioned* Ebony *as a news and photo magazine patterned much after* Life *magazine but specifically designed for African American readers.* Ebony *was immediately successful. It initially highlighted African American entertainers and sports figures but has since shifted its editorial focus to include black achievement of all sorts. By the beginning of the 21st century, its circulation had reached about 1.8 million. The circulation of* Jet, *another Johnson magazine with an emphasis on news as well as entertainment, was about 900,000.*

an African American family confronting the problems of upward mobility and integration, *A Raisin in the Sun* introduced not only the most brilliant playwright yet produced by black America but also an extraordinarily talented cast of African (or Bahamian, in the case of Sidney Poitier) American actors, including Poitier, Ruby Dee, and Lou Gossett, Jr., and the play's director, Lloyd Richards, the first black director of a Broadway show in more than 50 years. Hansberry's play was awarded the New York Drama Critics' Circle Award in 1959; she was the first African American writer to win this prestigious award. Hansberry completed another play, *The Sign in Sidney Brustein's Window* (produced 1964), and several screenplays, including the film version of *A Raisin in the Sun* (1961), before her death at age 34.

ALICE CHILDRESS

Another of black theatre's important voices was playwright and novelist Alice Childress, who is remembered for realistic stories that posited the enduring optimism of African Americans. Childress grew up in Harlem, where she acted with the American Negro Theatre in the 1940s. There she wrote, directed, and starred in her first play, *Florence* (produced 1949), about a black woman

LORRAINE HANSBERRY

Playwright Lorraine Hansberry, whose A Raisin in the Sun *(1959) was the first drama by an African American woman to be produced on Broadway, was interested in writing from an early age and while in high school was drawn especially to the theatre. She attended the University of Wisconsin in 1948–50 and then briefly the school of the Art Institute of Chicago and Roosevelt University (Chicago). After moving to New York City, she held various minor jobs and studied at the New School for Social Research while refining her writing skills. In 1958 she raised funds to produce her play* A Raisin in the Sun, *which opened in March 1959 at the Ethel Barrymore Theatre on Broadway, meeting with great success.*

A penetrating psychological study of the personalities and emotional conflicts within a working-class black family in Chicago, A Raisin in the Sun *was directed by actor Lloyd Richards, the first African American to direct a play on Broadway since 1907. It won the New York Drama Critics' Circle Award, and the film version of 1961 received a special award at the Cannes Festival. Hansberry's next play,* The Sign in Sidney Brustein's Window, *a drama of political questioning and affirmation set in New York's Greenwich Village, where she had long made her home, had only a modest run on Broadway in 1964. Her promising career was cut short by her early death.*

In 1969 a selection of her writings, adapted by Robert Nemiroff (to whom Hansberry was married from 1953 to 1964), was produced on Broadway as To Be Young, Gifted, and Black *and was published in book form in 1970.*

who, after meeting an insensitive white actress in a railway station, comes to respect her daughter's attempts to pursue an acting career. *Trouble in Mind* (produced 1955; revised and published 1971), *Wedding Band* (produced 1966), *String* (produced 1969), and *Wine in the Wilderness* (produced 1969) all examine racial and social issues. Among Childress's plays that feature music are *Just a Little Simple* (produced 1950; based on Langston Hughes's *Simple Speaks His Mind*), *Gold Through the Trees* (produced 1952), *The African Garden* (produced 1971), *Gullah* (produced 1984; based on her 1977 play *Sea Island Song*), and *Moms* (produced 1987; about the life of comedienne Jackie "Moms" Mabley).

Childress was also a successful writer of children's literature. *A Hero Ain't Nothin' but a Sandwich* (1973; film 1978) is a novel for adolescents about a teenage drug addict. Similarly, the novel *Rainbow Jordan* (1981) concerns the struggles of poor black urban youth. Also written for juveniles were the plays *When the Rattlesnake Sounds* (1975) and *Let's Hear It for the Queen* (1976). Her other novels include *A Short Walk* (1979), *Many Closets* (1987), and *Those Other People* (1989).

THE LITERATURE OF CIVIL RIGHTS

Declaring that "all art is ultimately social," Hansberry was one of several African American writers—most prominently Baldwin and Alice Walker—to take an active part in the civil rights movement and to be energized, imaginatively and socially, by the freedom struggles of the late 1950s and the '60s. The murder of Emmett Till, a black teenager visiting Mississippi in 1955, led Gwendolyn Brooks to compose *The Last Quatrain of the Ballad of Emmett Till*. Poets Margaret Esse Danner and Naomi Long Madgett began their careers publishing similar socially relevant work in the 1950s.

GWENDOLYN BROOKS

Brooks had graduated from Wilson Junior College in Chicago in 1936, and her early verses had appeared in the *Chicago Defender*, a newspaper written primarily for that city's African American community. Her first published collection, *A Street in Bronzeville* (1945), reveals her talent for making the ordinary life of her neighbours extraordinary. *Annie Allen* (1949), for which she won the Pulitzer Prize, is a loosely connected series of poems related to an African American girl's growing up in Chicago. The same theme was used for Brooks's novel, *Maud Martha* (1953).

Containing some of her best work, *The Bean Eaters* (1960) delivers the explicitly socially critical verse best embodied by *The Last Quatrain of the Ballad of Emmett Till*. Her *Selected Poems* (1963) was followed in 1968 by *In the Mecca*, half of which is a long narrative poem about people in the Mecca, a vast, fortresslike apartment building erected on the South Side of Chicago in

1891, which had long since deteriorated into a slum. The second half of the book contains individual poems, among which the most noteworthy are "Boy Breaking Glass" and "Malcolm X." Brooks also wrote a book for children, *Bronzeville Boys and Girls* (1956). She continued to write important poetry collections until her death in 2000.

AMIRI BARAKA

The development of an increasingly black-identified poetry in the 1960s, written deliberately to inspire black pride and to inflame black revolution, is epitomized in the evolution of LeRoi Jones into Amiri Baraka. Based in New York's East Village, Jones became known first as a Beat poet whose collection *Preface to a Twenty Volume Suicide Note* (1961) consisted largely of apolitical critiques of 1950s conventionality and materialism. By 1968, however, Jones had renamed himself Amiri Baraka and resettled in Harlem, where he became the fiery literary voice of a new black self-consciousness and social consciousness declaiming its freedom in original, sometimes shocking verse previewed in his *The Dead Lecturer* (1964, first published under the name of LeRoi Jones). In the same year, Baraka's play *Dutchman*, which climaxes in the death of an incipient black revolutionary poet at the hands of a white woman on a subway, won the 1964 Obie Award for the best off-Broadway production of the year. *Dutchman*'s polarized audience, including whites offended by

Amiri Baraka. Hulton Archive/Getty Images

the murderous and manipulative female lead in the play, foreshadowed the effect that most African American writers who sought to emulate Baraka had when the Black Arts movement, which Baraka advocated, came into full flower in the late 1960s.

THE BLACK ARTS MOVEMENT

The assassination of Malcolm X, eloquent exponent of black nationalism, in 1965 in New York and the espousal of "black power" by previously integrationist civil rights organizations such as SNCC and

CORE helped to galvanize a generation of young black writers into rethinking the purpose of African American art. Rejecting any notion of the artist that separated him or her from the African American community, the Black Arts movement (also called the Black Aesthetic movement) engaged in cultural nation building by sponsoring poetry readings, founding community theatres, creating literary magazines, and setting up small presses. In 1968 poetry, fiction, essays, and drama from writers associated with the movement appeared in the landmark anthology *Black Fire*, edited by Baraka and Larry Neal. One of the most versatile leaders of the Black Arts movement, Neal summed up its goals as the promotion of self-determination, solidarity, and nationhood among African Americans.

To Black Arts writers, literature was frankly a means of exhortation, and poetry was the most immediate way to model and articulate the new Black consciousness the movement sought to foster. Baraka's *Black Magic* (1969) and *It's Nation Time* (1970) typify the stylistic emphases of the poetry of this movement, particularly its preference for street slang, the rhythm of blues, jazz, and gospel music, and a deliberately provocative confrontational rhetoric. Important poets in this mode were Sonia Sanchez, Jayne Cortez, Etheridge Knight, Haki R. Madhubuti, Carolyn M. Rodgers, and Nikki Giovanni.

Sonia Sanchez lost her mother as an infant, and her father moved the family from Alabama to Harlem when she was nine. After graduating from Hunter College in 1955 with a degree in political science, she briefly studied writing at New York University. In the 1960s Sanchez was introduced to the political activism of the times and published poetry in such journals as *The Liberator, Journal of Black Poetry, Black Dialogue,* and *Negro Digest.* Her first book, *Homecoming* (1969), contains considerable invective against "white America" and "white violence"; thereafter she continued to write on what she called the "neoslavery" of blacks, as socially and psychologically unfree beings. She also wrote about sexism, child abuse, and generational and class conflicts. A good deal of Sanchez's verse is written in American black speech patterns, eschewing formal English grammar and pronunciations.

Unfulfilled love, unromantic sex, and jazz greats from ex-husband Ornette Coleman to Bessie Smith are subjects of *Pissstained Stairs and the Monkey Man's Wares* (1969), the first collection of poems by Jayne Cortez, who is noted for performing her own poetry, often accompanied by jazz. With the poems of *Festivals and Funerals* (1971), she turned to larger social issues, including the place of the artist in revolutionary politics. In *Scarifications* (1973) she examined aspects of the Vietnam War and wrote with a newfound romanticism about a journey to Africa. The frequent cruelty of Cortez's images and their startling juxtapositions often yield surrealistic effects. These elements and the rhythmic cadences of her lines enhance the impact of her poetry readings, as her recordings show, beginning with *Celebrations and Solitudes* (1975).

Etheridge Knight's poetry combined the energy and bravado of African American "toasts" (long narrative poems that were recited in a mixture of street slang, specialized argot, and obscenities) with a concern for freedom from oppression. After dropping out of high school, becoming addicted to drugs, and serving in the Army during the Korean War, Knight was convicted of robbery in 1960 and imprisoned for eight years—an experience that he recounted in verse in *Poems from Prison* (1968) and in prose in the anthology *Black Voices from Prison* (1970; originally published two years earlier in Italian as *Voce negre dal carcere*). Following his release from prison, Knight taught and worked as an editor. He experimented with rhythmic forms of punctuation in *Belly Song and Other Poems* (1973), which addressed the themes of ancestry, racism, and love. In *Born of a Woman* (1980)—a work that balances personal suffering with affirmation—he introduced the concept of the poet as a "meddler" who forms a trinity with the poem and the reader.

The poetry of teacher and publisher Haki R. Madhubuti (born Don Luther Lee), which began to appear in the 1960s, was written in black dialect and slang. His work is characterized both by anger at social and economic injustice and by rejoicing in African American culture. His first six volumes of poetry were published in the 1960s. The verse collection *Don't Cry, Scream* (1969) includes an introduction by poet Gwendolyn Brooks. Lee's poetry readings were extremely popular during this time. Lee founded the Third World Press in 1967, and he established the Institute of Positive Education in Chicago, a school for black children, in 1969.

Among the leading Black Arts playwrights, Baraka was joined by Ed Bullins, whose naturalistic plays concentrated on the gritty existence of urban African Americans, incorporating elements of black nationalism, "street" lyricism, and interracial tension. A high-school dropout who served in the Navy (1952–55) before resuming his studies at a variety of colleges (ultimately earning both undergraduate and graduate degrees later in life), Bullins made his theatrical debut in August 1965 with the production of three one-act plays: *How Do You Do?*; *Dialect Determinism, or The Rally*; and *Clara's Ole Man*. After helping to found a black cultural organization and briefly associating with the Black Panther Party, Bullins moved to New York City. His first full-length play, *In the Wine Time* (produced 1968), examines the scarcity of options available to the black urban poor. It was the first in a series of plays—called the Twentieth-Century Cycle—that centred on a group of young friends growing up in the 1950s. Other plays in the cycle are *The Corner* (produced 1968), *In New England Winter* (produced 1969), *The Duplex* (produced 1970), *The Fabulous Miss Marie* (produced 1971), *Home Boy* (produced 1976), and *Daddy* (produced 1977). In 1975 he received critical acclaim for *The Taking of Miss Janie,* a play about the failed alliance of an interracial group of political idealists in the 1960s.

Although fiction was not as important to the Black Arts movement as were poetry and drama, the novels of John A. Williams—particularly *The Man Who Cried I Am* (1967), a roman à clef about a dying black novelist intent on maintaining his political integrity in the face of government persecution—and the mythopoeic short stories of Henry Dumas communicate the spirit of the new Black Arts ideals. The vulnerability of black children amid the Southern white lynch-mob mentality, a young sharecropper encountering a civil-rights worker, and whites experiencing the mystical force of black music are among the subjects Dumas examined in his stories, many of which were collected in *Ark of Bones, and Other Stories* (1970) and *Rope of Wind* (1979). The "tell it like it is" temper of the 1960s spurred an unprecedented candour about race and placed a premium on authentic self-expression in African American autobiography. *The Autobiography of Malcolm X* (1965), a collaboration between Malcolm X and journalist-author Alex Haley, provided a standard that Anne Moody's *Coming of Age in Mississippi* (1968), George Jackson's *Soledad Brother* (1970), and Angela Davis's *Angela Davis: An Autobiography* (1974) sought to emulate. Leading theorists of the Black Arts movement included Houston A. Baker, Jr.;

Henry Louis Gates, Jr.; Addison Gayle, Jr., editor of the anthology *The Black Aesthetic* (1971); and Hoyt W. Fuller, editor of the journal *Negro Digest* (which became *Black World* in 1970).

RECONCEPTUALIZING BLACKNESS

Not all African American writers in the 1960s and early '70s subscribed to the new credo of blackness, however. While Gwendolyn Brooks switched publishers, from New York's Harper & Row to Detroit's Broadside Press, out of sympathy to the new movement, Robert Hayden was repelled by what he called "the chauvinistic and the doctrinaire." Ishmael Reed, who reserved the right to lampoon any attempts to impose artistic orthodoxy on African American writing, embarked on his iconoclastic career with a series of parodic novels, *The Free-Lance Pallbearers* (1967), *Yellow Back Radio Broke-Down* (1969), *Mumbo Jumbo* (1972), and *The Last Days of Louisiana Red* (1974), the latter one taking aim at black cultural nationalism.

Another 1960s writer more postmodernist than nationalist, Adrienne Kennedy made her avant-garde theatre debut with stunningly innovative, nightmarish one-act plays, most notably *Funnyhouse of a Negro* (produced 1962) and *The Owl Answers* (produced 1963), which featured surrealist spectacles of black women caught between African and European heritages. Offering no political solutions to her female characters' tormented

ISHMAEL REED

Ishmael Reed grew up in Buffalo, N.Y., and studied at the University of Buffalo. He moved to New York City, where he cofounded the East Village Other *(1965), an underground newspaper that achieved a national reputation. Also that year he organized the American Festival of Negro Art. His first novel,* The Free-Lance Pallbearers, *was published in 1967. The next year he began an intermittent teaching career at the University of California at Berkeley, where he made his home.*

Reed's novels are marked by surrealism, satire, and political and racial commentary. They depict human history as a cycle of battles between oppressed people and their oppressors; the characters and actions are an antic mixture of inverted stereotypes, revisionist history, and prophecy. In Pallbearers *Bukka Doopeyduk launches a rebellion in the miserable nation of Harry Sam, ruled by the despotic Harry Sam. A black circus cowboy with cloven hooves, the Loop Garoo Kid, is the hero of the violent* Yellow Back Radio Broke-Down *(1969).* Mumbo Jumbo *(1972) pits proponents of rationalism and militarism against believers in the magical and intuitive.* The Last Days of Louisiana Red *(1974) is a fantastic novel set amid the racial violence of Berkeley, Calif., in the 1960s.* Flight to Canada *(1976) depicts an American Civil War-era slave escaping to freedom via bus and airplane.*

Reed's later novels are The Terrible Twos *(1982), its sequel* The Terrible Threes *(1989), and* Japanese By Spring *(1993). He also wrote several volumes of poetry and collections of essays.*

struggles for unity and purpose, Kennedy dramatized the potent psychological and social symbolic value of black American women's emotions and personal lives. Less openly resistant to the strictures of the Black Arts aesthetic but no less dedicated to faithful and nuanced presentations of a wide range of African American experience, Ernest J. Gaines and James Alan McPherson also broke into print during the 1960s, demonstrating a mastery of the short story that yielded for Gaines the much-applauded stories in *Bloodline* (1968) and for McPherson the equally celebrated collection *Hue and Cry* (1968). Gaines went on to create in *The Autobiography of Miss Jane Pittman* (1971) one of the most famous female characters in African American fiction, whose first-person narrative testifies to the dauntless progress of the black folk whom she represents from bondage to the civil rights era. Jane Pittman joined Vyry Ware, the indomitable heroine of Margaret Walker's historical novel *Jubilee* (1966), in liberating black American women of the South from the stereotypes that had bound them to the "mammy" image while also serving notice to the male- and urban-oriented Black Arts movement that the voices and traditions of black women, Southern black culture, and the rural past offered much to the reconceptualizing of blackness that the 1960s and '70s had undertaken.

RENAISSANCE IN THE 1970S

A variety of literary, cultural, and political developments during the 1950s and '60s, including the heightened visibility of Hansberry, Kennedy, Walker, and Brooks, the expanding presence of black women's experience and expressive traditions in African American writing, and the impact of the women's movement on African American women's consciousness, fostered what has been termed the black women's literary renaissance of the 1970s.

Toni Morrison

Although this outpouring of creative energy by African American women, especially in fiction, had a long foreground, its founding text is generally considered *The Bluest Eye* (1970) by Toni Morrison. Born in Lorain, Ohio, and educated at Howard University and Cornell University, Morrison, a senior editor at Random House when she started her literary career, focused her first novel on the destructive effect of white ideals of beauty, symbolized by blue eyes, on a lonely black girl's attempt to find a positive sense of identity in a loveless family and a community prone to scapegoating. *The Bluest Eye*'s implicit endorsement of the "Black is beautiful" slogan of the 1970s made it topical, but its attention to the psychology of oppression affecting a poor, small-town black girl diverged from the norm of the Black Arts movement, which featured male protagonists in conflict with the larger white society. By 1974 *The Bluest Eye* was out of print, but in the previous year Morrison had brought out *Sula*, original for its portrayal of female friendship as the essential relationship in an African American novel and for its creation of the amoral, adventurous, and self-sanctioned Sula Peace, whose radical individualism Morrison traces with nonjudgmental detachment. More popular than *The Bluest Eye*, *Sula* whetted the appetite of Morrison's growing audience for her third major work of the 1970s, *Song of Solomon* (1977), the first African American novel since *Native Son* to be a Book-of-the-Month Club main selection. *Song of Solomon* blends African American folklore, history, and literary tradition to celebrate the moral and spiritual revival of Macon Dead, the first male protagonist in a Morrison novel, via the guidance and example of his aunt Pilate, another of Morrison's unconventional, soul-liberating heroines.

By the end of the decade, Morrison was the leading African American writer of the 1970s, an inspiration to a generation of younger novelists, especially Toni Cade Bambara and Gloria Naylor. Bambara's fiction, which is set in the rural South as well as the urban North, is written in black street dialect and presents sharply drawn characters whom she portrayed with affection. Bambara published the short-story collections *Gorilla, My Love* (1972) and *The Sea Birds*

Toni Morrison. Archive Photos/Getty Images

Are Still Alive (1977), as well as the novels *The Salt Eaters* (1980), which won an American Book Award, and *If Blessing Comes* (1987). Naylor's first novel, *The Women of Brewster Place* (1982), won her instant recognition for its powerful dramatization of the struggles of seven women living in a blighted urban neighbourhood. Using interconnecting stories to portray each woman's life, Naylor skillfully explored the diversity of the black female experience. The 1989 television dramatization of the novel starred Oprah Winfrey, Robin Givens, and Cicely Tyson.

EBONICS

Formerly known as Black English vernacular (BEV) and sometimes referred to as African American Vernacular English (AAVE), Ebonics is a dialect of American English spoken by a large proportion of African Americans. Many scholars hold that Ebonics, like several English creoles, developed from contacts between nonstandard varieties of colonial English and African languages. Its exact origins continue to be debated, however, as do the relative influences of the languages involved. Ebonics is not as extensively modified as most English creoles, and it remains in several ways similar to current nonstandard dialects spoken by white Americans, especially American Southern English. It has therefore been identified by some creolists as a semi-creole (a term that remains controversial).

Ebonics is a vernacular form of American English used in the home or for day-to-day communication rather than for formal occasions. It typically diverges most from standard American English when spoken by people with low levels of education. It should not be confused with language varieties spoken by such specialized subgroups as urban youth, in which one will come across words and phrases not typically used in the basic vernacular.

The structural similarities between Ebonics and American Southern English (e.g., double negatives, as in "I ain seen none"; relative clauses starting with what, as in "everything what he told you"; and double modals, as in "he might could help you") are attributable to their parallel development on the cotton plantations of the southeastern United States from the diverse varieties of English brought to the colonies by the original settlers. The emergence of Ebonics as a separate dialect may be correlated with the emergence of African American traditions in music, religious practices, and cooking styles, all of which developed separately from the practices of white American communities—although these other areas show less-inhibited influence from African cultures in ways that have still not been adequately explained. The influence of African languages on the structure of Ebonics has been rather elusive, limited to some features—such as copula omission, lack of subject-verb agreement, and absence of subject-auxiliary inversion in main clauses—that this dialect shares with Caribbean English creoles and Gullah. The origins of these peculiarities probably should not be located exclusively in black African languages.

Among the most commonly discussed features of Ebonics are: (1) omission of the copula be in such sentences as "Larry sick," "Sharon gon come," and "Glenn playin," (2) consonant cluster simplification, so that, for example, the pronunciation of passed or past is often indistinguishable from that of pass, *(3) double negatives, as in "She don wan nothin," (4) lack of subject-verb agreement, as in "He do," (5) absence of subject-auxiliary inversion in direct questions, such as "Why you don't like me?" and "Where he is?," (6) subject-auxiliary inversion in subordinate clauses, such as "He aks me did I do it?," (7) omission of the auxiliary* do *in questions such as "What you want?" (a feature germane to the absence of subject-auxiliary inversion and typologically related to the absence of the copula as a semantically empty verb), (8) consuetudinal or invariant* be, *such as "Billy don't be telling lies" (different in meaning from "Billy don't tell lies," because it refers to repeated processes rather than to a repeated activity), and (9) the use of* steady *to indicate persistence, in constructions such as "She steady talking" to mean "She persists in talking." Most of these features are not unique to Ebonics; they are shared, at lower frequencies, by other nonstandard varieties of English. They are said to be variable because they do not occur categorically; they alternate with their standard counterparts (when applicable), and they occur in frequencies that vary from one speaker to another—and sometimes within the same speaker, from one setting to another. Aside from the ethnic identity of its speakers, Ebonics is perhaps most distinctive in its intonation and some stress patterns, which it still shares with white American Southern English in such instances as the stress in the word* police *falling on the first rather than the second syllable.*

ALICE WALKER

Morrison was not the only black woman to exert a major influence on African American literature in the 1970s and '80s. Alice Walker punctuated the decade with a series of controversial books: *The Third Life of Grange Copeland* (1970), an epic novel that tracks three generations of a black Southern family through internal strife and a struggle to rise from sharecropping; *Revolutionary Petunias and Other Poems* (1973), a collection of poems that urges its reader to "[b]e nobody's darling; / Be an outcast"; and *Meridian* (1976), a novelistic redefinition of African American motherhood. In 1982 Walker's most famous novel, *The Color Purple*, an epistolary novel that depicted rape, incest, bisexuality, and lesbian love among African Americans,

won the Pulitzer Prize and the National Book Award. The successes of Morrison and Walker helped foster a climate for artistic explorations of race, gender, and class in a wide range of literary forms, such as the novels of Paule Marshall (who was previously published but not accepted as a major writer until the appearance of *Praisesong for the Widow* [1983]), Octavia E. Butler (a writer of science fiction novels, a genre generally considered to be the province of white males), Gayl Jones, and Jamaica Kincaid; the poetry of Audre Lorde, June Jordan, and Rita Dove; and the drama of Ntozake Shange. The remarkable sustained popularity of Maya Angelou's autobiography, *I Know Why the Caged Bird Sings* (1970), one of the most widely read and taught books by an African American woman, demonstrates the

Alice Walker. Harcourt Brace/Hulton Archive/Getty Images

lasting appeal to white as well as black American readers of much contemporary African American women's writing, especially when it is informed by the upbeat, woman-affirming outlook typified by Angelou's prose and poetry.

THE TURN OF THE 21ST CENTURY

Although women's writing claimed centre stage in the eyes of many critics and a large number of readers of African American literature from the 1970s to the end of the 20th century, African American male writers continued to receive important recognition for their work during this time. Seven years after Dove received the 1987 Pulitzer Prize for poetry for *Thomas and Beulah* (1986), her tribute to her maternal grandparents, Yusef Komunyakaa won the same prize for *Neon Vernacular* (1993), a collage of new and collected poems from seven previous volumes, ranging from *Dien Cai Dau* (1988), based on Komunyakaa's service in Vietnam, to *Magic City* (1992), a tense and lyrical evocation of the poet's boyhood in Bogalusa, La. When Butler, the first important African American woman science fiction writer, won that genre's prestigious Hugo and Nebula awards

JAMAICA KINCAID

Elaine Potter Richardson settled in New York City when she left her native Antigua at age 16, first working as an au pair in Manhattan. She later won a photography scholarship in New Hampshire but returned to New York within two years. In 1973 she took the name Jamaica Kincaid (partly because she wished the anonymity for her writing), and the following year she began regularly submitting articles to The New Yorker *magazine, where she became a staff writer in 1976. Kincaid's writings for the magazine often chronicled Caribbean culture. Her essays and stories were subsequently published in other magazines as well.*

In 1983 Kincaid's first book, At the Bottom of the River, *a collection of short stories and reflections, was published. Setting a pattern for her later work, it mixed lyricism and anger.* Annie John *(1984) and* Lucy *(1990) were novels but were autobiographical in nature, as were most of Kincaid's subsequent works, with an emphasis on mother-daughter relationships. A* Small Place *(1988), a three-part essay, continued her depiction of Antigua and her rage at its despoliation. Kincaid's treatment of the themes of family relationships, personhood, and the taint of colonialism reached a fierce pitch in* The Autobiography of My Mother *(1996) and* My Brother *(1997), an account of the death from AIDS of Kincaid's younger brother Devon Drew. Her "Talk of the Town" columns for* The New Yorker *were collected in* Talk Stories *(2001), and in 2005 she published* Among Flowers: A Walk in the Himalaya, *an account of a plant-collecting trip she took in the foothills of the Himalayas.*

for her 1984 short story *Bloodchild,* she retraced the path opened by Samuel R. Delany, who garnered Nebulas for *Babel-17* (1966) and *The Einstein Intersection* (1967) and a Hugo for the autobiographical *The Motion of Light in Water* (1988). The voices of novelist John Wideman (who twice won the PEN/Faulkner Award given by the international writers' organization Poets, Playwrights, Editors, Essayists, and Novelists [PEN]) and his incarcerated brother Robby in *Brothers and Keepers* (1984), one of the most innovative African American autobiographies of the late 20th century, previewed the success that awaited later women's collaborative first-person texts, such as the 1988 American Book Award winner *Tight Spaces* by Kesho Scott, Cherry Muhanji, and Egyirba High and the best-selling *Having Our Say* (1993) by centenarian sisters Sarah L. Delany and A. Elizabeth Delany.

In the last decades of the 20th century, African American drama soared into the highest echelon of American theatre, as Charles Gordone won the first Pulitzer Prize for an African American play with his depiction of a black hustler-poet in *No Place to Be Somebody* (produced 1969), Joseph A. Walker earned a prestigious Tony Award (presented by two American theatre organizations) for the best play of 1973 for the smash Broadway hit *The River Niger* (produced 1972), and Charles H. Fuller, Jr., claimed a Pulitzer Prize and the New York Drama Critics' Circle Award for *A Soldier's Play* (produced 1981), a tragedy set in a segregated military base in Louisiana. In the 1980s and '90s, George Wolfe won substantial acclaim both as a playwright, whose *The Colored Museum* (produced 1986) lampooned stereotypes and myths of black culture, and as the director of *Angels in America*, a Tony Award–winning drama by white playwright Tony Kushner.

AUGUST WILSON

The most accomplished of all African American dramatists in the last half of the 20th century, August Wilson created a remarkable cycle of plays that was designed to treat African American life in every decade of the century; the cycle included the Pulitzer Prize–winning *Fences* (1986) and *The Piano Lesson* (1990). Music, particularly jazz and

JOHN EDGAR WIDEMAN

Until the age of 10, John Edgar Wideman lived in Homewood, a black section of Pittsburgh, Pa., which later became the setting of many of his novels. An outstanding scholar and athlete at the University of Pennsylvania (B.A., 1963), he became the second black American to receive a Rhodes scholarship to the University of Oxford (B.Ph., 1966).

Wideman joined the faculty of the University of Pennsylvania in 1966, and the following year he published his first novel, A Glance Away, *about a day in the lives of a reformed drug addict and a homosexual English professor. His second novel,* Hurry Home *(1970), is the story of an intellectual alienated from his black ancestry and the black community. After serving as director of the university's Afro-American studies program from 1971 to 1973, Wideman published* The Lynchers *(1973), his first novel to focus on interracial issues.*

Wideman left Pennsylvania to become a professor at the University of Wyoming (1975–85). The so-called Homewood Trilogy, an historical exploration of family and community, comprised two novels, Hiding Place *(1981) and* Sent for You Yesterday *(1983), and a collection of short stories,* Damballah *(1981). In* Brothers and Keepers *(1984), his first nonfiction book, he contemplated the role of the black intellectual by studying his relationship with his brother, who was serving a life sentence in prison.*

Wideman joined the faculty at the University of Massachusetts in 1985. He was the first author to twice receive the PEN/Faulkner Award for Fiction, for the novels Sent for You Yesterday *and* Philadelphia Fire *(1990). He also wrote the short-story collections* Fever *(1989) and* The Stories of John Edgar Wideman *(1992), the nonfiction book* Fatheralong: A Meditation on Fathers and Sons, Race and Society *(1994), and the novel* The Cattle Killing *(1996).*

blues, is a recurrent theme in Wilson's works, and its cadence is echoed in the lyrical, vernacular nature of his dialogue. Wilson's early years were spent in the Hill District of Pittsburgh, a poor but lively neighbourhood that became the setting for most of his plays. Primarily self-educated, he quit school at age 15 after being accused of plagiarizing a paper. He later joined the Black Arts movement in the late 1960s, became the cofounder and director of Black Horizons Theatre in Pittsburgh (1968), and published poetry in such journals as *Black World* (1971) and *Black Lines* (1972).

In 1978 Wilson moved to St. Paul, Minn., and in the early 1980s he wrote several plays, including *Jitney* (first produced 1982). Focused on cab drivers in the 1970s, it underwent subsequent revisions as part of his historical cycle. His first major play, *Ma Rainey's Black Bottom*, opened on Broadway in 1984 and was a critical and financial success. Set in Chicago in 1927, the play centres on a verbally abusive blues singer, her fellow black musicians, and their white manager. *Fences*, first produced in 1985, is about a conflict between a father and son in the 1950s; it received a Tony Award for best play.

Wilson's chronicle of the black American experience continued with *Joe Turner's Come and Gone* (1988), a play about the lives of residents of a Pittsburgh boardinghouse in 1911 and a displaced Southern black man's quest for his wife; *The Piano Lesson*, in which

August Wilson. Brad Barket/Getty Images

competing ideas about their legacy threatens to rupture an African American family in the 1930s; and *Two Trains Running* (1992), whose action takes place in a coffeehouse in the 1960s and which provides a look at the black power ideals of that decade from the perspective of two decades removed. *Seven Guitars* (1996), the seventh play of the cycle, is set among a group of friends who reunite in 1948 following the death of a local blues guitarist. *King Hedley II* (produced 1999), an account of an ex-con's efforts to rebuild his life in the 1980s, and *Gem of the Ocean* (produced 2003), which takes place in 1904 and centres on Aunt Ester, a 287-year-old spiritual healer mentioned in previous plays, and a man who seeks her help. Wilson completed the cycle with *Radio Golf* (first produced 2005). Set in the 1990s, the play concerns the fate of Aunt Ester's house, which is slated to be torn down by real-estate developers.

African American Roots

The reclamation of African American history has propelled an unusual number of black novelists into an imaginative tour of the past, producing a new literary genre that many have called the neo-slave narrative. Building on historical novels such as *Jubilee* and *The Autobiography of Miss Jane Pittman*, African American fiction of the last quarter of the 20th century reopened the scars of slavery in search of keys to the meaning of freedom in the post-civil rights era. Alex Haley's *Roots* (1976), a fictionalized family history of seven generations traced back to Africa, took the United States by storm when, as a 1977 television miniseries, it attracted the largest audience yet for a feature film about black Americans. Subsequent novels returned to the slavery era to retrieve lost or suppressed heroes and heroines, as in Sherley Anne Williams's *Dessa Rose* (1986), or to effect healing and self-awareness in contemporary African Americans, exemplified by David Bradley's historian protagonist in *The Chaneysville Incident* (1981). Revisionist satire spurred Alice Randall to create *The Wind Done Gone* (2001), a parody of the 20th century's most extensively read historical novel, Margaret Mitchell's *Gone with the Wind* (1936).

Experiments with retelling the slave narrative in forms that would liberate its significance to today's African American struggle began with Ishmael Reed's exuberant *Flight to Canada* (1976) and extended into the metafiction of philosophical novelist Charles R. Johnson. In *Oxherding Tale* (1982), Johnson sends his biracial fugitive slave protagonist on a quest for emancipation that he can attain only by extricating himself, in Johnson's own words, from "numerous kinds of 'bondage' (physical, psychological, sexual, metaphysical)." Like the sophisticated, self-conscious trickster who narrates *Oxherding Tale*, the hero of Johnson's second novel, *Middle Passage*, which won the National Book Award in 1990, is also a product of slavery who must go on a dangerous journey—the infamous Middle Passage that brought Africans to enslavement in the Americas—to overcome his alienation from humanity and save himself from imprisoning ideas about self and race. The triumph of Rutherford Calhoun, the protagonist of *Middle Passage*, comes when he absorbs the enlightened moral and philosophical understanding of the Allmuseri, an African tribe of sorcerers who teach Calhoun to reject the materialism of the enslavers and adopt a holism free from the categories of self and other, on which exploitative hierarchies (such as race) are based. The most celebrated and distinguished of the neo-slave narratives, however, is Morrison's fifth novel, *Beloved* (1987), rivaled only by Ellison's *Invisible Man* as the most influential African American novel of the second half of the 20th century. A reinvocation of the Margaret Garner case of 1856, in which an escaped slave mother killed her infant daughter rather than allowing slave catchers to return her to slavery in Kentucky, *Beloved* won the Pulitzer Prize for fiction in 1988. Four years later, Morrison published *Jazz*, a novel of murder and reconciliation set in Harlem during the 1920s, and *Playing in the Dark*, a trenchant examination of whiteness as a thematic obsession in American literature. In 1993 Morrison became the first African American to be awarded the Nobel Prize for Literature. Her later works include *Paradise* (1998), which traces the fate of an all-black town in 1970s Oklahoma, and, with her son Slade, a children's book, *The Big Box* (1999).

In accepting the Nobel Prize, Morrison stated: "Word-work is sublime ... because it is generative; it makes meaning that secures our difference, our human difference—the way in which we are like no other life." Although Morrison was ostensibly speaking here of humanity's difference from the rest of creation, in light of the achievement of her African American literary predecessors from Wheatley forward, Morrison may well have been alluding also to the "word-work" of black America, which has generated through its literature the restoration of black racial "difference" from a sign of supposed absence or lack to a symbol of artistic mastery.

CHAPTER 4

JAZZ

Developed by African Americans and influenced by both European harmonic structure and African rhythms, jazz evolved partially from ragtime and blues and is often characterized by syncopated (offbeat) rhythms, polyphonic ensemble playing, varying degrees of improvisation, often deliberate deviations of pitch, and the use of original timbres.

Any attempt to arrive at a precise, all-encompassing definition of jazz is probably futile. Jazz has been, from its very beginnings at the turn of the 20th century, a constantly evolving, expanding, changing music, passing through several distinctive phases of development; a definition that might apply to one phase—for instance, to New Orleans style or swing—becomes inappropriate when applied to another segment of its history, say, to free jazz. Early attempts to define jazz as a music whose chief characteristic was improvisation, for example, turned out to be too restrictive and largely untrue, since composition, arrangement, and ensemble have also been essential components of jazz for most of its history. Similarly, syncopation and swing, often considered essential and unique to jazz, are in fact lacking in much authentic jazz, whether of the 1920s or of later decades. Again, the long-held notion that swing could not occur without syncopation was roundly disproved when trumpeter Louis Armstrong (among others) frequently generated enormous swing while playing repeated, unsyncopated quarter notes.

Jazz, in fact, is not—and never has been—an entirely composed, predetermined music, nor is it an entirely extemporized one. For almost all of its history it has employed both creative approaches in varying degrees and endless permutations. And yet, despite these diverse terminological confusions, jazz seems to be instantly recognized and distinguished as something separate from all other forms of musical expression. To repeat Armstrong's famous reply when asked what *swing* meant: "If you have to ask, you'll never know." To add to the confusion, there often have been seemingly unbridgeable perceptual differences between the producers of jazz (performers, composers, and arrangers) and its audiences. For example, with the arrival of free jazz and other latter-day, avant-garde manifestations, many senior musicians maintained that music that didn't swing was not jazz.

Classical composers such as Aaron Copland, John Alden Carpenter, and Igor Stravinsky were drawn to jazz by its instrumental sounds and timbres, the unusual effects and inflections of jazz playing (brass mutes, glissandos, scoops, bends, and stringless ensembles), and its syncopations, completely ignoring, or at least underappreciating, the extemporized aspects of jazz. Indeed, the sounds that jazz musicians make on their instruments—the way they attack,

inflect, release, embellish, and colour notes—characterize jazz playing to such an extent that if a classical piece were played by jazz musicians in their idiomatic phrasings, it would in all likelihood be called jazz.

Nonetheless, one important aspect of jazz clearly does distinguish it from other traditional musical areas, especially from classical music: the jazz performer is primarily or wholly a creative, improvising composer—his own composer, as it were—whereas in classical music the performer typically expresses and interprets someone else's composition.

Jazz has been dominated by the contributions of African Americans, but the list of white musicians who have played important roles in its development is long and includes Paul Whiteman, Benny Goodman, Gene Krupa, Bix Beiderbecke, Artie Shaw, Woody Herman, Gerrry Mulligan, Lennie Tristano, Django Reinhardt, Gil Evans, Bill Evans, Chet Baker, Dave Brubeck, and Keith Jarrett, among others. The following survey, however, has as its focus the African American musicians who have collectively made jazz one of the world's most complex and engaging art forms.

FIELD HOLLERS AND FUNERAL PROCESSIONS: FORMING THE MATRIX

Jazz, as it finally evolved as a distinct musical style and language, comprised what Max Harrison calls, in the *New*

Grove Dictionary of Music and Musicians, a "composite matrix" made up of a host of diverse vernacular elements that happened to come together at different times and in different regions. This matrix included the field hollers of the cotton plantations; the work songs on the railroads, rivers, and levees; hymns and spirituals; music for brass bands, funeral processions, and parades; popular dance music; the long-standing banjo performing tradition (starting in the 1840s), which culminated half a century later in the banjo's enormous popularity; wisps of European opera, theatre, and concert music; and, of course, the blues and ragtime. These last two forms began to flourish in the late 19th century—blues more as an informal music purveyed mostly by itinerant singers, guitarists, and pianists and ragtime becoming (by 1900) America's popular entertainment and dance music.

Ragtime evolved in the playing of honky-tonk pianists along the Mississippi and Missouri rivers in the last decades of the 19th century. It was influenced by minstrel-show songs, African American banjo styles, and syncopated dance rhythms of the cakewalk, and also elements of European music. Ragtime found its characteristic expression in formally structured piano compositions. The regularly accented left-hand beat, in $\frac{4}{4}$ or $\frac{2}{4}$ time, was opposed in the right hand by a fast, bouncingly syncopated melody that gave the music its powerful forward impetus.

Ragtime differs substantially from jazz in that it was (1) a through-composed, fully notated music intended to be played in more or less the same manner each time, much like classical music, and (2) a music written initially and essentially for the piano. Jazz, by contrast, became a primarily instrumental music, often not notated, and partially or wholly improvised. Ragtime had its own march-derived, four-part form, divided into successive 16-bar sections, whereas jazz, once weaned away from ragtime form, turned to either the 12-bar (or occasionally 8-bar) blues or the 32-bar song forms. What the two music genres had in common was their syncopated (thus "irregular") melodies and themes, placed over a constant "regular" $\frac{2}{4}$ or $\frac{4}{4}$ accompaniment.

The years from 1905 to 1915 were a time of tremendous upheaval for black musicians. Even the many musicians who had been trained in classical music but had found—as blacks—no employment in that field were now forced to turn to ragtime, which they could at least play in honky-tonks, bordellos, and clubs; many of these musicians eventually drifted into jazz. Hundreds of other musicians, unable to read and write music, nonetheless had great ability to learn it by ear, as well as superior musical talent. Picking up ragtime and dance music by ear (perhaps not precisely), they began almost out of necessity to embellish these syncopated tunes—loosening them up, as it

CAKEWALK

The cakewalk, as performed by African American dancers at the Pan-American Exposition, Buffalo, N.Y., 1901. Hulton Archive/Getty Images

The couples dance known as the cakewalk became a popular stage act for virtuoso dancers as well as a craze in fashionable ballrooms around 1900. Couples formed a square with the men on the inside and, stepping high to a lively tune, strutted around the square. Pairs were eliminated one by one by several judges, who considered the elegant bearing of the men, the grace of the women, and the inventiveness of the dancers; the last remaining pair was presented with a highly decorated cake.

The cakewalk originated earlier among slaves who, often in the presence of their masters, used the dance as a subtle satire on the elegance of white ballroom dances. It contributed to the evolution of subsequent American and European dances based on jazz rhythms, and its music influenced the growth of ragtime.

were—until ornamentation spilled over quite naturally into simple improvisation. This process took on a significantly increased momentum once the piano rags of such master composers as Scott Joplin, Joseph Lamb, and James Scott appeared in arrangements performed regularly by bands and orchestras. Joplin, called the King of Ragtime, published the most successful of the early rags, "The Maple Leaf Rag," in 1899.

Joplin, who considered ragtime a permanent and serious branch of classical music, composed hundreds of short pieces, a set of études, and operas in the style. Other important performers were, in St. Louis, Louis Chauvin and Thomas M. Turpin (father of St. Louis ragtime) and, in New Orleans, Tony Jackson.

That the pianist-composer Jelly Roll Morton was a braggart who claimed to be "the inventor of jazz" should not obscure

SCOTT JOPLIN

Studying piano with teachers near his childhood home in Texas, Scott Joplin traveled through the Midwest from the mid-1880s, performing at the Columbian Exposition in Chicago in 1893. Settling in Sedalia, Mo., in 1895, he studied music at the George R. Smith College for Negroes and hoped for a career as a concert pianist and classical composer. His first published songs brought him fame, and in 1900 he moved to St. Louis to work more closely with the music publisher John Stark.

Joplin published his first extended work, a ballet suite using the rhythmic devices of ragtime, with his own choreographical directions, in 1902. His first opera, A Guest of Honor (1903), is no longer extant and may have been lost by the copyright office. Moving to New York City in 1907, Joplin wrote an instruction book, The School of Ragtime, outlining his complex bass patterns, sporadic syncopation, stop-time breaks, and harmonic ideas, which

Scott Joplin. MPI/ Hulton Archive/Getty Images

were widely imitated. Joplin's contract with Stark ended in 1909, and, though he made piano rolls in his final years, most of Joplin's efforts involved Treemonisha, which synthesized his musical ideas into a conventional, three-act opera. He also wrote the libretto, about a mythical black leader, and choreographed it. Treemonisha had only one semipublic performance during Joplin's lifetime; he became obsessed with its success, suffered a nervous breakdown and collapse in 1911, and was institutionalized in 1916.

Joplin's reputation as a composer rests on his classic rags for piano, including Maple Leaf Rag and The Entertainer, published from 1899 through 1909, and his opera, Treemonisha, published at his own expense in 1911. Treemonisha was well received when produced by an Atlanta, Ga., troupe on Broadway in 1972, and interest in Joplin and ragtime was stimulated in the 1970s by the use of his music in the Academy Award–winning score to the film The Sting.

his major role in the development of that music. As early as 1902 Morton played ragtime piano in the vaunted bordellos of Storyville, New Orleans's famous red-light district, where prostitution was effectively legal from 1897 to 1917. (The district was unofficially named for Alderman Sidney Story, who responded to public protests against rampant prostitution in New Orleans by having the City Council adopt an ordinance in January 1897 limiting brothels, saloons, and other businesses of vice to a prescribed area, which came to include everything from cheap 25-cent brothels to extremely elegant establishments on North Basin Street.) Later, Morton began working as an itinerant musician, crisscrossing the South several times and eventually working his way to Los Angeles, where he was based for several years. As the first major composer of jazz, Morton seems to have assimilated (like a master chef making a great New Orleans bouillabaisse) most of the above-mentioned matrix, particularly blues and ragtime, into a single new, distinct, coherent musical style. Others, such as soprano saxophonist Sidney Bechet, trombonist Kid Ory, and

SIDNEY BECHET

Sidney Bechet began as a clarinetist at the age of six and by 1914 was a veteran who had worked in several semilegendary local bands, including those of Jack Carey and Buddy Petit. After working in New Orleans with Clarence Williams and King Oliver, pioneer jazz greats, he moved to Chicago and then, in 1919, to New York City. In that year he toured Europe with the Southern Syncopated Orchestra, becoming the first jazz musician ever to be praised by a distinguished classicist, the Swiss conductor Ernest Ansermet. Through the 1920s he gradually concentrated on the soprano saxophone, working briefly with his great admirer Duke Ellington in 1925 before touring Europe again. Intermittently, he worked in the Noble Sissle band (1928–38) and from the late 1940s based himself in Paris, where by the time of his death he had attained the kind of eminence granted to such world-famed Parisians as singer and actor Maurice Chevalier and poet, playwright, and film director Jean Cocteau.

Along with trumpeter Louis Armstrong, Bechet was one of the first musicians to improvise with jazz-swing feeling. He intelligently crafted logical lines atop the New Orleans-style ensemble, double-timing and improvising forcefully and with authority. Bechet produced a large, warm tone with a wide and rapid vibrato. It was his mastery of drama and his use of critically timed deviations in pitch ("note bending") that had the greatest long-lasting influence, because they were absorbed by his disciple Johnny Hodges, Duke Ellington's principal soloist from 1928 to 1970. With a style developed around Bechet's expressive techniques, Hodges became one of the two or three most influential alto saxophonists in the first half of the century.

cornetists Bunk Johnson and Freddie Keppard—four of the most gifted early jazz musicians—arrived at similar conclusions before 1920.

Bunk Johnson and others regarded themselves as ragtime musicians. In truth, in the cases of many musicians of that generation who grew up with ragtime, the listener would be hard put to determine when their playing turned from embellished rags to improvisatory jazz. Musicians confirmed the tenuousness and variety of these early developments in statements such as that of reedman Buster Bailey (speaking of the years before 1920): "I . . . was embellishing around the melody. At that time [1917–18] I wouldn't have known what they meant by improvisation. But embellishment was a phrase I understood." And reedman Garvin Bushell said, "We didn't call the music jazz when I was growing up [in Springfield, Ohio] . . . Ragtime piano was the major influence in that section of the country . . . The change to jazz began around 1912 to 1915."

RAGTIME INTO JAZZ: THE BIRTH OF JAZZ IN NEW ORLEANS

In spite of the wide dissemination and geographic distribution of these diverse musical traditions, New Orleans was where a distinctive, coherent jazz style evolved. Between 1910 and 1915 a systematization of instrumental functions within an essentially collective ensemble took shape, as did a regularization of the repertory. Despite the fact that a limited set of instruments was available to black musicians (at that time, typically, cornet, clarinet, trombone, tuba or bass, piano, banjo, and drums—the saxophone did not become common in jazz for about another decade), they arrived at a brilliant solution emphasizing independent but harmonically linked and simultaneous lines. Each of the seven instruments was assigned a clearly defined individual role in the established polyphonic collective ensemble. Thus, the cornet was responsible for stating and occasionally embellishing the thematic material—the tune—in the middle range, the clarinet performed obbligato or descant functions in a high register, the trombone offered contrapuntal asides in the tenor or baritone range, and the four rhythm instruments provided a unified harmonic foundation.

That this formation, which emphasized independent but harmonically linked simultaneous lines, was not only a brilliant solution but a necessity is confirmed by the inability in those early years of most players to read music. It was not long before musicians began to expand upon these materials and to improvise fresh new melodies and obbligatos of their own making. However, these explorations remained within the collective ensemble concept of New Orleans jazz. Few musicians before 1925 could have created independent, extended, improvised

NEW ORLEANS STYLE

Developed near the turn of the century, New Orleans–style jazz was not recorded first in New Orleans but rather in Chicago, Los Angeles, and Richmond, Ind. Divided by many experts into white (the Original Dixieland Jazz Band and the New Orleans Rhythm Kings, which first recorded in 1917 and 1922, respectively) and black (cornetist Joe "King" Oliver's Creole Jazz Band and Kid Ory's Spike's Seven Pods of Pepper Orchestra, which first recorded in 1923 and 1922, respectively) incarnations, it is traditionally said to have placed great emphasis on collective improvisation, all musicians simultaneously playing mutual embellishments. This was the case in the first recordings, but a portion was also given to solos and accompaniment in which a single instrument, such as cornet, occupied the foreground while others, such as clarinet and trombone, played obbligato with combinations of guitar and/or banjo and/or piano chording insistently on almost every beat. Many journalists use the term New Orleans style to designate those black musicians who performed in Chicago between 1915 and the early 1930s after having left their native New Orleans. Aside from Oliver and Ory, the strongest of these players were trumpeter Louis Armstrong, clarinetist–soprano saxophonist Sidney Bechet, clarinetist Jimmie Noone, drummer Warren "Baby" Dodds, and his brother, clarinetist Johnny Dodds. Armstrong and Bechet, in particular, helped to move the emphasis away from ensemble improvisation to a focus on solo improvisation, anticipating the later Dixieland style.

Revivals of the pre-1920s style included one with trumpeter Bunk Johnson, who was rediscovered by two jazz historians in 1939 and who reactivated his career in the 1940s; and another at Preservation Hall, an organization in New Orleans that into the 1990s presented improvised combo music by men who had lived in New Orleans during the music's formative period and that continued that tradition with a new generation of musicians.

solos. And when the solo as an integral element of a jazz performance arrived, the New Orleans format of a tightly integrated ensemble improvisation went out of fashion.

By approximately 1915 New Orleans had produced a host of remarkable musicians, mostly cornet and clarinet players, such as the legendary Buddy Bolden (legendary in part because he never recorded), Buddy Petit, Keppard, Johnson, and Bechet. Most New Orleans musicians, including scores of pianists, found steady employment in the entertainment palaces of Storyville, where, incidentally, the term *jazz*, initially spelled "jass," was the commonly used slang word for sexual intercourse. It is ironic that the first jazz recordings were made in New York City on Jan. 30, 1917, by a second-rate group of white musicians from New Orleans called the Original Dixieland Jazz Band, which present a misleading picture of true New Orleans jazz.

JAMES REESE EUROPE

James Reese Europe studied piano and violin in his youth and in about 1904 settled in New York City, where he directed musical comedies and, in 1910, helped organize the Clef Club, a union of African American musicians. The 125-member Clef Club orchestra that he conducted at Carnegie Hall featured an extraordinary instrumentation, including 47 mandolins and bandores and 27 harp-guitars.

Europe's Society Orchestra was probably the first African American band to record, as early as 1913, when it offered fast versions of ragtime works, typically in $^2/_4$ metre, with urgent rhythmic momentum. His band also regularly accompanied the popular white dance team of Irene and Vernon Castle, who popularized the fox-trot and a dance in $^5/_4$ metre, to scores by Europe and his collaborator, Ford Dabney.

During World War I Europe led the all-black 369th Infantry band, which toured France; it was noted for its syncopations and expressive colours. The band was nicknamed the "Hell Fighters" and was making a triumphal postwar tour of the United States when Europe was killed by one of his musicians.

VARIATIONS ON A THEME: JAZZ ELSEWHERE IN THE UNITED STATES

New Orleans was not the only place where jazz was being developed. Depending on how narrowly jazz is defined, some early form of it was practiced in places as far-flung as Los Angeles, Kansas City, Mo., Denver, and the Colorado mining towns—not to mention Baltimore, Md., and New York City. The two last-mentioned cities were major centres of ragtime, early pre-stride piano, vaudeville entertainment, large-sized dance orchestras, and musical theatre, including theatre created exclusively by black performers. Several other at least embryonic jazz groups and musicians were active in New York during 1913–19, such as James Reese Europe

and his various orchestras, Earl Fuller's Jass Band, Ford Dabney's band, and the pianists James P. Johnson, Abba Labba, and Willie "the Lion" Smith.

The closing of Storyville in 1917 was a disaster for New Orleans musicians, many of whom went on to play in Mississippi riverboat orchestras; Fate Marable's orchestra was the best and most famous of these and included, at times, the young Louis Armstrong. Others headed directly north to Chicago, which rapidly became the jazz capital of the United States. King Oliver, the much-heralded cornet champion of New Orleans, migrated to Chicago in 1918, and in 1922 he sent for his most talented disciple, Armstrong, to join his Creole Jazz Band as second cornetist. The two made history and astounded audiences with their slyly worked out duet breaks, and Armstrong had a chance to cut his musical teeth by freely improvising melodic counterpoint to Oliver's lead cornet. More important still, Oliver's band was able to forge a remarkably unified and disciplined style, integrating at a very high level the players' collective and individual instrumental skills, all couched in an irresistible, wonderfully stately, rolling momentum.

THE CORNETIST BREAKS AWAY: LOUIS ARMSTRONG AND THE INVENTION OF SWING

In late 1924 Armstrong was wooed away by Fletcher Henderson to New York City. In his year there Armstrong matured into a major soloist and at the same time developed—indeed, single-handedly invented—a compelling, propulsive, rhythmic inflection in his playing that came to be called swing. Early examples of this feeling can be heard in Henderson band recordings and even more clearly on Armstrong's Hot Five and Hot Seven recordings of 1926–27—e.g., "Potato Head Blues," "Big Butter and Egg Man," "S.O.L. Blues," "Hotter than That," and "Muggles." In effect, Armstrong taught the whole Henderson band, including the redoubtable tenor saxophonist Coleman Hawkins, how to swing.

More than that, Armstrong taught the whole world about swing and had a profound effect on the development of jazz that continues to be felt and heard. In that sense alone he can be considered the most influential jazz musician of all time. Beyond his artistic and technical prowess, Armstrong should be remembered as the first superstar of jazz. By the late 1920s, famous on recordings and in theatres, he more than anyone else carried the message of jazz throughout America; eventually, as entertainer supreme and jazz ambassador at large, he introduced jazz to the whole world. In this crusade Armstrong's unique singing style, in essence a vocalization of his improvisatory trumpet playing, played a crucial role. By often singing without words or texts, he popularized what came to be called scat, a universally comprehensible art form that needed no translation.

ARMSTRONG'S INFLUENCE

After Armstrong's spectacular breakthrough recordings, such as "West End Blues" (1928), he embarked on a solo career for 10 years, fronting bands whose general mediocrity made him sound by comparison even more brilliant. In the 1940s he formed the Armstrong All-Stars, a group of older New Orleans-style musicians. Although by then well past his prime, Armstrong, through his physical vitality and uncompromisingly high musical standards, was able to preserve his art almost to the end of his life in 1971.

That Armstrong's playing, both technically and conceptually, was many levels above that of most of his contemporaries can be heard on virtually every recording

SCAT

Scat, the jazz vocal style using emotive, onomatopoeic, and nonsense syllables instead of words in solo improvisations on a melody, was popularized by Louis Armstrong beginning in about 1927, but it also has dim antecedents in the West African practice of assigning fixed syllables to percussion patterns. The popular theory that scat singing began when a vocalist forgot the lyrics may be true, but this origin does not explain the persistence of the style. Earlier, as an accompanist to singers, notably the blues singer Bessie Smith, Armstrong played riffs that took on vocalization qualities. His scat reversed the process. Later scat singers fitted their styles, all individualized, to the music of their times. Ella Fitzgerald phrased her scat with the fluidity of a saxophone. Earlier, Cab Calloway became known as the "Hi-De-Ho" man for his wordless choruses. Sarah Vaughan's improvisations included bebop harmonic advances of the 1940s. By the mid-1960s Betty Carter was exploiting extremes of range and flexibility of time similar to those of saxophonist John Coltrane.

Louis Armstrong, 1953. New York World-Telegram and the Sun Newspaper Photograph Collection/Library of Congress, Washington, D.C. (Digital File Number: cph 3c27236)

he made between 1925 and 1940, whether he was paired with other soloists or with orchestras. He exerted a wide-ranging influence on all manner of players—not only trumpeters but trombonists, saxophonists, singers (such as Billie Holiday), and even pianists (such as Earl Hines and Teddy Wilson).

EARL HINES

Earl Hines was born into a musical family in Pittsburgh. As a child he learned trumpet from his father and then piano from his mother; his sister was also a pianist who led bands in the 1930s. After playing in trios during his high school years, Hines played in various bands throughout the Midwest. In 1925–26 he toured with Carroll Dickerson's orchestra. When Louis Armstrong took over Dickerson's band in 1927, Hines stayed on as pianist and musical director. He participated in several groundbreaking recording sessions at about this time, including several as a member of Armstrong's seminal quintet, the Hot Five, and others with clarinetist Jimmie Noone.

The Armstrong-Hines recordings (1927–29), which include the important "West End Blues," "Muggles," "Skip the Gutter," and their "Weather Bird" duet, are jazz classics. On these sides, Hines demonstrates a virtuosic piano technique that was far more advanced than that of his contemporaries. He developed a "trumpet style" of improvisation in which he eschewed the structured block-chord technique of stride pianists and played single-note solo lines, often with great speed, in the manner of a horn player. He overcame the piano's inherent background role in a band setting by playing with a forceful touch (sometimes breaking piano strings) and using octave voicing in his melody lines. His touch, plus his frequent use of tremolo (i.e., rapid alternation of notes), caused the piano to sound almost brassy. Hines's style set the standard for generations of jazz pianists, and even such comparatively modern players as Bud Powell and Oscar Peterson showed signs of his influence.

In the late 1920s Hines formed his own big band, noted for ensemble unity and hard-driving rhythm. From 1928 through the 1930s, this was the house band at Chicago's Grand Terrace Ballroom; regular radio broadcasts brought the music to millions of fans. In the early 1940s Hines formed a new West Coast band that included such bop pioneers as Charlie Parker and Dizzy Gillespie, as well as singers Sarah Vaughan and Billy Eckstine. Few recordings of this group survive because the musicians' union was on strike against the major record companies from 1942 to 1944. The band broke apart in 1947.

Hines resumed his partnership with Louis Armstrong in 1948 and played in Armstrong's small group, the All Stars, until 1951. He next formed a sextet that became a fixture at San Francisco's Hangover Club during the mid-1950s. Hines had a major career resurgence during the early 1960s, with concert performances and recordings (such as the albums Spontaneous Explorations *and* Legendary Little Theatre Concert, *both 1964) leading to renewed critical and popular appreciation. During his years as an elder statesman of jazz, Hines's dazzling technique remained as strong as ever, and his performance at the 1974 Montreux Jazz Festival (released on the album* West Side Story*) revealed his continued openness to new ideas.*

ORCHESTRAL JAZZ

It was in the 1920s that the first forms of true orchestral jazz were developed, most significantly by Fletcher Henderson and Duke Ellington. Although large aggregations had begun to appear in the late teens, these were dance orchestras playing the popular songs and novelty pieces of the day, with nary a smattering of jazz. The credit for being the first to perform and record orchestral jazz must go to Henderson, who, starting in about 1923, gathered together from the small beginnings of quintets and sextets a growing number of notable New York-based players and formed a full orchestra. By the mid- to late 1920s, Henderson could boast a 13- or 14-piece band and had the arranging services of the outstanding alto saxophonist and multi-instrumentalist Don Redman. It was Redman who developed antiphonal call-and-response procedures in orchestral jazz, juxtaposing the two main choirs of brass and reeds in ever more sophisticated and challenging arrangements.

Although he was very much aware of Redman's and Henderson's work, Duke Ellington took a somewhat different approach. From the start more truly a composer than an arranger, Ellington blended thematic material suggested to him by some of his players—in particular trumpeter Bubber Miley and clarinetist Barney Bigard—with his own compositional frameworks and backgrounds (e.g., "East St. Louis Toodle-oo" [1926] and "Black and Tan Fantasy" [1927]). Once ensconced

in Harlem's famous Cotton Club as the resident house band (a tenure that lasted three years, until early 1931), Ellington had the opportunity to explore, in some 160 recordings, several categories of compositions: (1) music for the club's jungle-style production numbers and pantomime tableaus, (2) dance numbers for the chorus line, (3) dance pieces for the club's patrons (all white—blacks were allowed only as entertainers), (4) arrangements of the pop tunes or ballads of the day, and (5) most important, independent nonfunctional instrumental compositions—in effect, miniature tone poems for presentation during the shows. The most celebrated of these was "Mood Indigo" (1930), the first of many pieces with a blueslike character, usually set in slow tempos. In these and in such other song and dance numbers as "Sophisticated Lady" (1932) and "Solitude" (1934), Ellington was able not only to exploit the individual talents of his musicians but to extend and vary the forms of jazz. In addition, he expanded upon his already highly developed feeling for instrumental timbres and colours and his extraordinary forward-looking harmonic sense. In early works such as "Mystery Song" (1931), "Delta Serenade" (1934), and "In a Sentimental Mood" (1935), Ellington experimented with never-before-heard brass sonorities (using mutes peculiar to jazz, including the lowly bathroom plunger) and unusual blendings of brass and reeds, as in his grouping of saxophones and Juan Tizol's light valve trombone sound. Ellington's instinctive genius for harmonic invention, using the outer extensions of basic triadic and dominant seventh chords, led him to use bitonality (two keys at once) or polytonality (several keys) at least a decade before anyone else. Striking examples of this aspect of his work are, to name only a few, "Eerie Moan" (1933), "Reminiscing in Tempo" (1935), "Alabamy Home" (1937), and "Azure" (1937), the last verging on atonality at several points.

All these Ellington innovations, nuanced and fulfilled as they were by the extraordinary cast of characters and individual soloists in his orchestra, served to create a more personal expression and emotional depth than had previously been achieved in jazz. The heterogeneity of personalities and talents in Ellington's orchestra virtually guaranteed that even the least of their efforts would be superior to the best of most other orchestras of the time. Motored by a remarkably cohesive rhythm section, each instrumental choir boasted dramatically different, individualistic personalities (e.g., Arthur Whetsol and Cootie Williams on trumpet; Rex Stewart on cornet; Lawrence Brown, Joe "Tricky Sam" Nanton, and Juan Tizol on trombone; and Johnny Hodges, Barney Bigard, Otto Hardwick, and Harry Carney on reeds) who nevertheless whenever needed would blend instantly into perfect ensembles.

As remarkable as Ellington's innovations were, they had relatively little impact on the field in general. In the racially still-very-divided world of the 1930s, not only were white bands such as the Casa Loma and Benny Goodman orchestras much more popular than the great black orchestras of Ellington, Jimmie Lunceford, Chick Webb, and Bennie Moten, but Ellington's music in particular was considered formally and harmonically too challenging and at the same time too subtle for the tastes of the average 1930s swing fan. Ellington's big, worldwide success with the public did not come until the 1960s, when he and his orchestra made lengthy annual tours all over the world, had some hugely popular successes with "Satin

JOHNNY HODGES

Renowned for the beauty of his tone and his mastery of ballads, Johnny Hodges was among the most influential sax players in the history of jazz. Initially Hodges was a self-taught musician, playing drums and piano before taking up the soprano saxophone at age 14. He then received instruction from Sidney Bechet, who was perhaps Hodges's only major influence. Hodges worked in Boston and New York during the mid-1920s, playing in bands led by Lloyd Scott, Chick Webb, Bobby Sawyer, Luckey Roberts, and Bechet. He joined Duke Ellington's orchestra in 1928 and was the band's most-featured soloist for the next four decades.

Hodges played lead alto in Ellington's sax section; his melody lines were an important component in the band's palette of sounds. He was featured on countless Ellington recordings, demonstrating his skill at ballads ("Warm Valley," "Passion Flower," "In a Sentimental Mood") and up-tempo numbers ("Things Ain't What They Used to Be," "The Jeep Is Jumpin'"). He projected sensuous elegance through a commanding sound and perfected the use of portamento (or "smearing" in jazz vernacular), in which the instrument glides from note to note in the manner of a slide trombone. His basic style did not change throughout the years, but his considerable technique and harmonic sense ensured that his solos always sounded fresh and contemporary.

Hodges was so closely associated with Ellington that jazz fans were taken by surprise when he left the band in 1951 to form his own combo. Other Ellington veterans such as Lawrence Brown and Sonny Greer, as well as the young John Coltrane, played in Hodges's band. They had one hit recording, Castle Rock, but lasting success proved elusive, and they disbanded in 1955. Hodges rejoined the Ellington orchestra and remained with Ellington until his death, although he continued to engage in side projects and lead occasional recording sessions under his own name.

Hodges's influence was so pervasive in American jazz that subsequent generations of saxophone players, even those who never heard him play, have emulated his style. He was a true original, about whom Ellington once said: "Johnny Hodges has complete independence of expression. He says what he wants to say on the horn, . . . in his language, from his perspective."

Duke Ellington (left) and Johnny Hodges confer during a Columbia Records recording session, Oct. 15, 1957. Sony BMG Music Entertainment/Getty Images

Doll" (1953) and other compositions, and began to consistently receive accolades—including a Presidential Medal of Freedom and the French Legion of Honour—from the broader musical, artistic, and intellectual community.

Two other musical groups led by African Americans met with outstanding success in the 1920s: Jelly Roll Morton's Red Hot Peppers and William McKinney's Cotton Pickers. The 17 sides Morton and his Red Hot Peppers recorded for RCA Victor in 1926–27 are among the finest classics of early jazz. Blending late ragtime with the rapidly burgeoning improvisational advances of the time, Morton gathered a group of veterans of New Orleans–style jazz, then in their prime. By avoiding a random succession of solos—indeed, by careful structural planning that astutely distributed the seven players' efforts over the three-minute limit allowed by a 10-inch 78-rpm disc—and by painstakingly rehearsing the group before the recording sessions, Morton achieved an almost perfect balance of ensemble and solo. Miraculously, the improvisations and compositions enhanced each other; thus, solos were integrated into arrangements in a way that remained uncommon in jazz for decades thereafter. Morton recorded both multithematic ragtime pieces (including "Black Bottom Stomp" and "Grandpa's Spells"), each piece with several strains in different chord progressions, and mono-thematic 12- and 32-bar pieces featuring a single passacaglialike repetitive harmonic

sequence (such as "Smokehouse Blues," "Jungle Blues," and "Dead Man Blues"). These recordings had nothing to do with the typical dance music of the period. Moreover, by balancing compositional unity with a maximum of textural and timbral variety—to an extent that was remarkable in a three-minute miniature form, with only a small band—and by reconciling composition and improvisation as well as polyphonic and homophonic ensembles in one fell swoop, Morton pointed a way toward the future of jazz. Alas, in the quasi-commercial and career-driven world of the late 1920s and 1930s, his comprehensive lesson was learned by only a handful of musicians. But Morton's example may have influenced Ellington, who for reasons never made clear considered Morton his musical archenemy.

Both Ellington and Henderson considered McKinney's Cotton Pickers, a Detroit-based band, their only serious rival. The distinctiveness of the Cotton Pickers' work during the band's heyday is attributable primarily to the remarkable leadership and the composing and arranging talents of John Nesbitt, whose work was mistakenly credited to Redman for many decades. Nesbitt was obviously aware and respectful of Ellington's fast-tempo "stomp" pieces. And like Morton, Nesbitt was intent on utilizing his 10- or 11-piece jazz orchestra to produce the most varied yet balanced integration of solo improvisation and arranged ensemble, as well as a maximum of textural and structural variety. In such

CHICK WEBB

Drummer Chick Webb went to New York City in 1924 and formed his own big band in 1926; in its early years it included such players as alto saxophonists Benny Carter and Johnny Hodges. Throughout the 1930s, steady engagements at the Savoy Ballroom in Harlem helped Webb maintain a stable roster of band personnel and develop ensemble discipline. His drumming, noted for swing, taste, and virtuoso technique, was the band's foundation. His work was perhaps particularly impressive in light of his short physical stature owing to a curved spine. From 1933 Edgar Sampson's arrangements ("Blue Lou," "Stompin' at the Savoy") gave the band distinctive character. Though it included no major soloists, Webb's band regularly defeated the other major swing bands in musical contests. It reached its heights of popularity after the teenaged Ella Fitzgerald began recording novelty songs with it in 1935. After Webb's death from tuberculosis in 1939, Fitzgerald led the band for two years.

recordings as "Put It There," "Crying and Sighing," and "Stop Kidding," esbitt and the band demonstrated their virtuosic command of what were for their time rather complex scores, replete with implied metre permutations, challenging rhythmic overlays, hard-driving solos, daring modulations, and—as Morton often urged—"plenty of solo breaks."

In these ways the orchestras of Morton and McKinney (as well as that of Ellington) went considerably beyond Henderson's and Redman's method of setting solos off against arranged ensembles, showing that composition, and not mere arrangement, was completely compatible with jazz.

THE PRECURSORS OF MODERN JAZZ AND THE POPULARIZATION OF SWING

In the early 1930s two bands made important contributions to jazz: Bennie Moten's,

with the recordings of "Toby," "Lafayette," and "Prince of Wails," and the Casa Loma Orchestra, with "Casa Loma Stomp" and "San Sue Strut." The black Moten band had little immediate effect on the greater jazz scene, instead influencing an inner circle of black contemporaries, rivals, and jazz insiders. The driving, explosive, rhythmic energy of the Moten pieces, combined with an unprecedented instrumental virtuosity as well as a splendid balance of solos—by saxophonists Ben Webster and Eddie Barefield, trumpeter "Hot Lips" Page, and others—with riff-based ensembles, forged a breakthrough in orchestral jazz that can be seen as a precursor of modern jazz.

The white Casa Loma band exerted a tremendous influence on a host of dance bands (including, temporarily, some black orchestras, notably those of Jimmie Lunceford, Fletcher Henderson, and Earl Hines). The Casa Lomans' role in the history of jazz remains controversial, but it is clear that they were, at the very least, the first white orchestra to try to swing, though their rhythms were more often peppy than swinging. By the mid-1930s another white musician, bandleader Benny Goodman, was being hailed as the "King of Swing." That must have been interesting news to the bands of such black bandleaders as Ellington, Moten, Lunceford, Webb, Cab Calloway, and especially Henderson, who had been swinging for some five to seven years. Scores that Henderson had introduced in the late 1920s and early 1930s—"King Porter Stomp," "Wrappin' It Up," and "Down South Camp Meeting"—suddenly became big hits for Goodman, who had acquired both Henderson's arrangements of these numbers and the services of Henderson himself when Henderson's orchestra was forced to disband in 1934. As reinterpreted and energized by the Goodman forces, these pieces suddenly took on a new life. The Henderson-Redman formula of pitting soloists against ensembles and constantly juxtaposing the different choirs of the orchestra in call-and-response patterns became the widely emulated norm. When the Count Basie band from Kansas City, the successor to Moten's orchestra, reintroduced the riff as another extremely useful structural element, the scene was set for the hundreds of orchestras that had sprung up in the wake of Goodman's success to feed the enormous appetite for swing music of a generation of dance-crazy college-age jazz fans.

By the late 1930s the country was awash with dance bands, all adhering to generic swing tenets: antiphonal section work, juxtaposition of solos and ensembles, and increasingly riff-based tunes. Though this led to a great quantity of dross, many talented young arrangers now rushed into the field and produced an impressive amount of astonishingly good music. This excellence is all the more remarkable since the music was created primarily to be danced to, with no pretensions to anything one might call art.

Among the innumerable orchestras that populated the jazz scene, Count Basie's achieved enormous importance. Perhaps the most magnificent "swing machine" that ever was, the Basie band strongly emphasized improvised solos and a refreshing looseness in ensemble playing that was usually realized through "head arrangements" rather than written-out charts. Its incomparable rhythm section—Walter Page (bass), Freddie Green (guitar), Jo Jones (drums), and Basie (piano)—supported an outstanding cast of soloists, ranging from the great innovative tenor saxophonist Lester Young and his section mate Herschel Evans to trumpeters Buck Clayton and Harry "Sweets" Edison, trombonists Dicky Wells and Vic Dickenson, and blues singer Jimmy Rushing. The Basie band's steadfast popularity can be measured by the fact that, except for a brief period in the early 1950s, it performed and toured successfully right up to Basie's death in 1984. Even after the height of the swing era, Basie continued to introduce swing masterpieces (including "Shiny Stockings," "The Kid from Red Bank," "Li'l Darling," and "April in Paris"),

Jazz Dance

Jazz dance paralleled the birth and spread of jazz itself from roots in African American society and was popularized in ballrooms by the big bands of the swing era (1930s and '40s). It radically altered the style of American and European stage and social dance in the 20th century. The term is sometimes used more narrowly to describe (1) popular stage dance (except tap dance) and (2) jazz-derived or jazz-influenced forms of modern dance. It excludes social dances lacking jazz accompaniment—e.g., the rumba and other Latin-American dances.

Jazz dance developed from both 19th- and 20th-century stage dance and traditional black social dances and their white ballroom offshoots. On the stage, minstrel show performers in the 19th century developed tap dancing from a combination of Irish jigging, English clog dancing, and African rhythmic stamping. Tap dance and such social dances as the cakewalk and shuffle became popular vaudeville acts and appeared in Broadway revues and musical comedies as these replaced vaudeville early in the 20th century. In addition, comedy, specialty, and character dances to jazz rhythms became standard stage routines. By the 1940s elements of jazz dance had appeared in modern dance and in motion picture choreography.

Although the stage popularized certain social dances, many others were transmitted mainly in social gatherings. The dances that gave rise to social forms of jazz dance developed from rural slave dances. In both early dances and 20th-century jazz dances, there is a noticeable continuity of dance elements and motions. The eagle rock and the slow drag (late 19th century) as well as the Charleston and the jitterbug have elements in common with certain Caribbean and African dances. In addition, the slow drag contributed to the fish of the 1950s; the ring shout, which survived from the 18th into the 20th century, in isolated areas, influenced the cakewalk.

In about 1900 the cakewalk, popularized through stage shows, became a craze in European and American ballrooms. In its wake appeared other social dances such as the Charleston (1920s), the jitterbug (1930s and '40s), the twist (1960s), and disco dancing (1970s). Some dances, such as the fox-trot, borrowed European dance steps and fitted them to jazz rhythms. The growth of radio, television, and recording, which popularized black music among wide audiences, greatly aided the diffusion of these dances.

often featuring extraordinary solos by trumpeter-arranger Thad Jones and vocals by Joe Williams.

It was perhaps inevitable that in the excitement of the burgeoning swing era, jazz fans became obsessed with the reigning bandleaders, the new superstars of music. Little did swing fans realize that the music to which they kicked up their heels was the creation not of orchestra leaders but of arrangers who, behind the scenes, forged each band's distinctive style. The history of jazz has too often been described as the story of the improvising soloists, virtually ignoring the important contributions of the composer-arrangers who provided the soloists' framework. These included Sy Oliver (with the Jimmie Lunceford and Tommy Dorsey bands), Mary Lou Williams (with Andy Kirk's band), Walter Thomas (with Cab Calloway), Eddie Durham, Fletcher Henderson, Jimmy Mundy, Edgar Sampson, Eddie Sauter, Jerry Gray, and Benny Carter.

Major swing soloists also emerged in the 1930s—most notably tenor saxophonists Coleman Hawkins, Lester Young, and Ben Webster; pianists Art Tatum and Teddy Wilson; and singer Billie Holiday. Hawkins had left the Henderson band in 1933 for what turned out to be a six-year stay in Europe, during which he not only taught most Europeans about jazz and swing but honed and perfected his personal style, which culminated—upon his return to the United States in 1939—in his recorded masterpiece, "Body and Soul." During that period Hawkins's slightly younger contemporaries Young and Webster developed quite divergent and highly distinctive improvisational styles. Webster exerted a powerful influence on Ellington during his 1939–42 tenure with the Ellington orchestra, while Young spawned an important new school of saxophone playing. In contrast to Hawkins's hyperenergetic, primarily chord-based approach, Young featured a more relaxed, sleek, linear, Southwestern blues-oriented style. Unlike Hawkins's pre-1940s improvisations, which were solidly anchored to their underlying harmonies, Young's lines glided over the harmonies and thereby freed those lines rhythmically.

Tatum and Wilson were both initially inspired by Hines but soon moved in directions different from Hines and from each other. Tatum, the supreme virtuoso technician, developed an astonishingly rich and advanced harmonic vocabulary, which he lavished on his solo improvisations on popular songs. Wilson, more of an ensemble player, led a memorable series of recordings between 1935 and 1937, featuring not only an elite of swing soloists in spontaneously created performances but also the incomparable Holiday.

Holiday's singing style was crafted out of an original amalgam of the vocal stylings of Armstrong and Bessie Smith as well as her own vocal-technical limitations—her range was barely more than an octave. With her unique timbre and diction, she reconstructed dozens of popular songs, streamlining and contracting the original melodies and embellishing them with highly personal ornamentations, many of which she absorbed from some of the great instrumentalists of her time. In this sense she was a true jazz singer, constantly re-creating, improvising, and inventing. Moreover, Holiday brought to her art a level of emotion, expression, and philosophical depth unprecedented in jazz,

BEN WEBSTER

Ben Webster began playing the violin in childhood and then played piano accompaniments to silent films; after learning to play alto saxophone, he joined the family band led by Lester Young's father. By 1930 he had switched to tenor saxophone, and he quickly became a leading soloist on that instrument. Through the decade he was a fixture in after-hours jam sessions in Kansas City, and he worked briefly in the bands of Fletcher Henderson, Benny Carter, Cab Calloway, and Teddy Wilson, among others. Although initially Webster's sound was nearly indistinguishable from that of his idol, Coleman Hawkins, he soon began to develop a personal style.

A full-time engagement as the first featured tenor saxophonist with Duke Ellington (1940–43) brought Webster into his own, and he matured as a soloist and unique musician. He often played raspy, growling solos on up-tempo numbers, yet he displayed a rich, breathy tone on ballads. His melodies were direct, and his sound was immediately recognizable. Recordings of Ellington numbers such as "Cotton Tail," "Chelsea Bridge," "Blue Serge," and "All Too Soon" showcase solos by Webster that are considered classics.

Through most of the 1940s Webster worked in small bands out of New York and Chicago. Heavy drinking (which earned him the nickname "The Brute") caused him many problems throughout his career, and for a time (1950–52) personal problems kept him off the scene. After this break he resumed his freelance activity, touring and recording with several of the most respected jazz artists. His sessions with Art Tatum in 1956 were particularly important. Webster moved to Europe in 1964 (living first in the Netherlands, later in Denmark); he performed and recorded very actively throughout Europe until his death.

ranging from abject melancholia and tragedy to the most joyous evocations.

THE RETURN OF THE COMBO AND THE INFLUENCE OF THE TERRITORY BANDS

In the first decade of jazz, roughly 1915–25, almost all forms worth considering had been played by small groups, but these were driven away in the 1930s by the arrival of the big bands. Later in the decade there was a return to smaller groups, ranging in size from trios to septets. Foremost among these new small groups were the various Goodman-led combos, starting in 1935. These were the first racially mixed jazz groups to tour the United States: Goodman and drummer Gene Krupa were white; Wilson and vibraphonist Lionel Hampton were black. By 1939–40 permutations of Goodman's small groups included guitarist Charlie Christian and trumpeter Cootie Williams. Among the several dozen recordings produced by these groups, the superb "Body and Soul," "Avalon," "Breakfast Feud," and "Seven Come Eleven" must be singled out.

In 1937 the 20-year-old Nat King Cole formed a trio, initially featuring himself as pianist; it was not until 1940 that Cole began singing and the trio began recording. Their big hits "Straighten Up and Fly Right" (1943) and "Route 66" (1946) made the group one of the top attractions of the mid-1940s, a success that eventually led to Cole's equally brilliant solo singing career. Piano trios and quartets—such as those of Clarence Profit, Dorothy Donegan, and Art Tatum—were among the many successful small groups of the 1940s.

The success of these small groups not only affirmed the artistic and commercial viability of a true chamber-jazz concept but inaugurated the notion of extracting a small combo from a larger orchestra. This "band within a band" idea spawned many successful groups, such as Basie's Kansas City Seven and, Ellington's many small ensembles led alternately by Hodges, Williams, Stewart, and Bigard. Possibly the most perfect small group recordings are the four sides recorded in Paris in 1939 by three Ellingtonians—Stewart, Bigard, and Billy Taylor (bass)—and the great Belgian Roma guitarist Django Reinhardt.

Also important in the 1930s were the territory bands, notably Walter Page's Blue Devils (out of Oklahoma City, Okla.), the Jeter-Pillars band (based in St. Louis), and those of Nat Towles (Omaha, Neb.), Alphonse Trent (Dallas), Don Albert (San Antonio, Texas), Jesse Stone and Jay McShann (Kansas City, Mo.), and others. Although their music was only sporadically recorded, these nomadic orchestras had considerable influence, for by roaming the Midwestern and Southern hinterlands in trains and broken-down buses and cars, they brought superb jazz to the public, especially the black population. In addition, these bands functioned as traveling music conservatories in which young talent could grow, develop, and gain vital experience.

Several major innovative soloists emerged during this period, among them trumpeters Roy Eldridge and Dizzy Gillespie, singer Pearl Bailey, alto saxophonist Charlie Parker, and Ellington's bassist Jimmy Blanton. With this roster of solo talent and the era's orchestral, compositional, and arranging developments—all inspired by a high sense of professionalism and an unprecedented artistic (but often also commercial) competitiveness—it was inevitable that a new jazz idiom would soon evolve. Ellington's harmonic lessons were finally beginning to be appreciated as arrangers forged beyond simple triadic and dominant harmonies into the various types of 9th, 11th, and 13th chords, all manner of substitute harmonizations, and wide-ranging modulations. On the rhythmic side, $^4/_4$ swing had by now completely taken over, providing the basis for a new fluency, freedom, and (as desired) complexity in rhythm sections; this in turn freed the soloists and ensembles to explore new structural territories—and all of these developments were expressed with a radically new virtuosity.

JAZZ AT THE CROSSROADS

While much of what happened between 1941 and 1945 may have appeared revolutionary to musicians and the public alike, the process was actually evolutionary and inevitable. The older guard held on as long as possible, dominating the airwaves well into the mid-1940s. But ultimately the experiments and forward thrusts of bebop—many of them initiated in such places as Minton's Playhouse in Harlem, in small lounges and obscure nightclubs, on tours, and in even more private situations such as homes and hotel rooms—had to break through to an expanding public via record companies and the larger, more popular club venues.

The leading figure in jazz was now Charlie Parker, who, along with his colleagues Dizzy Gillespie (trumpet), Bud Powell and Thelonious Monk (piano), Kenny Clarke and Max Roach (drums), Oscar Pettiford and Ray Brown (bass), and later Lucky Thompson (tenor saxophone), Milt Jackson (vibraphone), J.J. Johnson (trombone), and Miles Davis (trumpet), reshaped jazz on all three important fronts: harmonically, melodically, and rhythmically. Perhaps the most radical advance was rhythmic, when Parker, with his dazzling technique and fluency, turned the former $^4/_4$ metric substructures into $^8/_8$; quavers now superseded the basic quarter-note beats, and in effect the audible speed of the music doubled. Parker was, for all his startling innovations, a great blues player, as can be heard not only in his constant reference to earlier blues traditions but also in the depth and beauty of his tone and its often anguished expression. His coinnovators Gillespie and Powell, equipped with both a prodigious technical mastery and a keen sense for harmonic exploration, set dramatically new standards of improvisation. Drummers, too, became more intrinsically involved in the total ensemble effect by introducing a certain contrapuntal independence, expressed polyrhythmically and even melodically.

The new, onomatopoetically named bebop, or bop, used more chromatically convoluted melodic lines. Played at high speed, it was no longer aurally related to the sedate song repertory of the 1930s, and it required a greater variety of chord substitutions and passing harmonies. It also built a whole new jazz repertory by superimposing brand new themes onto older, well-known chord progressions, particularly on such standards as "I Got Rhythm" and "How High the Moon." This new repertoire was created mostly for small combos but also for larger ensembles such as Gillespie's and Billy Eckstine's, orchestras.

As bebop took hold after World War II, the entire jazz scene changed dramatically. Many big bands, even those that tried to make the transition to modern jazz, began to falter both financially and

BILLY ECKSTINE

Billy Eckstine left Howard University after winning an amateur contest in 1933 and began singing in nightclubs and with dance bands. From 1939 to 1943 he sang with Earl Hines's band, and at Eckstine's urging Hines hired such newcomers as Sarah Vaughan, Dizzy Gillespie, and Charlie Parker. In 1944 Eckstine formed his own band, which in its three-year existence gave strong impetus to the new bebop style by featuring the talents of Gillespie, Parker, Miles Davis, Fats Navarro, Gene Ammons, Dexter Gordon, Tadd Dameron, Art Blakey, and others. From 1947 on Eckstine was a successful popular singer; among his recordings were "Caravan," "Prisoner of Love," "You Go to My Head," and "That Old Black Magic."

Billy Eckstine. Hulton Archive/Getty Images

artistically. Touring costs and musicians' salaries skyrocketed. The best musicians preferred to stay in Los Angeles, New York, and Chicago, where they could do the suddenly lucrative studio work. In any case, bebop was played mostly by small combos—quartets, quintets, and sextets. And bebop was made for listening, not dancing; it was not intended to be played to the accompaniment of clinking glasses and nightclub merrymaking.

Essentially, the audience for the more or less homogeneous jazz of the 1930s and early '40s (swing) was split three ways. A majority rejected bop and clung to swing, if and wherever they could still find it, or to even earlier styles, such as Dixieland and Chicago-style jazz. Another segment shifted its allegiance entirely to a new breed of singers—the principal African Americans being Nat King Cole, Sarah Vaughan, Ella Fitzgerald, and Billy Eckstine—who came out of the bands and embarked on full-time careers as highly paid "single" acts. The third and smallest faction stayed with the boppers, relishing the music's technical and conceptual challenges and returning jazz to a minority art.

Two singular pianists emerged at this time: Thelonious Monk and Erroll Garner. After Morton and Ellington, Monk was the first major composer to enter the field, contributing to such pieces as "Criss Cross," "Misterioso," and "Evidence" (all 1948) a uniquely individual repertory. Partly because he had developed a totally unorthodox piano technique, Monk created an inimitable style and touch, as well as highly unusual voicings and chord formations, as can be heard on his Blue Note quartet and quintet recordings of 1947–51 and on his later solo piano recordings of 1957 and 1959.

Equally sui generis yet completely different in intent, technique, and feeling, Garner had developed from his earliest professional days a prodigious both-hands technique (rivaled or surpassed only by Tatum) that allowed him to play asymmetrical rhythmic and melodic configurations and contours with his right hand while maintaining an absolutely steady beat with his left. Not a composer at all in the Monk or Ellington sense and given at times to a certain pianistic pomposity, Garner nevertheless brilliantly recomposed the hundreds of Broadway songs he played during his long career into astonishingly fresh, extemporized pieces.

COOL JAZZ ENTERS THE SCENE

Perhaps in reaction to the hot, more strident, more frenetic expressions of the postwar bands, a cool strain entered the jazz scene in the late 1940s. Generated by Young, cool jazz, along with its structural corollary—contrapuntal, harmonically slimmed-down (often pianoless) chamber jazz—was suddenly in. Understatement and a more relaxed expression replaced extroversion and high-tension virtuosity. Examples abound, beginning with the Miles Davis Nonet (1948–50). In such pieces as "Boplicity," "Israel," "Move," and "Moondreams," fine improvised solos by Davis and white reed players Lee Konitz and Gerry Mulligan were meaningfully integrated into the arrangers' scores. Various octets, nonets, and other small ensembles soon followed suit.

On a slightly different tack, the Modern Jazz Quartet (made up of John Lewis, piano; Milt Jackson, vibraphone; Percy Heath, bass; and Kenny Clarke, soon replaced by Connie Kay, drums) was formed in 1953. After his years with Gillespie, Lewis had been inspired further by his study of classical music, especially the work of Johann Sebastian Bach. Thus, Lewis brought a new kind of compositional (often contrapuntal) integration to the group's repertory, particularly in fugal or quasi-fugal pieces, such as the early "Vendome" or the later "Three Windows" and the album-length work "The Comedy." Above all, in these performances Lewis sought to bring collective improvisation back from earlier times; many striking examples can be heard on the recordings made by the Modern Jazz Quartet over a period of 20 years, especially in the frequent, remarkable same-register duets of Lewis and Jackson.

It was also in the 1950s that a greater rapprochement between jazz and classical music began to emerge. Like Lewis, many other jazz musicians were studying much of the great classical music, from Bach to Béla Bartók, to expand their musical horizons. Classical musicians, too, were listening more seriously to jazz and taking a professional interest in it. The ideological and technical barriers between jazz and classical music were beginning to break down. In that climate an apparently new concept or style, termed "third stream" by Gunther Schuller arose. But third stream music was only apparently new, since European and American composers—including Claude Debussy, Igor Stravinsky, Charles Ives (using ragtime), Darius Milhaud, Maurice Ravel, Aaron Copland, John Alden Carpenter, Kurt Weill, and many others—had employed elements of jazz since early in the century. The difference in the 1950s and '60s was that (1) the third stream amalgams began to include improvisation and (2) the traffic was now no longer on a one-way street from classical music toward jazz but was flowing in both directions. The movement produced a wide variety of works and varying approaches to the process of cross-fertilization.

Though the term is now seldom used, the concept of third stream remains alive and well; Randy Weston and Melba Liston's African-influenced compositions are cases in point. Third stream music is also called by other names: crossover, fusion, or world music. So lively and penetrating has the stylistic intercourse been that it is nowadays often impossible to identify a piece as jazz, classical, or ethnic, proof that the third stream ideal of a true and complete fusion (not always technically possible in the 1960s) has at least partially been achieved.

In the meantime, the jazz mainstream continually broadened and expanded through the contributions of a wide range of talented African Americans from saxophonists Sonny Rollins, John Coltrane, Eric Dolphy and bassist-composer Charles Mingus, to pianist Cecil Taylor.

ERIC DOLPHY

Eric Dolphy began playing clarinet, oboe, and alto saxophone in his youth and attended Los Angeles City College. He was in Roy Porter's big band during the late 1940s. He then spent a few years in a U.S. Army band, after which he transferred to the U.S. Naval School of Music. Upon returning to Los Angeles Dolphy played locally, and he first became nationally recognized when he toured and recorded with the Chico Hamilton quintet in 1958–59.

Settling in New York by early 1960 led to Dolphy's most noted performing associations, with Charles Mingus, trumpeter Booker Little, and John Coltrane. He recorded often, but opportunities to play in public were erratic. He died of complications of diabetes.

Dolphy's impact resulted largely from his brilliant playing of not only alto saxophone but also flute (then uncommon in jazz) and bass clarinet (which he virtually introduced into jazz improvisation). Besides his thorough mastery of these woodwinds, he introduced an unprecedented range of unique expressive techniques on them. While his phrasing usually resembled Charlie Parker's in rhythmic terms, Dolphy harmonically was given to wide, angular leaps and distant relations to fixed harmonic structures, so that his chromatic lines at times seemed to approach atonality. Typically, his solos proceeded by free association. By 1963–64, however, he had discovered unique ways of organizing his improvising, using original themes and radical harmonic means, as in his major album Out to Lunch.

Miles Davis and Coltrane exerted the greatest influence, Coltrane especially; he inadvertently bred thousands of clones who copied his sound and turned his every move into a cliché. Much more difficult to imitate and to absorb was the music of Dolphy, who, along with his unequaled mastery of alto saxophone and flute, was the first to conquer the bass clarinet as a jazz instrument. "Stormy Weather" (1960), his nearly 14-minute-long duet improvisation on alto with Mingus, must be counted as one of the greatest creative efforts in all of jazz.

The great wonder of jazz is its open-endedness, allowing truly talented musicians to explore new stylistic and conceptual avenues. Such was the case with Rollins, who—instead of merely releasing a string of unrelated musical ideas—was the first to develop thematic improvisation in such a way that themes or motifs were varied and revisited within a single performance. Although he was a remarkably gifted musician with a deep humility regarding jazz and his art, Coltrane (probably under the influence of Davis) abandoned his earlier fascination with the burgeoning harmonic language of bop—especially Monk's unique tonal explorations—and fell into the trap of modal and single chord confinement. This led to extended improvisations, often lasting as long as an hour, that some observers regarded as "practicing in public."

Art Blakey's Jazz Messengers, the most renowned and respected of the "traveling conservatories," held forth in the world's jazz clubs and concert halls for more than three decades, hatching a long line of talented players ranging from Horace Silver, Kenny Dorham, and Lee Morgan (in the 1950s) to Freddie Hubbard, Woody Shaw, and (in the 1980s) Wynton Marsalis.

Initially a loyal disciple of Gillespie, Davis by the late 1950s knew that he had neither the embouchure nor the ear for Gillespie's pyrotechnics. Under the benign influence of John Lewis, white jazzman Gil Evans, and others, he turned to an opulent, more lyrical style with which he and Evans were to make dramatic musical history in such recordings as *Miles Ahead* (1957) and Evans's inspired recomposing of George Gershwin's *Porgy and Bess* (1958). Davis abandoned conventional major and minor harmonies for modal and pentatonic patterns (first fully aired in 1959 on the album *Kind of Blue*), a plunge into a vagrant harmonic no-man's-land that unfortunately infected much of jazz. Modal playing, with its endless pedal points and one-chord bass ostinatos, allowed by definition no harmonic progression or forward movement and resulted in a structural stasis that only, maybe, the greatest improvisers could overcome.

Mingus, together with Parker and Gillespie, was among the most gifted of all the postwar giants. A major composer in the full creative sense as well as a brilliant bass virtuoso and formidable bandleader, Mingus experimented with extended forms as early as the late 1940s ("Mingus Fingers" with Lionel Hampton). His oeuvre ranges from early simple blues and atonal free-form pieces to such poetically named jazz instrumentals as "Pithecanthropus Erectus" (1956), "Haitian Fight Song" (1957), "Fables of Faubus" (1959), and "Peggy's Blue Skylight" (1961) to the monumental two-and-a-half-hour, posthumously premiered "Epitaph." Accumulated between the early 1940s and 1962 and composed for 31 instruments, "Epitaph" is a gigantic summation of everything Mingus felt and heard in music, from the gentlest lyric ballads and earthy blues to the most complex and advanced Ivesian and Stravinskian orchestral excursions.

FREE JAZZ: THE EXPLORATIONS OF ORNETTE COLEMAN

Whereas most of these postwar musicians worked out their individual styles through personal explorations within the central modern tradition, the arrival of saxophonist Ornette Coleman and trumpeter Donald Cherry constituted an even more radical break from the recent past. Eschewing conventional key and time signatures, Coleman also abandoned all the traditional jazz forms, arriving quickly at something that was to be called free jazz.

Art Ensemble of Chicago

Among the important innovators of sound, structure, and form in free jazz was the Art Ensemble of Chicago, a group of musicians who embraced a diversity of African and African American styles and sources in their creation of what they preferred to call Great Black Music. In 1966 composer-woodwind player Roscoe Mitchell began forming small Chicago jazz units that he called art ensembles, which included bassist Malachi Favors and trumpeter Lester Bowie. Often they were joined by composer-woodwind player Joseph Jarman, who became a permanent member of the Art Ensemble in 1968, turning it into a cooperative quartet. Their international fame began in 1969–71, when they recorded and toured prolifically in Europe and added a percussionist, Don Moye. Subsequently they toured almost annually as a quintet in Europe, Japan, and the United States.

At a time when the dominant trend in free jazz was intense, loud, very fast music, the Art Ensemble by contrast began featuring group and solo improvising in a wide range of freely changing tempos, dynamics, and textures. Its members played many instruments; their virtuosity included mastery of their instruments' overtone and multiphonics ranges, and Bowie became especially noted for his expressive concepts. They all played percussion instruments, including bells, gourds, and gongs, and the addition of Moye broadened their use of exotic percussion. While the Art Ensemble incorporated traditional jazz, classical, and popular works, music composed by its members was the source of its improvising in recordings such as A Jackson in Your House *(1969),* People in Sorrow *(1969), and* Urban Bushmen *(1980).*

The five musicians also pursued independent careers; Bowie, for example, was a featured soloist with his Brass Fantasy band and the New York Organ Ensemble, and Mitchell composed extended works such as Nonaah *(1976–77) and* The Maze *(1978).*

Although partially inspired by the Parker revolution, Coleman's music also harkened back in its linear fragmentation, wailing blues sonorities, and unconventional intonation to a much older, primitive, folklike blues and work song tradition, incidentally more or less cleansed of jazz's earlier European borrowings. Given Coleman's abandonment of traditional forms such as 12-bar blues and 32-bar song forms, it would be wrong to conclude that such works as *Change of the Century* (1959) or *Free Jazz* (1960) are therefore formless. Rather, they are simply subject to a new kind of organization where—in *Free Jazz*, for example—the eight players are each assigned "solo" sections accompanied by all the other players, with the various sections partitioned from each other by predetermined, collectively played motivic materials and the overall formal subdivisions thus clearly delineated.

Though others who followed in Coleman's footsteps—for example, the saxophonists Albert Ayler, Archie Shepp,

ASSOCIATION FOR THE ADVANCEMENT OF CREATIVE MUSICIANS

Of the approximately three dozen Chicago musicians who formed the Association for the Advancement of Creative Musicians (AACM), most had played in an early 1960s rehearsal band led by pianist-teacher Muhal Richard Abrams that had experimented with polytonal and atonal jazz and used then-new free jazz techniques of improvisation and composition. They founded the AACM to produce their own concerts in 1965; however, a shared spirit of musical exploration quickly came to dominate their ventures. AACM members were expected to be adept at composition and improvisation and to present concerts that included only original music. Abrams was the organization's leader in its early years; the Art Ensemble of Chicago, drummer Steve McCall, trumpeter Leo Smith, and saxophonists Fred Anderson, Anthony Braxton, and Henry Threadgill were among its other notable performers and composers.

Also in the 1960s the AACM began a school to provide free musical instruction to inner-city youth. After the Art Ensemble and Braxton's ensemble began appearing in Europe in 1969, the AACM became internationally known. As older members moved away from Chicago, AACM school graduates—including woodwind virtuoso Douglas Ewart and trombonist George Lewis—took their places. The AACM musicians' discoveries in terms of sound colour, fluid rhythms, structure, and free jazz lyricism continued to be influential in the 1990s.

and George Adams—sought to expand on his free-form innovations, they lacked his innate talent and inherent musical discipline. A creative stasis set in during the 1970s and '80s that eventually led, on the one hand, to a gigantic eclecticism where no style or conception took priority and, on the other hand, to a profound sea change that dramatically altered the face of jazz. This fundamental shift can be seen in the fact that, in contrast to past decades when jazz produced a succession of highly individual artists whose musical styles and personalities could be recognized instantly, by the end of the 20th century jazz had no such distinctive artists.

JAZZ AT THE TURN OF THE 21ST CENTURY

Whether the past was inherently better than the present is questionable. Something was gained and something was lost. The personal, instantly recognizable distinctiveness of jazz's early greats was replaced by an astonishing technical assurance and stylistic flexibility. Most younger players in the 1990s sounded very much alike—with the exception of a few standouts such as trumpeter Wynton Marsalis. Whereas later players functioned well in any stylistic context—even beyond jazz in ethnic and classical realms—the earlier players, great as they were, could not reach out into other stylistic regions. The players of yore did not—could not, in most cases—go to music schools and were in essence self-taught, having learned on the job and to a large extent from each other and from their seniors.

Whether the eclectic versatility of these later generations is good for the

JAZZ-ROCK

Since the recordings of 1920s bands, there have been fusions of jazz and popular music, usually presenting jazz's "hot," swinging, staccato qualities in contrast to "sweet," legato popular music characteristics. With the slow development of a unique identity in rock music, occasional jazz tunes also began including rock rhythms in the 1960s. Beginning in 1969, trumpeter Miles Davis and an interracial group of associates such as drummer Tony Williams, guitarist John McLaughlin, saxophonist Wayne Shorter, and electric keyboardists Joe Zawinul, Herbie Hancock, Larry Young, and Chick Corea broke through to distinctive fusion musics. Jazz and rock elements contrasted, even competed with or enhanced each other, in bands of the early 1970s such as Davis's increasingly African-music-oriented groups, Williams's Lifetime quartet, McLaughlin's fiercely loud and energetic Mahavishnu Orchestra, the light, danceable music of Hancock's Headhunters and Corea's Return to Forever, and the mobile sound and rhythmic colours of Zawinul's and Shorter's Weather Report.

The most important work by these musicians dates from the early 1970s; since then, most have alternated between periods of playing fusion music and playing mainstream jazz. The jazz-rock idiom gained one of the largest jazz audiences since the swing era ended in the mid-1940s. The style was also known as crossover because sales of the music crossed over from the jazz market to the popular music market.

Meanwhile, two other kinds of fusion music were also current. The most popular jazz-rock strain grew out of hard bop: the funky 1960s jazz of musicians such as flutist Herbie Mann, alto saxophonist Hank Crawford, and the Crusaders. Their repertoires included original and standard rock tunes over which they improvised jazz. In the 1970s the CTI record label in particular offered this kind of fusion music on albums by Stanley Turrentine, Freddie Hubbard, and others. Less commercially successful was the free jazz fusion of Ornette Coleman's Prime Time group (beginning in 1973) and his associates, guitarist James Blood Ulmer, bassist Jamaaladeen Tacuma, and drummer Ronald Shannon Jackson, though all led valuable bands in the 1980s. One problem was that the recurring rhythmic-harmonic patterns of rock tended to dominate, reducing jazz improvisation to mere decoration.

A later development of jazz-rock—contemporary jazz, or light jazz—appeared on the radio in the 1980s and '90s. The most popular kind of fusion music, it abandoned jazz elements almost completely and frequently used a minimum of improvisation. Two jazz-rock fashions of the 1990s were acid jazz, a catchall term for bop and free jazz improvising over funk and hip-hop rhythms; and neo-swing, which revived the shuffle rhythms of small 1940s swing ("jump") bands.

future of jazz is as yet hard to say. One fact, however, is clear: in the wake of these changes, composition moved much more into the front and centre of activities—as in the works of Wadada Leo Smith and Henry Threadgill—suggesting that the long-standing conflict between improvisation and composition may have finally been resolved. A good part of the reason for this is that most later jazz musicians went to music school—conservatories and university or college music departments—where they took theory, music history, and general music survey courses, and in most cases they also studied with teachers who were themselves major jazz figures. In addition, starting in the 1970s, the enormously expanding number of recordings made available an infinite variety of musical traditions encompassing all jazz styles as well as a rainbow of ethnic, popular, and vernacular musics of all persuasions and philosophies. The younger generations took advantage of this plethora of musical and stylistic resources.

Where this leaves jazz and where jazz goes in the future—indeed, whether jazz can endure as a distinct musical idiom or language—were unanswerable questions at the end of the 20th century. The one truism about jazz is that it remains distinguishable not by what is played but by how it is played.

CHAPTER 5

GOSPEL, BLUES, R&B, AND DOO-WOP

In his deeply insightful book *A Change Is Gonna Come: Music, Race & the Soul of America* (1999), Craig Werner borrows the notion of musical "impulses" from James Baldwin to offer an explanation of "black music's refusal to simplify reality or devalue emotion." Werner characterizes jazz, the subject of the previous chapter, as innovation: jazz "refuses," he writes, "to accept the way things are, envisions ways of reaching a higher ground we're only beginning to imagine." The "jazz impulse" is revolutionary, a process of constant redefinition that stretches minds and transgresses boundaries. Though it demands a knowledge of tradition and of its roots in gospel and the blues, jazz tells people that they do not have to do things the way they have always done them.

Gospel and blues—considered in this chapter along with two genres based on them, rhythm and blues and doo-wop—are the other two impulses that Werner identifies. Grounded in the "belief that life's burdens can be transformed into hope, salvation, [and] the promise of redemption," the "gospel impulse" in Werner's model is made up of a three-step process: (1) acknowledging the burden; (2) bearing witness; (3) finding redemption. Gospel relishes the promise of a better day; getting there relies upon the support of one's beloved community and the faith in something bigger than oneself. In gospel music, that something is God; in gospel's secular offshoot, soul music (covered in the next chapter), it is the power of love.

In its unvarnished recognition of life's unavoidable problems, the "blues impulse" can be seen as a catalyst for the other two impulses. In the blues, says Werner, "all you can do is reach down inside the pain, finger the jagged grain, tell your story, and hope you can find the strength to go on." The blues are sung not to wallow in self-pity but as a life-affirming exercise. "You sing the blues," according to Werner, "so you can live to sing the blues again."

GOSPEL MUSIC

The tradition that came to be recognized as black American gospel music emerged in the late 19th and early 20th centuries alongside ragtime, blues, and jazz. The progenitors of the tradition, however, lie in both black and white musics of the 19th century, including, most notably, black spirituals, slave songs, and white hymnody.

The roots of black gospel music can be ultimately traced to the hymnals of the early 19th century. *A Collection of Spiritual Songs and Hymns Selected from Various Authors* (1801) was the first hymnal intended for use in black worship. It contained texts written mostly by 18th-century British clergymen, such as Isaac Watts and Charles Wesley, but also included a number of poems by black American Richard Allen—the founder of the African Methodist Episcopal Church—and his parishioners. The volume contained no music, however, leaving the congregation to sing the texts to well-known hymn tunes. After the Civil War, black hymnals began to include music, but most of the arrangements employed the rhythmically and melodically straightforward, unembellished style of white hymnody.

In the last decade of the 19th century, black hymnody experienced a stylistic shift. Colourful and allusive texts, reminiscent in many respects of the older black spirituals, were set to melodies composed by white hymnodists. The arrangements, however, were adjusted to reflect black American musical sensibilities. Most significantly, the hymns were syncopated; that is, they were recast rhythmically by accentuating normally weak beats. Among the first hymnals to use this modified musical style was *The Harp of Zion*, published in 1893 and readily adopted by many black congregations.

The immediate impetus for the development of this new, energetic, and distinctly black gospel music seems to have been the rise of Pentecostal churches at the end of the 19th century. Pentecostal shouting is related to speaking in tongues and to circle dances of African origin. Recordings of Pentecostal preachers' sermons were immensely popular among black Americans in the 1920s, and recordings of them along with their choral and instrumental accompaniment and congregational participation persisted, so that ultimately black gospel reached the white audience as well. The voice of the black gospel preacher was affected by black secular performers and vice versa. Taking the scriptural direction "Let everything that breathes praise the Lord" (Psalm 150), Pentecostal churches

Mahalia Jackson. Keystone/Hulton Archive/Getty Images

welcomed tambourines, pianos, organs, banjos, guitars, other stringed instruments, and some brass into their services. Choirs often featured the extremes of female vocal range in call-and-response counterpoint with the preacher's sermon. Improvised recitative passages, melismatic singing (singing of more than one pitch per syllable), and an extraordinarily expressive delivery also characterize black gospel music.

Among the most prominent black gospel music composers and practitioners have been the Rev. C.A. Tindley (1851–1933), composer of "I'll Overcome Someday," which may have served as the basis for the anthem of the American civil rights movement, "We Shall Overcome";

blind Rev. Gary Davis (1896–1972), a wandering preacher and guitar soloist; Thomas A. Dorsey (1899–1993), a prolific and best-selling songwriter whose works include, most notably, "Precious Lord, Take My Hand"; and the Rev. C.L. Franklin (1915–84) of Detroit (father of soul music singer Aretha Franklin), who issued more than 70 albums of his sermons and choir after World War II. Important women in the black gospel tradition have included Roberta Martin (1907–69), a gospel pianist based in Chicago with a choir and a school of gospel singing; Mahalia Jackson (1911–72), who toured internationally and was often broadcast on television and radio; and Sister Rosetta Tharpe (1915–73), whose guitar and vocal

SPIRITUAL

Black spirituals developed mostly from white rural folk hymnody. (Blacks and whites attended the same camp meetings, for instance, and black performance style possibly counterinfluenced the revival songs.) Many black spirituals thus exist in the white folk music tradition also, and many others have melody analogues in secular white American and British folk music. The borrowing of melodies with pentatonic (five-note) and major scales is especially prominent. In voice quality, vocal effects, and type of rhythmic accompaniment, black spirituals differ markedly from white ones. Black spirituals were sung not only in worship but also as work songs, and the text imagery often reflects concrete tasks.

Musically, it is believed that a complex intermingling of African and white folk-music elements occurred and that complementary traits of African music and white U.S. folksong reinforced each other. For example, the call-and-response pattern occurs in both, as do certain scales and the variable intonation of certain notes. Most authorities see clear African influence in vocal style and in the complex polyrhythmic clapped accompaniments. African tradition also included polyphonic and choral singing. The ring shout (a religious dance usually accompanied by the singing of spirituals and clapped rhythms) is of African ancestry.

After the Civil War the black spirituals were "discovered" by Northerners and either developed toward harmonized versions, often sung by trained choirs, or, conversely, preserved the older traditional style, especially in rural areas and certain sects.

performances introduced gospel into nightclubs and concert theatres.

BLUES

From its origin in the South in the early 20th century, the blues' simple but expressive forms had become by the 1960s one of the most important influences on the development of popular music in the United States. Although instrumental accompaniment is almost universal in the blues, the blues are essentially vocal. Blues songs are lyrical rather than narrative; blues singers are expressing feelings rather than telling stories. The emotion expressed is generally one of sadness or melancholy, often due to problems in love. To express this musically, blues performers use vocal techniques such as melisma and syncopation and instrumental techniques such as "choking" or bending guitar strings on the neck or applying a metal slide or bottleneck to the guitar strings to create a whining, voicelike sound.

As a musical style, the blues is characterized by expressive pitch inflections (blue notes), a three-line textual stanza of the form AAB, and a 12-measure form. Typically the first two and a half measures of each line are devoted to singing, the last measure and a half consisting of an instrumental "break" that repeats, answers, or complements the vocal line. In terms of functional (i.e., traditional European) harmony, the simplest blues harmonic progression is described as follows (I, IV, and V refer respectively to the first or tonic, fourth or subdominant, and fifth or dominant notes of the scale):

Phrase 1 (measures 1–4) I–I–I–I
Phrase 2 (measures 5–8) IV–IV–I–I
Phrase 3 (measures 9–12) V–V–I–I

African influences are apparent in the blues tonality, the call-and-response pattern of the repeated refrain structure of the blues stanza, the falsetto break in the vocal style, and the imitation of vocal idioms by instruments, especially the guitar and harmonica.

The origins of the blues are poorly documented. Blues developed in the southern United States after the Civil War. It was influenced by work songs and field hollers, minstrel show music, ragtime, church music, and the folk and popular music of whites. Blues derived from and was largely played by southern black men, most of whom came from the milieu of agricultural workers. The earliest references to blues date back to the 1890s and early 1900s. In 1912 black bandleader W.C. Handy's composition "Memphis Blues" was published. It became very popular, and thereafter many other Tin Pan Alley songs entitled blues began to appear.

The rural blues developed in three principal regions, Georgia and the Carolinas, Texas, and Mississippi. The blues of Georgia and the Carolinas is noted for its clarity of enunciation and regularity of rhythm. Influenced by ragtime and white folk music, it is more melodic than the Texas and Mississippi styles. Blind Willie McTell and Blind Boy Fuller were representative of this style.

The Texas blues is characterized by high, clear singing accompanied by supple guitar lines that consist typically of single-string picked arpeggios rather than strummed chords. Blind Lemon Jefferson was by far the most influential Texas bluesman. Blind from birth and the youngest of seven children, Jefferson became an itinerant entertainer in his teens, learning a repertoire of prison songs, blues, moans, spirituals, and dance numbers. He worked in the streets and in brothels, saloons, and parties in Texas, Louisiana, Mississippi, Alabama, and Virginia. In the 1920s he went to Chicago.

Jefferson's high voice, shouting style, and advanced guitar technique, which used melodic lead lines, bent notes, and imitative effects, as well as his lyrics and themes, became staples of the blues through such disciples as Leadbelly (Huddie Ledbetter), who worked with Jefferson for a time, and through his recordings for the Paramount label (1926–29).

Jefferson also recorded spiritual songs, using the pseudonym Deacon L.J. Bates. Among his best-known songs are "Black Snake Moan," "Matchbox Blues," and "See That My Grave Is Kept Clean."

Mississippi Delta blues, which developed in the Delta region of northwestern Mississippi, is the most intense of the three styles and has been the most influential. Vocally, it is the most speechlike, and the guitar accompaniment is rhythmic and percussive; a slide or bottleneck is often used. The Mississippi style is represented by Charley Patton, Willie Brown, Eddie ("Son") House, Robert Johnson, and Johnny Shines.

Singer-guitarist Patton spent most of his life in the Delta region, and from about 1900 he was often based at Dockery's plantation in Sunflower county. There he and other early blues performers, such as Brown and Tommy Johnson, shared songs and ideas. Patton spent most of his career playing blues and ragtime-based popular songs for dancers at rural parties and barrelhouses, where his singing and clowning made him a popular entertainer.

WDIA

When WDIA went on the air in Memphis in 1948, its white owners, Bert Ferguson and John R. Pepper, were anything but blues aficionados; however, deejay Nat D. Williams was. A former high-school history teacher and journalist, Williams brought his own records and his familiarity with Memphis's blues hotbed Beale Street with him. But rather than aspiring to be a hipster, Williams acted as a cultural historian and gatekeeper, watching for lyrics that might be deemed offensive to WDIA's (largely white) audience. The popularity of his show helped open WDIA to more black performers. B.B. King deejayed and sang commercial jingles at the station, and Rufus Thomas, a former student of Williams, joined the on-air staff in 1950. Together the three transformed WDIA into the South's first African American-oriented radio station, soon to be known throughout the region as the "Mother Station of the Negroes."

In the nearly 70 recordings he made between 1929 and 1934, Patton sang in a coarse, strained, sometimes unintelligible voice while providing himself with a changing, heavily percussive guitar accompaniment. His lyrics range from personal to topical. He also recorded some gospel songs. His best-known recording is "Pony Blues," among the first of his to be issued, and others such as "Down the Dirt Road," "Shake It and Break It," "High Water Everywhere," and "Moon Going Down" helped secure his popularity.

The aggressive intensity of Patton's performances is particularly notable, a quality that influenced his successors such as Howlin' Wolf (Chester Arthur Burnett), Son House, and Bukka White.

The first blues recordings were made in the 1920s by black women such as Mamie Smith, Ma Rainey, Ida Cox, and Bessie Smith. These performers were primarily stage singers backed by jazz bands; their style is known as classic blues.

The Great Depression and the World Wars caused the geographic dispersal of the blues as millions of blacks left the South for the cities of the North. The blues became adapted to the more sophisticated urban environment. Lyrics took up urban themes, and the blues ensemble developed as the solo bluesman was joined by a pianist or harmonica player and then by a rhythm section consisting of bass and drums. The electric guitar and the amplified harmonica created a driving sound of great rhythmic and emotional intensity.

Among the cities in which the blues initially took root were Atlanta, Memphis, and St. Louis. On the West Coast Aaron ("T-Bone") Walker developed a style later adopted by Riley ("B.B.") King.

LITTLE WALTER

Raised on a Louisiana farm, Little Walter (born Marion Walter Jacobs) began playing harmonica in childhood, and by the time he was 12 he was playing for a living on New Orleans street corners and in clubs. In his teens he gradually worked northward, settling in Chicago about 1946; there he began recording in 1947 and played in Muddy Waters' blues band (1948–52). After Little Walter's 1952 harmonica solo "Juke" became a popular record, he successfully led his own bands in Chicago and on tours. In the 1960s alcoholism curtailed his career, and he died following a street fight.

Little Walter was one of the major figures in postwar Chicago blues. Influenced by guitarists as well as by senior harmonica players, he brought a singular variety of phrasing to the blues harmonica. His solos were cunningly crafted, alternating riffs and flowing lines; he was a pioneer of playing a harmonica directly into a handheld microphone and developed expressive techniques to enhance his playing. Though his vocal range was small, his singing often emulated Waters' style. His most popular recording was "My Babe," and his finest work included "Sad Hours," "Off the Wall," and "Can't Hold Out Much Longer."

Born into a Mississippi sharecropping family, John Lee Hooker moved to Detroit in 1943, and it was there that he made his mark as a blues musician. On such early records as "Boogie Chillen," "Crawling King Snake," and "Weeping Willow (Boogie)" (1948–49), Hooker, accompanied only by an electric guitar, revealed his best qualities: aggressive energy in fast boogies and no less intensity in stark, slow blues. A primitive guitarist, he played simple harmonies, pentatonic scales, and one-chord, modal harmonic structures. Later hits included "Dimples" (1956) and "Boom Boom" (1962).

It was Chicago, however, that played the greatest role in the development of urban blues. In the 1920s and '30s Memphis Minnie, Tampa Red, Big Bill Broonzy, and John Lee ("Sonny Boy") Williamson were popular Chicago performers. After World War II they were supplanted by a new generation of bluesmen that included Muddy Waters, Howlin' Wolf, Elmore James, Otis Spann, and Little Walter Jacobs.

The blues have influenced many other musical styles. Blues and jazz are closely related; such seminal jazzmen as Jelly Roll Morton and Louis Armstrong employed

BOOGIE-WOOGIE

Boogie-woogie, the heavily percussive style of blues piano in which the right hand plays riffs (syncopated, repeating phrases) against a driving pattern of repeating eighth notes (ostinato bass), was played in honky-tonks and rent parties on the South Side of Chicago in the 1920s but gained national attention only in the late 1930s. The height of its popularity was marked by a 1938 concert in Carnegie Hall, New York City, featuring its most prominent interpreters. It declined rapidly after World War II.

Among the greatest popularizers of boogie-woogie were Jimmy Yancey, Pinetop Smith, who is generally credited with inventing the term itself, Albert Ammons, Pete Johnson, and Meade "Lux" Lewis.

Boogie-woogie pianist Meade "Lux" Lewis. Frank Driggs Collection/Hulton Archive/ Getty Images

blues elements in their music. Soul music and rhythm and blues also show obvious blues tonalities and forms. The blues have had their greatest influence on rock music. Early rock singers such as Elvis Presley often used blues material. British rock musicians in the 1960s, especially the Rolling Stones, Eric Clapton, and John Mayall, were strongly influenced by the blues, as were such American rock musicians as Mike Bloomfield, Paul Butterfield, and the Allman Brothers Band.

RHYTHM AND BLUES

Rhythm and blues is the term used for several types of postwar African American popular music. The term was coined by Jerry Wexler in 1947, when he was editing the charts at the trade journal *Billboard* and found that the record companies issuing black popular music considered the chart names then in use (Harlem Hit Parade, Sepia, Race) to be demeaning. The magazine changed the chart's name in its June 17, 1949, issue, having used the term *rhythm and blues* in news articles for the previous two years. Although the records that appeared on *Billboard*'s rhythm-and-blues chart thereafter were in a variety of different styles, the term was used to encompass a number of contemporary forms that emerged at that time.

THE ORIGINS OF
RHYTHM AND BLUES

Perhaps the most commonly understood meaning of the term *rhythm and* *blues* (often also referred to as rhythm & blues or R&B) is as a description of the sophisticated urban music that had been developing since the 1930s, when Louis Jordan's small combo started making blues-based records with humorous lyrics and upbeat rhythms that owed as much to boogie-woogie as to classic blues forms. This music, sometimes called jump blues, set a pattern that became the dominant black popular music form during and for some time after World War II. Among its leading practitioners were Jordan, Amos Milburn, Roy Milton, Jimmy Liggins, Joe Liggins, Floyd Dixon, Wynonie Harris, Big Joe Turner, and Charles Brown. While many of the numbers in these performers' repertoires were in the classic 12-bar A-A-B blues form, others were straight pop songs, instrumentals that were close to light jazz, or pseudo-Latin compositions.

Within this genre there were large-group and small-group rhythm and blues. The former was practiced by singers whose main experience was with big bands and who were usually hired employees of bandleaders such as Lucky Millinder (for whose band Harris sang) or Count Basie (whose vocalists included Turner and Jimmy Witherspoon). The small groups usually consisted of five to seven pieces and counted on individual musicians to take turns in the limelight. Thus, for instance, in Milton's group, Milton played drums and sang, Camille Howard played piano and sang, and the alto and tenor saxophonists (Milton went through several

LOUIS JORDAN

The bouncing, rhythmic vitality of saxophonist-singer Louis Jordan's music, coupled with clever lyrics and an engaging stage presence, enabled him to become one of the few African American artists of the 1940s to enjoy crossover popularity with a white audience. Jordan's father was a professional musician, and it was through him that Jordan absorbed the black musical traditions of the American South. As a teenager Jordan toured as a singer, dancer, comedian, and woodwind player with a variety of performing troupes including the Rabbit Foot Minstrels. He joined drummer-bandleader Chick Webb's orchestra in 1936, remaining (alongside the young Ella Fitzgerald) for two years before forming his own band. Though Jordan had developed into an accomplished alto saxophonist in the mold of Benny Carter, he did not set out to

Louis Jordan. George Pickow/Hulton Archive/ Getty Images

form a jazz group. His goal, instead, was to create a music that would have a broader appeal.

Jordan and his Tympany Five (a name chosen despite the fact that he was normally accompanied by six musicians, none of whom played tympani) became by 1942 one of the most popular recording acts in the country. They often combined Count Basie-style riffs with a buoyant, boogie-based shuffle, and hits such as "Ain't Nobody Here But Us Chickens" and "Choo Choo Ch'Boogie" inspired countless "jump blues" combos. Though largely retaining the sound and subject matter of his African American roots, he enjoyed celebrity status among both blacks and whites, starring in numerous Hollywood short films and receiving equal billing on recorded collaborations with Louis Armstrong and Bing Crosby.

Jordan's musical style exerted a profound influence on a wide range of performers, most notably Chuck Berry, Ray Charles, and Bill Haley. Among many others who covered his material were Woody Herman, Muddy Waters, and Eric Clapton.

of them) each would be featured at least once. Another hallmark of small-group rhythm and blues was the relegation of the guitar, if indeed there was one, to a time-keeping status, because guitar soloing was considered "country" and unsophisticated. The most extreme example of this was Brown, both in his early work with Johnny Moore's Three Blazers and in his subsequent work as a bandleader; in both cases the band consisted of piano, bass, and guitar, but solos almost totally were handled by Brown on the piano.

Independent Record Labels

In the wake of World War II, a shortage of shellac (then the principal raw material of record manufacture) caused the major recording companies to economize. When they ignored the so-called "race" market, a new wave of entrepreneurs moved in to capitalize on the growing audience for rhythm and blues. Most of them were already involved with music in one way or another: owning a record shop (Syd Nathan of King Records in Cincinnati, Ohio) or a nightclub (the Chess brothers in Chicago), working in the jukebox business (the Bihari brothers of Modern Records in Los Angeles) or in radio (Lew Chudd of Imperial Records in Los Angeles, Sam Phillips of Sun Records in Memphis, Tenn.), or, in one case, turning a hobby into a living (Ahmet Ertegun of Atlantic Records in New York City).

Several companies set up studios in their office buildings, and label owners efficiently doubled as producers in an era when recording sessions lasted only three hours (according to union requirements). With the notable exception of Phillips, they had no experience in the studio. Some bluffed, telling the musicians to play the next take harder or faster or with more feeling. Others preferred to delegate studio supervision to experienced arrangers or engineers while dealing themselves with the logistics of pressing, distributing, and promoting their records and trying to collect money from sales.

Although the term *producer* did not come into currency until the mid-1950s, several arrangers had been performing that function for 10 years by then, most notably Maxwell Davis in Los Angeles, Dave Bartholomew in New Orleans, Willie Dixon in Chicago, Henry Glover in Cincinnati, Ohio, and Jesse Stone in New York City. Veterans of the big-band era who created rhythm-based arrangements for rhythm and blues, they acted as midwives for what is now called rock and roll.

For all concerned, the experience was a crash course in economics, and practices ranged from the honourable to the disreputable. When label bosses discovered that whoever published the song was legally entitled to receive two cents per title on each record sold, they soon became song publishers too. But some bought out the writers' share for a few dollars, thereafter taking all the proceeds from both sales and airplay.

Specialty Records

Specialty Records was founded in Los Angeles by Art Rupe, a graduate of the University of California, Los Angeles, who started out by recording local black artists for the jukebox market. He soon built a strong roster of small combos led by Roy Milton and brothers Jimmy and Joe Liggins as well as gospel groups such as the Soul Stirrers and the Pilgrim Travelers. Specialty scored three of the biggest rhythm-and-blues hits of the early 1950s with "Please Send Me Someone to Love" by Percy Mayfield (1950), "Lawdy Miss Clawdy" by Lloyd Price (1952), and "The Things That I Used to Do" by Guitar Slim (1954), the last two recorded in New Orleans with musicians from Fats Domino's session band. When Rupe added Little Richard to his roster in 1955, newly appointed artists-and-repertoire man Robert ("Bumps") Blackwell went to New Orleans for the label's first session with Richard, which resulted in "Tutti Frutti."

Richard turned out to be Specialty's biggest artist. Rupe missed a chance for even greater success with Sam Cooke. The young lead singer of the Soul Stirrers recorded "You Send Me" at Specialty's studio under the supervision of Blackwell, but an unconvinced Rupe (determined not to lose his gospel star to secular music) terminated the contracts of both singer and producer. Rupe then watched ruefully as the single topped the pop charts on another local label, Keen, and Cooke emerged as one of the biggest artists of the era. The scrupulous Rupe stayed in business for several more years but was never comfortable with the practice of payola (paying disc jockeys to play his records).

ATLANTIC RECORDS

Formed in 1947 by jazz fans Ahmet Ertegun, son of a Turkish diplomat, and Herb Abramson, formerly the artists-and-repertoire director for National Records, Atlantic became the most consistently successful New York City-based independent label of the 1950s, with an incomparable roster of rhythm and blues performers including Joe Turner, Chuck Willis, Ruth Brown, the Clovers, Ray Charles, Clyde McPhatter and the Drifters, and LaVern Baker. At Atlantic, Charles (who had been imitating Charles Brown) found a new direction, which eventually would evolve into soul. Apart from Charles none of these singers regularly wrote their own songs, which were provided by freelance writers including Jesse Stone, Rudolph Toombs, and Winfield Scott. Stone was also a vital part of the production team in his capacity as rehearsal coach and session arranger. Jerry Wexler joined the company in 1953, just in time to take part in a golden era when many of the label's classic records were recorded at evening sessions in the 56th Street office after the desks had been stacked on top of each other to make room for engineer Tom Dowd to set up his recording equipment. Atlantic hired jazz musicians as studio players and, because of Dowd, paid particular attention to the sound quality of their recordings. As the roster expanded, Atlantic set a precedent by hiring Jerry Leiber and Mike Stoller as producers of records by the Coasters and the Drifters.

CLYDE McPHATTER

Clyde McPhatter (centre) surrounded by The Drifters, (l-r) Bill Pinkney, Willie Ferber, Andrew Thrasher, and Gerhart Thrasher. Michael Ochs Archives/Getty Images

One of the most dramatic vocalists of his generation, Clyde McPhatter grew up in a devout Christian family that moved from North Carolina to New Jersey in the mid-1940s. There, together with some high school friends (including two of author James Baldwin's brothers), he formed the Mount Lebanon Singers, who quickly found success on the gospel circuit. In 1950 a talent contest brought him to the attention of vocal coach Billy Ward, whose group he joined. With McPhatter singing lead, Billy Ward and the Dominoes became one of the era's preeminent vocal groups, but the martinetish Ward fired McPhatter in 1953 (replacing him with Jackie Wilson). Shortly thereafter, Atlantic Records' Ahmet Ertegun sought to establish a new group around McPhatter, eventually recruiting former members of the Thrasher Wonders. As Clyde McPhatter and the Drifters, this group soon had a hit with "Money Honey," which perfectly showcased McPhatter's melismatic, gospel-derived style. In 1954 their recording of Irving Berlin's classic "White Christmas" was banned from the radio because of alleged lewdness, yet it became a perennial seller. That fall McPhatter was drafted into the army but, stationed in New Jersey, was able to continue recording and appear in the film Mister Rock and Roll (1957).

Upon his discharge he became a soloist, with the Drifters continuing with other lead singers (most notably Ben E. King). Thereafter, McPhatter began to record increasingly pop-oriented material, including the pop Top 20 hits "Without Love (There Is Nothing)" (1956) and "A Lover's Question" (1958) as well as the rhythm-and-blues hit "Lovey Dovey." In 1960 he switched record labels, signing first with MGM, then with Mercury. His new material was so pop-oriented that his 1962 hit "Lover Please" did not even show up on the rhythm-and-blues charts, and, after a mild success in 1965 with "Crying Won't Help You Now," the hits stopped coming, although his voice would have been perfect for the emerging style of soul. Slipping into alcoholism, he played the oldies circuit and died before his 40th birthday.

KING RECORDS

Record store owner Syd Nathan established King Records in Cincinnati, Ohio, in 1943. Situated just across the Ohio River from more rural, Southern-oriented Kentucky, Nathan recorded country acts who came to town to play on WLW's *Midwestern Hayride* and the touring black singers and bands who included Cincinnati on their itinerary. By reputation irascible and penny-pinching, the single-minded Nathan created a uniquely self-sufficient operation with not only a recording studio and publishing company but his own pressing plant, printing press (for labels and sleeves), and distribution system.

Despite being incapable of actually writing a song himself, Nathan regularly bought out the composer rights for nominal sums and claimed authorship under the name Lois Mann. To supervise recordings he hired Henry Glover and Ralph Bass, who pulled together an incomparable roster of performers that included big band refugees Earl Bostic (alto sax) and Bill Doggett (organ), blues shouters Wynonie Harris and Roy Brown, blues ballad singers Little Esther and Little Willie John, and vocal groups Billy Ward and the Dominoes (featuring first Clyde McPhatter and later Jackie Wilson) and Hank Ballard and the Midnighters. But by far the biggest artist to record for King was the maverick James Brown, who succeeded despite Nathan's initial skepticism at Bass's decision to record

and release Brown's first single, "Please, Please, Please" (1956), which launched his remarkable career.

CHESS RECORDS

In 1947 brothers Leonard and Phil Chess became partners with Charles and Evelyn Aron in the Aristocrat Record Company. The Chesses had operated several taverns on Chicago's South Side—the last and largest of which was the Mocamba Lounge—and their desire to record one of the singers who performed in their nightclub led them into the record business. In 1950, after buying out the Arons, they changed the name of their company to Chess and attracted an unparalleled roster of blues artists who had come to the city from the Mississippi Delta, including Muddy Waters, Howlin' Wolf, the second Sonny Boy Williamson (Alex ["Rice"] Miller), Little Walter, and Bo Diddley. Bassist-arranger Willie Dixon was a vital presence at these blues sessions, writing several classic songs, including "I'm Your Hoochie Coochie Man." He also was versatile enough to help deliver Chuck Berry's version of rock and roll. As rhythm and blues began to infiltrate the pop market, Chess and its subsidiary label, Checker, recorded such vocal groups as the Moonglows and the Flamingos and administered the Arc and Jewel publishing companies through Maurice Levy. Levy managed disc jockey Alan Freed and assigned to him a share of the songwriting royalties for the Moonglows' "Sincerely" and Berry's "Maybellene."

VEE JAY RECORDS

Record store owners Vivian Carter ("Vee") and James Bracken ("Jay"), later husband and wife, formed Vee Jay Records in 1953. (At various times the company's labels also read VJ or Vee-Jay.) With Carter's brother Calvin as producer and Ewart Abner in charge of promotion, Vee Jay became the most successful black-owned record company of its period. Jimmy Reed made more commercial blues records than Chess managed to produce; without ever sounding like rock and roll, his simple, hypnotic grooves were jukebox staples through the early 1960s, when both he and John Lee Hooker became bedrock influences on the emerging British blues movement.

Vee Jay reached the pop charts mostly through vocal groups, starting in 1954 with "Goodnite, Sweetheart, Goodnite" by the Spaniels, continuing with "For Your Precious Love" by Jerry Butler and the Impressions in 1958, and reaching a pinnacle with a string of hits by the Four Seasons in the early 1960s. When Capitol refused its option to release several Beatles singles—as well as their first American album, *Introducing…the Beatles* (1964)—Vee Jay jumped at the opportunity, taking the album to number two and four singles to the Top Five. Ironically, overexpansion in the wake of this success contributed to the bankruptcy that befell the company soon after.

DUKE AND PEACOCK RECORDS

A decade before the ascendance of Motown, Houston's Duke and Peacock record labels flourished as an African American–owned company. Don Robey, a nightclub owner with reputed underworld connections, founded Peacock Records in 1949 and ran it with an iron hand. In 1952 Robey and James Mattias of Duke Records (founded in Memphis, Tenn., earlier in the year) formed a partnership. A year later Robey became the outright owner of Duke and centralized its operation in Houston. The company's staples were gospel (the Five Blind Boys of Mississippi) and gospel-oriented blues (Bobby "Blue" Bland and Junior Parker, with arrangements by Joe Scott and Bill Harvey, respectively). In 1953 Willie Mae ("Big Mama") Thornton recorded the first version of "Hound Dog," which Elvis Presley turned into a rock-and-roll anthem three years later. In 1954 Duke's ballad singer Johnny Ace became the first martyr of the new teen era, losing at Russian roulette after a concert; his posthumous hit "Pledging My Love" became one of the most-played "oldies" in the decades that followed.

RHYTHM AND BLUES IN THE ERA OF ROCK AND ROLL

By mid-decade rhythm and blues had come to mean black popular music that was not overtly aimed at teenagers, since the music that was becoming known as rock and roll sometimes featured lyrics that concerned first love and parent-child conflict, as well as a less subtle approach to rhythm. Many doo-wop vocal groups, therefore, were considered rock-and-roll acts, as were performers such as Little Richard and Hank Ballard and the Midnighters. Because the distinction between rock and roll and rhythm and blues was not based on any hard-and-fast rules, most performers issued records that fit in both categories. Moreover, some vocalists who were later considered jazz performers—in particular, Dinah Washington—also appeared on the rhythm-and-blues charts, and a steady stream of saxophone-led instrumentals firmly in the rhythm-and-blues tradition continued to be produced by performers such as Joe Houston, Chuck Higgins, and Sam ("The Man") Taylor but were considered rock and roll and were often used as theme music by disc jockeys on rock-and-roll radio.

The division based on the age of the intended audience for black popular music also meant that, by the mid-1950s, much of the guitar-led electric blues music coming from Chicago and Memphis was now considered rhythm and blues, since it appealed to older buyers. Thus, although they had little to nothing in common with the earlier generation of band-backed blues shouters, performers such as Muddy Waters, Howlin' Wolf, and B.B. King (who, because he used a horn section when he could, was perhaps more like the older generation than the Chicago bluesmen) became regarded as rhythm-and-blues performers. One important figure in

this transition was Ike Turner, a piano-player-turned-guitarist from Mississippi who worked as a talent scout for several labels and fronted a band called the Kings of Rhythm, which backed many of his discoveries on records. When Turner married the former Anna Mae Bullock and rechristened her Tina Turner, the Ike and Tina Turner Revue became a significant force in the modernization of rhythm and blues, dispensing with the horn section but including a trio of female backing singers who were modeled on Ray Charles's Raelettes.

By 1960 rhythm and blues was, if not a spent force, at least aging with its audience. Performers such as Washington, Charles, and Ruth Brown were appearing more in nightclubs than in the multiperformer revues in which they had made their names. Although younger performers such as Jackie Wilson and Sam Cooke clearly owed a debt to the previous generation of rhythm-and-blues performers, they were more transitional figures who were, like Charles, establishing the new genre of soul. Significantly, in the Aug. 23, 1969, issue of *Billboard,* the black pop chart's name was changed again, to soul. Although *soul* then became the preferred term for black popular music, in some quarters *rhythm and blues* continued to be used to refer to nearly every genre of post–World War II black music.

The term *rhythm and blues,* however, attained a new meaning thanks to the British bands that followed in the wake of the Beatles. Most of these groups, notably the Rolling Stones, played a mixture of Chicago blues and black rock and roll and described their music as rhythm and blues. Thus, the Who, although a quint-essential mod rock band, advertised their early performances as "Maximum R&B" to attract an audience. Although bands that followed this generation—John Mayall's Bluesbreakers and Fleetwood Mac, for example—called themselves blues bands, rhythm and blues remained the rubric for the Animals, Them, the Pretty Things, and others. Today a band that advertises itself as rhythm and blues is almost certainly following in this tradition rather than that of the early pioneers.

DOO-WOP

A style of vocal music popular in the 1950s and '60s, doo-wop took its name from the sounds made by a group as they provided harmonic background for the lead singer. The structure of doo-wop music generally featured a tenor lead vocalist singing the melody of the song with a trio or quartet singing background harmony. The roots of the doo-wop style can be found as early as the records of the Mills Brothers and the Ink Spots in the 1930s and '40s. The Mills Brothers turned small-group harmony into an art form when, in many of their recordings, they used their vocal harmony to simulate the sound of string or reed sections. The Ink Spots established the preeminence of the tenor and bass singer as members of the pop vocal ensemble, and their influence can be heard in rhythm-and-blues music beginning in the 1940s (in records by the Ravens), throughout the '50s, and well into

THE INK SPOTS

One of the first African American groups, along with the Mills Brothers, to reach both black and white audiences, the Ink Spots exerted great influence on the development of the doo-wop vocal style. The principal members were Orville ("Hoppy") Jones, Charles Fuqua, Ivory ("Deek") Watson, Bill Kenny, Jerry Daniels, Herb Kenny, and Billy Bowen.

Formed in 1932 as the King, Jack and the Jesters, the group became the Ink Spots when they relocated to New York City. After Herb Kenny replaced original member Jerry Daniels, the group began a slow evolution toward its distinctive sound. In 1939 the Ink Spots scored a huge hit with "If I Didn't Care," on which Bill Kenny's tenor lead contrasted with Jones's deep bass. In establishing the prominence of the high tenor lead and adding spoken bass choruses to the backing harmonies, the Ink Spots laid the groundwork for countless doo-wop and rhythm-and-blues vocal groups, from the Ravens and the Orioles to Motown's Temptations. Among their many hits in the 1940s were "Address Unknown," "My Prayer" (later rerecorded by the Platters), "Into Each Life Some Rain Must Fall" (a collaboration with Ella Fitzgerald), "We Three," "To Each His Own," and "The Gypsy." In the early 1950s the group split into two, and multiple incarnations of the Ink Spots continued to perform through the 1990s.

the '70s. This influence is best exhibited in the remakes of the Ink Spots' hit records "My Prayer" (1956) by the Platters and "If I Didn't Care" (1970) by the Moments. In fact, Motown's premier male group of the 1960s and '70s, the Temptations, had a vocal sound that was based in this classic doo-wop style, with the Ink Spots' tenor lead singer, Bill Kenny, and bass singer, Hoppy Jones, serving as inspiration for the Temptations' lead singers, Eddie Kendricks and David Ruffin, and their bass singer, Melvin Franklin. There also was a school of female doo-wop, best exemplified by the Chantels, the Shirelles, and Patti LaBelle and the Bluebelles.

The popularity of doo-wop music among young singers in urban American communities of the 1950s such as New York City, Chicago, and Baltimore, Md., was due in large part to the fact that the music could be performed effectively a cappella. Many young enthusiasts in these communities had little access to musical instruments, so the vocal ensemble was the most popular musical performing unit. Doo-wop groups tended to rehearse in locations that provided echoes—where their harmonies could best be heard. They often rehearsed in hallways and high school bathrooms and under bridges; when they were ready for public performance, they sang on stoops and street corners, in community centre talent shows, and in the hallways of the Brill Building, the songwriting "factory" on Broadway in New York City. As a result many doo-wop records had such remarkably rich vocal harmonies that they virtually overwhelmed their minimalist instrumental accompaniment. Doo-wop's appeal for much of the public lay in its artistically powerful simplicity, but this "uncomplicated" type of record also was an ideal, low-budget investment for a small record company to produce. The absence of strings and horns ("sweetening") in their production gave many of

THE PLATTERS

One of the foremost singing groups of their era, the Platters (Tony Williams, Zola Taylor, David Lynch, Paul Robi, Herb Reed, and Sonny Turner) were managed by songwriter Buck Ram, who had been so taken with Williams's dramatic, soaring voice that he had the singer form a group around himself in 1953 in Los Angeles. Ram wrote or cowrote some of the Platters' biggest hits, including "Only You (and You Alone)" (1955), "The Great Pretender" (which topped the pop and rhythm-and-blues charts in 1956), and "(You've Got) The Magic Touch" (1956). The Platters sustained their career by specializing in rock-and-roll renditions of old big-band hits, notably "My Prayer" (1956) and "Twilight Time" and "Smoke Gets in Your Eyes" (both 1958). The group also appeared in two rock-and-roll movies, The Girl Can't Help It *and* Rock Around the Clock *(both 1956). Williams left the Platters in 1961, but during the late 1960s, with Turner as the lead vocalist, the group achieved moderate success with soul-style hits.*

the doo-wop records of the early 1950s an almost haunting sparseness. The Orioles' "What Are You Doing New Years Eve?" (1949) and "Crying in the Chapel" (1953), the Harptones' "A Sunday Kind of Love" (1953), and the Penguins' "Earth Angel" (1954) are excellent examples of this effect.

An unfortunate by-product of the poetic simplicity of doo-wop records was that it was relatively easy for major labels to cover (rerecord) those records with greater production values (including the addition of strings and horns) and with a different vocal group. Consistent with the racial segregation of much of American society in the 1950s, the practice of major record labels producing cover records usually involved doo-wop records that were originally performed by African American artists being re-created by white artists, the objective being to sell these covers to a broader, "pop" (white) audience. Among the legion of doo-wop records that suffered this fate were the Chords' "Sh-Boom" (covered by the Crew-Cuts in 1954) and the Moonglows' "Sincerely" (covered by the McGuire Sisters in 1955). A number of white singing groups adopted the doo-wop style—particularly Italian-American ensembles who shared the same urban environment with the African Americans who originated doo-wop. Like the phenomenon of cover records, the advent of the "clean-cut" teen idols who prospered on *American Bandstand,* and the popularity of blue-eyed soul, this version of doo-wop further exemplified how black music was co-opted by the white recording industry. Prominent practitioners of the "white doo-wop" sound were the Elegants ("Little Star" [1958]), Dion and the Belmonts ("I Wonder Why" [1958]), and the Four Seasons' ("Sherry" [1962]). Ultimately, the musical power of doo-wop has flowed from the original groups through the Motown music of the 1960s and the Philly Sound of the '70s and continued into the urban contemporary music of the '90s.

CHAPTER 6

SOUL, MOTOWN, DISCO, FUNK, HIP-HOP, AND HOUSE

From the 1960s on to the beginning of the 21st century, African Americans continued to create new styles of popular music, all of which eventually exploded to win huge diverse audiences. Studio mastery progressed in leaps and bounds as the technical side of musicmaking grew in importance on its way to the postmodern aesthetic of hip-hop and house music. Likewise black music increasingly became black-owned and -managed as African Americans founded their own labels and rose through the management ranks of major recording companies.

SOUL MUSIC

Soul music was the term adopted to describe black popular music in the United States as it evolved from the 1950s to the '60s and '70s. Some view soul as merely a new term for rhythm and blues. In fact a new generation of artists profoundly reinterpreted the sounds of the rhythm-and-blues pioneers of the 1950s—Chuck Berry, Little Richard, Bo Diddley, Sam Cooke, and Ray Charles—whose music found popularity among whites and was transformed into what became known as rock and roll.

If rock and roll, represented by performers such as Elvis Presley, can be seen as a white reading of rhythm and blues, soul is a return to black music's roots—gospel and blues. The style is marked by searing vocal intensity, use of church-rooted call-and-response, and extravagant melisma. If in the 1950s Charles was the first to secularize pure gospel songs, that transformation realized its full flowering in the work of Aretha Franklin, the "Queen of Soul," who, after six years of notable work on Columbia Records, began her glorious reign in 1967 with her first hits for Atlantic Records—"I Never Loved a Man (the Way I Love You)" and "Respect." Before Franklin, though, soul music had exploded largely through the work of Southern artists such as James Brown and Southern-oriented labels such as Stax/Volt.

The Motown sound, which came of age in the 1960s, must also be considered soul music. In addition to its lighter, more pop-oriented artists such as the Supremes, the Motown label produced artists with genuine gospel grit—the Contours ("Do You Love Me" [1962]), Marvin Gaye ("Can I Get a Witness" [1963]), and Stevie Wonder ("Uptight [Everything's Alright]" [1966]). But Motown packaged its acts as clean-cut and acceptable, as it sought to sell to white teens. As the civil rights movement gained

Aretha Franklin, pictured in 1968. Express Newspapers/Hulton Archive/Getty Images

steam, black artists grew more politically aware. Rooted in personal expression, their music resonates with self-assertion, culminating in Brown's "Say It Loud—I'm Black and I'm Proud (Part 1)" (1968).

In Memphis, Stax/Volt Records was built on an unshakable foundation of straight-up soul. Founded in 1960 by country music fiddle player Jim Stewart and his sister Estelle Axton, following a previous false start with Satellite Records, Stax maintained a down-home, family atmosphere during its early years. Black and white musicians and singers worked together in relaxed conditions, where nobody looked at a clock or worried about union session rates, at the recording studio in a converted movie theatre at 926 East McLemore. They created records from ideas jotted down on bits of paper, phrases remembered from gospel songs, and rhythm licks that might make the kids on *American Bandstand* dance. Steve Cropper, organist Booker T. Jones, bassist Donald ("Duck") Dunn, and drummer Al Jackson, Jr., had numerous hits as Booker T. and the MG's, and they made many more records as the rhythm section (and, in effect, producers) for most of the recordings at Stax during the decade, sometimes with the help of pianist Isaac Hayes and lyricist David Porter, who teamed up as writer-producers in 1964.

Many Stax records featured a distinctive horn sound, and their bass-heavy bottom end had a powerful impact when played on jukeboxes and in dance clubs. Atlantic's Jerry Wexler, who had participated in the earliest phase of soul music with his productions for Solomon Burke ("Just out of Reach" [1961]), was the earliest industry figure to recognize the potential of this Memphis Sound.

Wexler made a deal that allowed Atlantic to distribute Stax both nationally

SOLOMON BURKE

Born into a family that established its own church, Solomon Burke was both a preacher and the host of a gospel radio program by age 12. He began recording in 1955 but did not have his first national hit until 1961, with a rhythm-and-blues version of a country ballad, "Just out of Reach." His recordings, most of which were produced in New York City, incorporated gospel-derived vocal techniques—shouted interjections, an exhortatory recitation, melisma, and rasping timbre. At Atlantic Records, under producer Bert Berns, Burke became one of the first rhythm-and-blues performers to be called a soul artist, based on his success with "Cry to Me" (1962), "If You Need Me" (1963), "Goodbye Baby (Baby Goodbye)" (1964), "Got to Get You off My Mind" (1965), and his last Top 40 pop hit, "Tonight's the Night" (1965). After the mid-1960s Burke continued to record but with lessening success, last placing a record on the rhythm-and-blues chart in 1978. In the 1980s and '90s he remained a popular performer on the blues festival and club circuit.

and internationally; he also was the catalyst for several milestone records made by singers from out of town, including "Respect" (1965) by Otis Redding (from Georgia), whose records were released on the subsidiary label Volt; and "Soul Man" (1962) by Sam and Dave (from Florida). Wexler also began recording Aretha Franklin as well as Wilson Pickett, one of soul's premier vocalists, in Fame Studios in Florence, Ala., where the arrangements were largely spontaneous and surprisingly sparse—strong horn lines supported by a rhythm section focused on boiling funk.

Other artists and producers followed Wexler's lead. Etta James, with her earth-shaking delivery and take-no-prisoners approach, traveled to Muscle Shoals, Ala., to record "Tell Mama" (1967), one of the decade's enduring soul anthems, written by singer and songwriter Clarence Carter. Percy Sledge's supersmooth "When a Man Loves a Woman" (1966), recorded in nearby Sheffield, became the first Southern soul song to reach number one on the pop charts.

Toward the end of the 1960s, the interracial harmony at Stax was disturbed by the social and political tension sweeping the country. Still under its original management but represented publicly by Al Bell, the black promotion man who became vice-president and co-owner, Stax achieved its greatest commercial success during the early 1970s with hits recorded in Detroit, Chicago, and Muscle Shoals, Ala., as well as in its own studios,

by Johnnie Taylor, Hayes, the Staple Singers, the Dramatics, and others.

In the early 1970s Memphis's chain of racially mixed musics made by integrated musicians—from the output of Sun Records to that of Stax/Volt and Chips Moman's American Sound Studios—was broken, largely as a consequence of urban blight and the coalition-splintering shock of the assassination of the Rev. Martin Luther King, Jr. In the aftermath Willie Mitchell created a new soul style with vocalist Al Green at Hi Records. Hi had been around since the late 1950s, with instrumental hits by Elvis Presley's former bassist, Bill Black, and by Mitchell, a former jazz bandleader who took over as artists-and-repertoire man.

Hi's Royal Recording Studios, at 1320 South Lauderdale Street, just off Highway 61 in a predominantly African American portion of the city, were, like Stax's, located in a former movie theatre. Mitchell used the unusual acoustics caused partly by the theatre's sloping floor to construct a new sound. He slowed soul's tempo and emphasized a percussive $^4/_4$ beat, utilizing the talents of drummer Al Jackson (formerly of Booker T. and the MG's) and the Hodges brothers—Leroy (bass), Charles (keyboards), and Teenie (guitar). The first hint of the new sound was Ann Peebles's "Part Time Love" (1970), but its full glory was revealed in a sublime series of hits by Green (remembered for his trademark white suit) from 1971 to 1975. These sexy songs for adults were the cornerstone of some of soul's most

WILSON PICKETT

Singer-songwriter Wilson Pickett's explosive style helped define the soul music of the 1960s. Pickett was a product of the Southern black church, and gospel was at the core of his musical manner and onstage persona. He testified rather than sang, preached rather than crooned. His delivery was marked by the fervour of religious conviction, no matter how secular the songs he sang.

Along with thousands of other Southern farmworkers, Pickett migrated in the 1950s to industrial Detroit, where his father worked in an auto plant. His first recording experience was in pure gospel. He sang with the Violinaires and the Spiritual Five, modeling himself after Julius Cheeks of the Sensational Nightingales, a thunderous shouter.

Wilson Pickett at Muscle Shoals Recording Studios, Nov. 24, 1969 in Sheffield, Ala. Michael Ochs Archives/Getty Images

Pickett's switch to secular music came quickly. As a member of the Falcons, a hardcore rhythm-and-blues vocal group, he sang lead on his own composition I Found a Love (1962), one of the songs that interested Jerry Wexler in Pickett as a solo artist. "Pickett was a pistol," said Wexler, who nicknamed him "the Wicked Pickett" and sent him to Memphis, to write with Otis Redding's collaborator, guitarist Steve Cropper of Booker T. and the MG's. The result was a smash single, "In the Midnight Hour" (1965). From that moment on, Pickett was a star. With his dazzling good looks and confident demeanour, he stood as a leading exponent of the Southern-fried school of soul singing. His unadorned straight-from-the-gut approach was accepted, even revered, by a civil-rights-minded pop culture.

After his initial string of smashes—"Land of 1000 Dances" (1966), "Mustang Sally" (1966), "Funky Broadway" (1967)—Pickett was successfully produced by Philadelphians Kenny Gamble and Leon Huff, who took a bit of the edge off his fiery style on "Engine Number 9" (1970) and "Don't Let the Green Grass Fool You" (1971). Before leaving Atlantic, Pickett enjoyed another run of smashes, including "Don't Knock My Love" (1971), "Call My Name, I'll Be There" (1971), and "Fire and Water" (1972). The advent of funk bands and disco resulted in a decline in Pickett's popularity, although there are critics who consider "Groove City" (1979) on EMI, his one nod to disco, a dance groove of monumental stature. Although his output began to slow in the 1980s, Pickett continued to perform into the early 21st century, and his influence on younger generations of soulful singers remained strong.

luxuriant music. It may have been the last great innovation of the Memphis music scene, but its erotic mix of the sacred and the profane remained influential. Talking Heads had a hit with a cover version of Green's "Take Me to the River" in 1978, and glimpses of Hi's slinky rhythms could be heard in the more overtly eroticized house music of Chicago in the 1980s.

Soul was not restricted to the South and Detroit. Berry Gordy, Jr., and his Motown Records overshadowed Chicago during the 1960s, but several black music producers—including Roquel ("Billy") Davis and Carl Davis (who were not related), Johnny Pate (who also was an arranger), and Curtis Mayfield, who added his own sense of social consciousness to the soul music movement—developed a recognizable Windy City sound that flourished from the late 1950s to the mid-1970s. This lightly gospelized rhythm and blues, which came to be known as Chicago soul, replaced the raucous blues of South Side bars with sophisticated, jazzy arrangements confected in recording studios and featuring melodic vocals backed by brass sections and strings.

The first record from the city with a distinctly soulful sound was Jerry Butler and the Impressions' "For Your Precious Love" (1958). Butler and the Impressions parted company to pursue parallel careers but remained in contact, and the group's guitarist, Mayfield, provided Butler's next big hit, "He Will Break Your Heart" (1960); its gospel structure established the blueprint for the sound of the city for the next 10 years. The Impressions' own career was launched the following year with "Gypsy Woman." In addition to writing a series of uplifting anthemic hits for the Impressions (produced by Pate for ABC Records), Mayfield also provided songs for numerous other artists, including "Um, Um, Um, Um, Um, Um" and "Monkey Time" for Major Lance. Most of these records were released on out-of-town labels, and Mayfield's status as a lyricist and innovative guitarist was not fully recognized until he formed his own Curtom label in 1968 in partnership with his longtime manager, Eddie Thomas.

Billy Davis had been Gordy's songwriting partner before joining the artists-and-repertoire (A&R) staff at Chess, where he worked with most of the label's roster, including Etta James and Sugar Pie DeSanto. Following the success of Gene Chandler's "Duke of Earl" (1961), producer Carl Davis was appointed head of A&R for OKeh Records, where he recruited Mayfield to write for several artists including Lance. Davis then moved to Brunswick Records, where he produced one of Jackie Wilson's finest records, "(Your Love Keeps Lifting Me) Higher and Higher" (1967). He subsequently set up his own Dakar label, whose singles by Tyrone Davis—"Can I Change My Mind?" (1969) and "Turn Back the Hands of Time" (1970)—were classics of wistful regret.

Meanwhile, as Chicago's blues men were losing their slots on the city's jukeboxes to these new soul artists, their songs were being recycled in Britain by white musicians—most prominently the

Rolling Stones, who made a pilgrimage to the Chess studios in 1965 to record the backing track for their epochal single "(I Can't Get No) Satisfaction."

Soul also flowered in New Orleans, in the ultrafunky work of Art Neville's group the Meters. Atlantic Records produced smoldering soul smashes in New York City, notably by Aretha Franklin and Donny Hathaway; and Stevie Wonder and the Jackson 5 created some of the era's great soul records in Los Angeles. Meanwhile the Sound of Philadelphia in the 1970s was the bridge between Memphis soul and international disco and between Detroit pop and Hi-NRG (high energy; the ultrafast dance music popular primarily in gay clubs in the 1980s). African American–run Philadelphia International Records was the vital label of the era; its sound was a timely mix of swishing high-hat cymbals and social awareness, of growling soul vocals and sweeping strings. The founding fathers were Philadelphian Kenny Gamble and New Jersey–born Leon Huff, writer-producers who had made their way through the collapsing Philadelphia music industry of the 1960s. They were reinforced by singer-turned-writer Linda Creed and writer-arranger Thom Bell, who had helped create the sound of the Delfonics at the city's other main label, Philly Groove. Together they created a new kind of pop soul, which can appear cliché when dissected but was immensely popular on the dance floor. Based on the rhythmic talents of the Sigma Studios session men, who had a hit of their own

as MFSB, Philadelphia International music featured unusual instrumentation—French horns, for example—and adult sensibilities delivered by adult vocalists.

"Me and Mrs. Jones" (1972), a tale of implied infidelity, launched nightclub balladeer Billy Paul. After nearly 20 years in the business, Harold Melvin and the Bluenotes became stars, and lead vocalist Teddy Pendergrass became an archetypal 1970s sex symbol. The O'Jays, also veterans with a 10-year recording history behind them, reached the Top Ten with "Back Stabbers" (1972) and "Love Train" (1973), both social commentaries in a successfully naive vein. Where Gamble and Huff led, disco followed—the Ritchie Family's "Best Disco in Town" (1976) was recorded at Sigma, as was the Village People's "YMCA" (1978). Philadelphia's final big hit, the anthemic "Ain't No Stoppin' Us Now" (1979) by (Gene) McFadden and (John) Whitehead, came as dance music underwent one of its episodic black-white schisms. A couple of years later, Daryl Hall and John Oates—the favourite white sons of Philadelphia soul—grafted their traditional rhythm-and-blues voicings onto the new black rhythms of hip-hop.

Soul became a permanent part of the grammar of American popular culture. Its underlying virtues—direct emotional delivery, ethnic pride, and respect for its own artistic sources—live on as dynamic and dramatic influences on musicians throughout the world. To varying degrees, the power and personality of the form were absorbed in disco, funk, and hip-hop, styles that owe their existence to soul.

MOTOWN

The tale of the founding and flourishing of Detroit's Motown Record Corporation under the leadership of Berry Gordy, Jr., is one of the most compelling success stories in African American history. Moving from Georgia to Detroit, Gordy's family was part of the massive migration of hundreds of thousands of African Americans from the South during and after World War I, lured largely by the promise of work in Northern manufacturing industries such as Detroit's auto plants. Gordy's parents, hardworking entrepreneurs, instilled in their children the gospel of hard work and religious faith. They also played a major role in financing Gordy in his early years in the music business.

Berry Gordy at a gala reunion/celebration of Motown's 50th anniversary, Oct. 20, 2007, Detroit, Mich. Bill Pugliano/Getty Images

Following an attempt at a professional boxing career and a stint in the army during the Korean War, Gordy entered the music business. He briefly owned a jazz record store, but his true love was songwriting. Although he could not read music, he demonstrated an unerring ability to gauge whether a song had the elements of popular appeal. Before forming Motown, Gordy tried to make it as an independent songwriter and record producer, cowriting hit songs for Jackie Wilson, another former boxer and Detroiter, and Marv Johnson. Despite his success, Gordy remained on the fringes of the popular music business, making very little money, until he discovered William ("Smokey") Robinson, a Detroit high schooler with a soothing falsetto and an ear for sweet lyrics.

In 1959, not long after recording Robinson's group, the Miracles, for New York–based End Records and establishing Jobete Publishing Company, Gordy began Motown Records (its name derived from Detroit's nickname, "Motor City"). A number of factors came together to make Motown's success possible at this time. First, after World War II, big-band swing, the dominant popular dance music in the United States during the Great Depression, became passé. Big musical units were no longer economically feasible. Jazz had been taken over by a new group of Young Turk stylists; calling themselves beboppers, they were inclined to play music for listening rather than dancing.

Second, a new urban dance music, rhythm and blues, was ascendant. Emerging primarily from inner-city ghettos and popularized by such bandleaders as Louis Jordan and Lionel Hampton, rhythm and blues was almost exclusively recorded by small independent labels. Of the three major recording companies—Columbia, Capitol, and Decca—only the last showed any interest in the exciting new music that would spawn rock and roll. During the 1950s it was possible for a young entrepreneur with an ear for this music to start a moderately successful independent company producing a sound that appealed to young people and inner-city African Americans.

Third, by the late 1950s two other black-owned independent record companies that specialized in rhythm and blues and rock and roll—Peacock Records and Vee Jay Records—had been enjoying considerable success for nearly a decade. Therefore Gordy was not going into completely uncharted territory as a black music entrepreneur. In 1959, the year Gordy founded Motown, Harry Belafonte became the first black to produce a Hollywood film, *Odds Against Tomorrow,* through his own company. The social

change promised by the *Brown v. Board of Education of Topeka* decision and the new civil rights activism made this a heady time indeed to be an enterprising African American—anything seemed possible. Moreover, black radio had become a force in the marketing of popular music after World War II. This gave black listeners great clout as consumers and made it possible for black record company owners to market their wares directly to this growing audience.

During the 1960s Motown became one of the reigning presences in American popular music, along with the Beatles. Gordy assembled an array of talented local people (many of whom had benefited from the excellent music education program at Detroit public schools in the 1950s) at 2648 West Grand Boulevard, destined to become the most famous address in Detroit. Serving as both recording studio and administrative headquarters, this two-story house became the home of "Hitsville." Motown's roster included several successful solo acts, such as Marvin Gaye, Stevie Wonder (a star as both a child and an adult), and Mary Wells. In addition to the Miracles, who notched Motown's first million-selling single, "Shop Around" (1960), there were several young singing groups, including the Temptations, Martha and the Vandellas, and the Marvelettes. There also were a number of somewhat older groups that scored big, such as the Four Tops, the Contours, and Junior Walker and the All-Stars.

MARTHA AND THE VANDELLAS

Martha and the Vandellas were founded in 1960 as the Del-Phis by school friends from Detroit: Martha Reeves, Annette Beard Sterling-Helton, Gloria Williams, Rosalind Ashford. Their big break came in 1962 when Reeves, then working as a secretary at Motown, landed them the chance to provide backing vocals for recording sessions by Marvin Gaye. So impressed was Motown head Berry Gordy, Jr., that he signed the group (a trio as a result of Williams's departure) to his label. The group's new name, Martha and the Vandellas, was derived from the names of a Detroit street (Van Dyke) and one of Reeves's favourite singers (Della Reese). Their raw, soulful sound flourished under the guidance of the renowned songwriting-production team Holland-Dozier-Holland and produced a string of hits, including "Come and Get These Memories" (1963), "(Love Is Like a) Heat Wave" (1963), "Nowhere to Run" (1965), and "Jimmy Mack" (1967). Their biggest hit, "Dancing in the Street" (1964), was cowritten by Gaye. A shifting lineup of Vandellas had limited success into the 1970s, and Reeves embarked on a solo career in 1974.

A number of acts that were not developed by Motown wound up enjoying hit records during a stint with the company, including the Isley Brothers and Gladys Knight and the Pips.

Yet, despite the considerable acclaim these performers garnered, no Motown act of the 1960s matched the success of the Supremes, a girl group that scored number one hits with "Where Did Our Love Go," "Baby Love," "Come See About Me" (all 1964), "Stop! In the Name of Love," "Back in My Arms Again," "I Hear a Symphony" (all 1965), and "You Can't Hurry Love" (1966). Not only were they the second most successful singing group of the decade—surpassed only by the Beatles—they remain the most successful female singing group of all time. The group's glamorous lead singer, Diana Ross, went on to a remarkable solo career

as a singer and a moderately successful career as an actress.

As Motown's acts became increasingly famous, its songwriters and producers became household, or at least familiar, names. Brian Holland, Lamont Dozier, and Eddie Holland, who wrote and produced most of the Supremes' mid-1960s hits, were nearly as famous as the Supremes themselves, and their squabble with Gordy over money, which resulted in a nasty lawsuit and their departure from the company, was major industry news. Robinson was an important songwriter at Motown, as were Sylvia Moy, Norman Whitfield, Mickey Stevenson, Ivy Joe Hunter, and Gordy himself. All these songwriters were also producers. Some were assigned by Gordy to work with specific acts. Such fame did some of Motown's writers achieve and such problems did their fame cause for Gordy that, when the Jackson 5 were signed by the company in 1969, the team that wrote the group's early hits was credited simply as the Corporation.

Motown had an extraordinary house band (known as the Funk Brothers) made up of some of the best nightclub and bar musicians in black Detroit, including Earl Van Dyke on keyboards, Benny Benjamin and Uriel Jones on drums, and James Jamerson on bass. They played a huge role in the development of the Motown sound, a branch of soul music that featured more sophisticated arrangements and orchestration than the grittier Southern soul that contemporaneously flourished at Stax Records as the Memphis Sound. Motown brought together rhythm-and-blues, gospel, and pop influences as it sought to "cross over" (i.e., move beyond single-genre listeners) to reach a wide audience that included white teenagers. Motown records were specifically mixed to sound good on car radios and were characterized by a thumping backbeat that made dancing easy for everyone. Motown sought to be and became the "Sound of Young America."

Despite its great number of hits, Motown was actually a small company, but it was run with unmatched efficiency. Gordy prided himself on having learned

Berry Gordy poses with the Supremes, (top to bottom) *Cindy Birdsong, Mary Wilson, and Diana Ross.* Apic/Hulton Archive/Getty Images

about producing a quality product from a brief stint on the assembly line at an auto plant. He had rigorous quality control meetings, and only records that could pass the harsh criticism of his assembled brain trust were released. As a result of Gordy's stringent measures, at the height of its popularity (in the mid- to late 1960s), Motown enjoyed the highest hit

HOLLAND-DOZIER-HOLLAND

The production and songwriting team of Brian Holland, Lamont Dozier, and Eddie Holland crafted hits for nearly every major Motown artist—including Martha and the Vandellas ("[Love Is Like a] Heat Wave"), the Miracles ("Mickey's Monkey"), and Marvin Gaye ("How Sweet It Is to Be Loved by You")—but they were most closely associated with the Four Tops ("I Can't Help Myself [Sugar Pie, Honey Bunch]") and the Supremes.

Prior to the trio's teaming, Dozier and Eddie Holland had both pursued careers as singers, while Holland's brother Brian had collaborated with other Motown producers and songwriters, including Dozier. In 1963 Motown chief Berry Gordy, Jr., matched Holland-Dozier-Holland with the then hitless Supremes. Beginning with "Where Did Our Love Go" (1964) and continuing through "In and Out of Love" (1967), the trio wrote and produced more than a dozen U.S. Top Ten singles for the Supremes. Dozier's forte was melodies, Eddie Holland's was lyrics, and Brian Holland's was producing. Leaving Motown in 1968 after battling with Gordy over royalties, they began their own record company, Invictus/Hot Wax, for which Freda Payne, Honey Cone, and the Chairmen of the Board recorded.

ratio for its released singles of any record company in history. In truth, Gordy had to employ these extraordinary means if a company as small as his was to survive against bigger companies in the popular music business.

Artist development at Motown was comprehensive. Equal parts finishing school and academy of popular arts, the company provided its acts with elaborate choreography under the tutelage of Cholly Atkins. Young women raised in public housing projects, such as the Supremes, were schooled in the social graces, and chaperones accompanied the package-tour bus cavalcades that brought Motown to other parts of the United States during the company's early years.

Motown enjoyed its greatest success between 1965 and 1968, when it dominated

the *Billboard* charts. Although the company was never quite the force in the 1970s that it had been in the '60s (having lost several key performers), it was still a formidable enterprise with the Jackson 5, the Commodores, Wonder, and Ross. In 1971 Motown released what became, arguably, the most influential soul record ever, Gaye's *What's Going On*. In the late 1960s Detroit was wracked with violent race riots, and in the early '70s the company relocated to Los Angeles, where its move into filmmaking was generally fruitful. Motown's most famous film, *Lady Sings the Blues* (1972), starred Ross and was loosely based on the career of jazz singer Billie Holiday.

In the 1980s Gordy found it difficult to prosper in a music industry increasingly dominated by multinational conglomerates, and in 1988 he sold Motown to

Marvin Gaye poses during a record cover portrait session for his seminal soul album, What's Going On. Michael Ochs Archives/Getty Images

MCA, which later sold the company to PolyGram. Motown remained a force in popular music—a vital, near-primal influence with stunning longevity. No one since has quite been able to reproduce the classic Motown sound.

DISCO

Disco, the beat-driven style of popular music that was the preeminent form of dance music in the 1970s, took its name from *discotheque*, a type of dance-oriented nightclub that first appeared in the 1960s. Initially ignored by radio, disco received its first significant exposure in deejay-based underground clubs that catered to black, gay, and Latino dancers.

Deejays were a major creative force for disco, helping to establish hit songs and encouraging a focus on singles: a new subindustry of 12-inch, 45-rpm extended-play singles evolved to meet the specific needs of club deejays. The first disco qua disco hit was Gloria Gaynor's "Never Can Say Goodbye" (1974), one of the first records mixed specifically for club play. While most of disco's musical sources and performers were African American, the genre's popularity transcended ethnic lines, including both interracial groups (e.g., KC and the Sunshine Band) and genre-blending ensembles (e.g., the Salsoul Orchestra).

As disco evolved into its own genre in the United States, its range of influences included upbeat tracks from Motown, the choppy syncopation of funk, the sweet melodies and polite rhythmic pulse of Philadelphia soft soul, and even the most compelling polyrhythms of nascent Latin American salsa. Its lyrics generally promoted party culture. As the dance-floor mania developed into a more upscale trend, the cruder sensuality of funk was eclipsed by the more polished Philadelphia sound and the controlled energy of what came to be known as Eurodisco.

European disco—rooted in Europop, with which it is largely synonymous—evolved along somewhat different lines. Notably, producer Giorgio Moroder, working primarily at Musicland Studios in Munich, conceived of whole album sides as a single unit and arrived at a formula that became the standard approach

DONNA SUMMER

An admirer of gospel singer Mahalia Jackson, Donna Summer (born Donna Adrian Gaines) sang in church and later in clubs in Boston. At age 18 she joined the German production of the musical Hair. *While in Europe she studied with the Vienna Folk Opera and performed in productions of* Godspell *and* Showboat. *She also married actor Helmut Sommor, keeping his name after their divorce but Anglicizing it for the stage. While doing session work at Musicland studios in Munich, Summer met producer-songwriters Giorgio Moroder and Pete Bellotte. The three collaborated on several Europop hits before creating the historic single "Love to Love You Baby" (1975), the first of more than a dozen hits in the United States for Summer, most on Casablanca. Nearly 17 minutes long, the club version of the erotically charged song introduced the 12-inch disco mix. Over the next 14 years Summer, dubbed the "Queen of Disco," wrote or cowrote most of her material, including "I Feel Love," "Bad Girls," and "She Works Hard for the Money." She also scored big hits with "MacArthur Park"; "Hot Stuff"; "No More Tears (Enough Is Enough)," a duet with Barbra Streisand; and her signature song, "Last Dance," from the film* Thank God It's Friday *(1978).*

to European dance music in the 1980s and '90s. These continental differences did not prevent intercultural collaborations such as that between Moroder and American singer Donna Summer, nor did they close off input from other sources: Cameroonian artist Manu Dibango's "Soul Makossa," first a dance-floor hit in Paris, helped usher in the disco era in 1973.

Disco moved beyond the clubs and onto the airwaves in the mid-1970s. From 1976 the American Top 40 lists burst with disco acts such as Hot Chocolate, Wild Cherry, Chic, Heatwave, Yvonne Elliman, and Summer. Key to the commercial success were a number of savvy independent labels such as TK in Miami and Casablanca in Los Angeles. In 1977 the *Saturday Night Fever* soundtrack, dominated by the English-Australian group the Bee Gees, made disco fully

mainstream. Its popularity was matched by an equally ferocious criticism as the genre's commercialization overwhelmed its subversively homoerotic and interracial roots. As a result, in the 1980s disco returned to its club roots, with a few performers providing radio listeners with glimpses of its continuing development. In the clubs it mutated into house and techno and by the mid-1990s even began to resurface once again.

FUNK

Funk, the rhythm-driven musical genre popular in the 1970s and early 1980s, linked soul to later African American musical styles. Like many words emanating from the African American oral tradition, *funk* defies literal definition, for its usage varies with circumstance.

As a slang term, *funky* is used to describe one's odour, unpredictable style, or attitude. Musically, *funk* refers to a style of aggressive urban dance music driven by hard syncopated bass lines and drumbeats and accented by any number of instruments involved in rhythmic counterplay, all working toward a "groove."

The development of the terms *funk* and *funky* evolved through the vernacular of jazz improvisation in the 1950s as a reference to a performance style that was a passionate reflection of the black experience. The words signified an association with harsh realities—tales of tragedy and violence, erratic relationships, crushed aspirations, racial strife—and flights of imagination that expressed unsettling yet undeniable truths about life.

James Brown's band established the "funk beat" and modern street funk in the late 1960s. The funk beat was a heavily syncopated, aggressive rhythm that put a strong pulse on the first note of the musical measure ("on the one"), whereas traditional rhythm and blues emphasized the backbeat (the second and fourth beats of the measure). Brown and others, such as Sly and the Family Stone, began to use funk rhythms as their musical foundation while their lyrics took on themes of urgent social commentary.

In the early 1970s funk became the musical standard for bands such as Kool and the Gang and soul singers such as the Temptations and Stevie Wonder, its driving beat accompanied by lush, melodic arrangements and potent, thoughtful

KOOL AND THE GANG

Kool and the Gang (whose principal members were Khalis Bayyan, Robert "Kool" Bell, Claydes "Charles" Smith, George "Funky" Brown, Dennis "DT" Thomas, Robert "Spike" Mickens, Ricky West, and James "JT" Taylor) was one of the first self-contained black bands of the 1970s. The group's first charting single, "Kool and the Gang," a horn-driven, highly rhythmic instrumental dance track, was followed by a steady string of similar singles through 1976. The band's commercial breakthrough came in 1973 with the album Wild and Peaceful, *which featured the singles "Funky Stuff," "Jungle Boogie," and "Hollywood Swinging," all of which reached the rhythm-and-blues Top Ten. Kool and the Gang's sound was an innovative fusion of jazz, African rhythms, and street funk that established the band as an innovator in black music until the onset of the disco era. However, when the group's single "Open Sesame" was reissued on the soundtrack for the motion picture* Saturday Night Fever *in 1977, Kool and the Gang shifted emphasis toward pop and disco.*

In 1979 the band added lead vocalist Taylor and producer Eumir Deodato, which led to a cleaner, pop-driven sound and to the crossover single "Ladies' Night." Numerous hits followed, including the number one hit "Celebration" in 1980, as well as the sentimental pop songs "Joanna" in 1983 and "Cherish" in 1985. Kool and the Gang charted more pop singles than any other act in the 1980s. The band continued to record and tour into the early 21st century.

lyrics. Parliament-Funkadelic and other bands sang the praises of funk as a means of self-development and personal liberation, while established jazz artists such as Miles Davis and Herbie Hancock adapted and explored the funk groove.

One of the most vibrant centres of funk creativity was Dayton, Ohio, a small industrial city of approximately 200,000 people that produced some of the genre's most prolific hitmakers. Dayton funk bands all featured dance music with an emphasis on heavy bass, aggressive rhythms, complex horn arrangements, ensemble vocals, and showstopping choreography. During the 1970s, industries such as a Chrysler plant, the Harrison Radiator factory, and Wright-Patterson Air Force Base provided a stable income base for a population that was roughly 50 percent African American. From this base came high-school bands who sought the stardom first achieved by the founders of Dayton funk, the Ohio Players. Their number one pop hits "Fire" (1974) and "Love Rollercoaster" (1975) set the standard for local bands. Heatwave had a global hit, "Boogie Night," in 1977, the same year that Slave scored with "Slide"; crosstown rival Lakeside moved to Los Angeles before striking it big with "It's All the Way Live" in 1978. Roger Troutman and his band, Zapp, lasted into the 1990s with a slick, high-tech sound and dynamic show.

Go-Go

Go-go, a style of funk heavy on bass and percussion, originated in Washington, D.C., in the late 1970s. Go-go bands were large ensembles with multiple percussionists who could maintain a steady beat for hours at a time. By 1982 go-go was the most popular music of the dance halls (called go-gos) in the black parts of the capital. The go-go pioneers were Chuck Brown and the Soul Searchers, who cultivated the steady, rigid use of the funk beat, and Trouble Funk, who packaged their powerful shows into some of the best studio recordings of the go-go era. Other steady go-go acts were Redds and the Boys, E.U. (Experience Unlimited), and Rare Essence.

Go-go bands were influenced by George Clinton and Parliament-Funkadelic, who frequently played four-hour concerts in the region. The tireless percussive rhythms of go-go also have connections to the Caribbean dance styles of soca and reggae. The rigid beats served some of the early rap sides for New York City hip-hop acts Afrika Bambaataa and Kurtis Blow; and rappers of the mid-1980s, such as Doug E. Fresh, Run-D.M.C., and the Beastie Boys, utilized the distinctive go-go beat in their music. The zenith of go-go's popularity was E.U.'s "Da Butt," from Spike Lee's film School Daze *(1988).*

Go-go recordings were almost exclusively released on independent labels, the most successful of which was D.E.T.T. Records, founded by Maxx Kidd. In 1985 Island Records made a brief attempt to record and market go-go groups, but the style never became nationally known, and its associations with hip-hop faded as urban rap styles changed in the 1990s.

In the 1980s the sexually expressive aspects of funk were popularized through the works of Rick James and Prince, while the funk beat became the primary rhythm in black popular music. The influence of funk spread to other styles in the 1980s—mixing with the gritty realism of hard rock and punk and the experimentation of much of the electronic music of the time. With the rise of rap music in the 1980s and its "sampling" of 1970s funk songs, funk grew in stature and significance in hip-hop culture. It became associated with ancient mysteries in the black tradition, providing hip-hop with a historical link to artists and cultural movements of the past. As part of hip-hop's influence on popular culture, funk provided the rhythmic basis for most American dance music of the 1990s.

HIP-HOP

By the late 1990s hip-hop music had replaced country and western as the best-selling music in the United States. Indeed, it was so ubiquitous that the Feb. 8, 1999, cover of *Time* magazine proclaimed "Hip-Hop Nation." Almost from hip-hop's inception mainstream media and many people, both black and white, criticized the violence and misogyny at the heart of a good number of its songs; however, in its now decades-long history, hip-hop has taken on just about every subject and attitude imaginable from calls to political action, such as "Don't Believe the Hype" by Public Enemy (whose Chuck D famously characterized rap as the "black CNN") and celebrations of roots and community such as Arrested Development's "Tennessee" (1992) to positive affirmations like Lauryn Hill's "Everything is Everything" (1998).

ORIGINS AND THE OLD SCHOOL

Although widely considered a synonym for rap music, the term *hip-hop* refers to a complex culture comprising four elements: deejaying, or "turntabling"; rapping, also known as "MCing" or "rhyming"; graffiti painting, also known as "graf" or "writing"; and "B-boying," which encompasses hip-hop dance, style, and attitude, along with the sort of virile body language that philosopher Cornel West described as "postural semantics." Hip-hop originated in the predominantly African American, economically depressed South Bronx section of New York City in the late 1970s. As the hip-hop movement began at society's margins, its origins are shrouded in myth, enigma, and obfuscation.

Graffiti and break dancing, the aspects of the culture that first caught public attention, had the least lasting effect. Reputedly, the graffiti movement was started about 1972 by a Greek American teenager who signed, or "tagged," Taki 183 (his name and street, 183rd Street) on walls throughout the New York City subway system. By 1975 youths in the Bronx, Queens, and Brooklyn were stealing into train yards under cover of darkness to spray-paint colourful mural-size renderings of their names, imagery from underground comics and television, and even Andy Warhol-like Campbell's soup cans onto the sides of subway cars. Soon, influential art dealers in the United States, Europe, and Japan were displaying graffiti in major galleries. New York City's Metropolitan Transit Authority responded with dogs, barbed-wire fences, paint-removing acid baths, and undercover police squads.

The beginnings of the dancing, rapping, and deejaying components of hip-hop were bound together by the shared environment in which these art forms evolved. The first major hip-hop deejay was DJ Kool Herc (Clive Campbell), an 18-year-old immigrant who introduced the huge sound systems of his native Jamaica to inner-city parties. Using two turntables, he melded percussive fragments from older records with popular dance songs to create a continuous flow of music. Kool Herc and other pioneering hip-hop deejays, such as Grand Wizard Theodore, Afrika Bambaataa, and Grandmaster Flash, isolated and extended the break beat (the part of a dance record where all sounds but the drums drop out), stimulating improvisational dancing. Contests developed in which the best dancers created break dancing, a style whose repertoire of acrobatic and occasionally

GRANDMASTER FLASH AND THE FURIOUS FIVE

Formed in the Bronx, N.Y., in 1976, Grandmaster Flash and the Furious Five—Grandmaster Flash (born Joseph Saddler), Cowboy (Keith Wiggins), Melle Mel (Melvin Glover), Kid Creole (Nathaniel Glover), Mr. Ness (also called Scorpio; born Eddie Morris), and Raheim (Guy Williams)—were one of the first multimember rapping crews. They were a staple of the earliest hip-hop shows in the Bronx and Harlem, and nonrapping member Grandmaster Flash was credited with being an inventor and innovator of many of the techniques and performing gimmicks associated with hip-hop deejaying. He also jury-rigged a drum machine into his turntable and created miniature audio dramas on his legendary 12-inch single "The Adventures of Grandmaster Flash on the Wheels of Steel" (1981)—a 15-minute epic that sampled sections of Chic's "Good Times" (1979) and showcased the new sound of scratching. As recording artists on hip-hop's flagship label, Sugar Hill, the group was originally known for high-energy singles such as "Freedom" (1980) and "Birthday Party" (1981), which combined their rhyme skills with slick production. With their depiction of the harsh realities of ghetto life in "The Message" (1982), they became the pioneers of socially conscious protest rap, inspiring the likes of Public Enemy's Chuck D and Boogie Down Production's KRS-One to create provocative social commentary in the manner of Bob Dylan and Bob Marley. The group also tackled drug abuse in "White Lines" (1983). By the mid-1980s the group had disbanded, and later reunions were short-lived.

airborne moves included the "helicopter," whereby dancers spun on the tops of their heads.

In the meantime, deejays developed new techniques for turntable manipulation. Needle dropping, created by Grandmaster Flash, prolonged short drum breaks by playing two copies of a record simultaneously and moving the needle on one turntable back to the start of the break while the other played. Sliding the record back and forth underneath the needle created the rhythmic effect called "scratching."

Kool Herc was widely credited as the father of modern rapping for his spoken interjections over records, but among the wide variety of oratorical precedents cited for MCing are the epic histories of West African griots, talking blues songs, jailhouse toasts (long rhyming poems recounting outlandish deeds and misdeeds), and the dozens (the ritualized word game based on exchanging insults, usually about members of the opponent's family). Other influences cited include the hipster-jive announcing styles of 1950s rhythm-and-blues deejays such as Jocko Henderson; the black power poetry of Amiri Baraka, Gil Scott-Heron, and the Last Poets; rapping sections in recordings by Isaac Hayes and George Clinton; and the Jamaican style of rhythmized speech known as toasting.

Rap first came to national prominence in the United States with the release of the Sugarhill Gang's song "Rapper's Delight" (1979) on the independent African American–owned label Sugar Hill. Within weeks of its release, it had become a chart-topping phenomenon and given its name to a new genre of pop music. The major pioneers of rapping were Grandmaster Flash and the

SUGAR HILL RECORDS

Launched in 1979 by industry veterans Sylvia and Joe Robinson as a label for rap music (at that time a new genre), Sugar Hill Records, based in Englewood, N. J., was named after the upmarket section of Harlem and funded by Manhattan-based distributor Maurice Levy. Sylvia (born Sylvia Vanderpool) had a national hit in 1957 with "Love Is Strange" as half of the duo Mickey and Sylvia; Robinson was a former promotions man. Together they ran the All-Platinum label with some success during the 1970s.

At Sugar Hill a core session team of guitarist Skip McDonald, bass player Doug Wimbish, drummer Keith Leblanc, and percussionist Ed Fletcher provided the compulsive rhythm for most of the label's releases, including three milestone 12-inch (long-playing) singles in the genre that came to be called hip-hop. "Rapper's Delight" (1979) by the Sugarhill Gang was the first to make the Top 40. The label is also remembered for its landmark recordings by Grandmaster Flash.

Furious Five, Kurtis Blow, and the Cold Crush Brothers, whose Grandmaster Caz is controversially considered by some to be the true author of some of the strongest lyrics in "Rapper's Delight." These early MCs and deejays constituted rap's old school.

THE NEW SCHOOL

In the mid-1980s the next wave of rappers, the new school, came to prominence. At the forefront was Run-D.M.C., a trio of middle-class African Americans who fused rap with hard rock, defined a new style of hip dress, and became staples on MTV as they brought rap to a mainstream audience. Run-D.M.C. recorded for Profile, one of several new labels that took advantage of the growing market for rap music. Rick Rubin and Russell Simmons managed several pioneer hip-hop acts, including Run-D.M.C., through their Rush Management agency, and in 1984 they set up their own Def Jam label; shortly thereafter, Columbia Records made a deal with the label and became its distributor. Def Jam's initial success was hip-hop's first romantic superstar, LL Cool J, a soft-spoken "love" rapper whose style was compatible with black radio's still-conservative ideas of itself and its audience. Next up were the Beastie Boys, a trio of white New Yorkers who popularized digital sampling and who helped broaden hip-hop's audience by redefining rap as a cool alternative for white suburban kids, notably with the infectious, tongue-in-cheek anthem "(You Gotta) Fight for Your Right (to Party)" in 1986. Def Jam's next substantial act, Public Enemy, was altogether

LL COOL J

Taking the stage name LL Cool J ("Ladies Love Cool James") at age 16, James Todd Smith, a native of Queens, N.Y., signed with the then-fledgling label Def Jam in 1984. Distinguished by hard, fast, sinuous rhymes and artfully arrogant phrasing, his first single, "I Need a Beat," sold more than 100,000 copies. His first album, Radio, was released in 1985, the year he appeared in Crush Groove, the movie celebrating Def Jam's origins. Thereafter he outlasted most of his competition by constantly creating daring, fresh modes of expression—gaining airplay with rap's first romantic ballad, "I Need Love" (1987), and prefiguring West Coast rap with "Going' Back to Cali" (1988), recorded in California. Criticized by some for his crossover success, LL responded by teaming with producer Marley Marl for the musically and thematically innovative album Mama Said Knock You Out (1990).

Following the huge commercial success of that album, the increasingly versatile LL began acting in films and on television. He starred in the situation comedy In the House (1995–99), and he continued to record, releasing the double-platinum Mr. Smith (1995); a string of solid albums followed.

more confrontational. Building on the social consciousness of Grandmaster Flash and the Furious Five's *The Message*, they invested rap with radical black political ideology, while stoking the flames of antiwhite and antipolice rhetoric. Rubin went off to form Def American, leaving Simmons to sustain the most successful of the first generation of rap labels.

Rap's classical period (1979–93) also included significant contributions from De La Soul—whose debut album on Tommy Boy, *3 Feet High and Rising* (1989), pointed in a new and more playful direction—and female rappers such as Queen Latifah and Salt-n-Pepa, who offered an alternative to rap's predominantly male, often misogynistic viewpoint. Hip-hop artists from places other than New York City began to make their mark, including the provocative 2 Live Crew from Miami; M.C. Hammer,

from Oakland, Calif., who experienced short-lived but massive crossover success with a pop audience; and DJ Jazzy Jeff and the Fresh Prince (Will Smith) from Philadelphia.

Schoolly D, also from Philadelphia, presented graphic tales of gangs and violence, such as "PSK—What Does It Mean?" (1985), that were a reflection and product of the often violent lifestyle of American inner cities afflicted with poverty and the dangers of drug use and drug dealing. In Houston the Geto Boys' sex- and violence-dominated music was the subject of outrage in some corners. The most significant response to New York hip-hop, though, came from Los Angeles, beginning in 1989 with N.W.A.'s dynamic album *Straight Outta Compton*. N.W.A. (Niggaz With Attitude) and former members of that group—Ice Cube, Eazy E, and Dr. Dre—led the way as West Coast rap grew in prominence in the early 1990s.

TOMMY BOY RECORDS

Dance Music Report editor Tom Silverman started Tommy Boy Records in 1981 in his apartment on Manhattan's West 85th Street. Producer Arthur Baker helped put the label on the map with hits by Afrika Bambaataa —"Looking for the Perfect Beat" (1982) and "Planet Rock" (1983)— whose robotic rhythms were inspired by European groups like Kraftwerk. With radio slow to recognize this new idiom, exposure for hip-hop came mostly through 12-inch singles in dance clubs, but Tommy Boy's focused approach to artists-and-repertoire and promotion led to commercial breakthroughs with quirky character acts. Based in California, Digital Underground was led by the eccentric Shock-G, who brought a George Clinton-like sense of the absurd to the group's repertoire; their radio hit "The Humpty Dance" (1989) paved the way for the amusing and friendly vibe of De La Soul, hippielike rappers from Long Island, N.Y., whose album 3 Feet High and Rising (1989) sampled the entire panoply of pop and had a particularly big impact in Britain and continental Europe.

Their graphic, frequently violent tales of real life in the inner city, as well as those of other Los Angeles rappers such as Ice-T and Snoop Dogg and East Coast counterparts such as Schoolly D, gave rise to the genre known as gangsta rap.

The most distinguishing characteristic of N.W.A.'s approach was the very plain way that violence was essayed: as plainly as it occurred in the streets of south-central Los Angeles and neighbouring Compton, argued the group. Hyperrealism was often conflated with myth and declarations of immortality; exaggeration became a kind of self-protective delusional device for listeners who were actually involved in the dangerous lifestyle N.W.A. was chronicling.

In the mainstream press and among African Americans nationwide, N.W.A., by virtue of their name, single-handedly reignited a debate about the word *nigger*. Its appropriation by black youth transformed it into a positive appellation, argued Ice Cube. For many, the persistent misogyny in N.W.A.'s work, which was alternately cartoonish and savage in its offensiveness, was less defensible.

As N.W.A. splintered, the group's importance multiplied with each solo album. Ice Cube's *AmeriKKKa's Most Wanted* (1990) employed Public Enemy's

NEW JACK SWING

New jack swing (also known as swingbeat) was the most pop-oriented rhythm-and-blues music since 1960s Motown. Its performers were unabashed entertainers, free of artistic pretensions; its songwriters and producers were commercial professionals. Eschewing the fashion for sampling (using sounds and music from other recordings), the makers of new jack swing discovered their rhythms on the newly available SP1200 and 808 drum machines (which had already been used by hip-hop producers). They laid an insistent beat under light melody lines and clearly enunciated vocals. In contrast to the sex-and-drugs-and-guns messages of gangsta rap, this was music that the industry preferred to promote as the Sound of Young Black America.

The key producers were L.A., Babyface, and Teddy Riley, who crafted romantic songs for the dance floor. L.A. (Antonio Reid, whose nickname was derived from his allegiance to the Los Angeles Dodgers baseball team) and Babyface (youthful-looking Kenneth Edmonds) had been members of the Deele, a group based in Cincinnati, Ohio, before becoming writer-producers. Their million-selling hits for Bobby Brown in 1988 ("Don't Be Cruel" and "My Prerogative") led to work with Paula Abdul, Whitney Houston, and Boyz II Men. In the early 1990s the duo relocated to Atlanta, where their LaFace label launched soul diva Toni Braxton and the female trio TLC. A native of New York City's Harlem district and influenced by the Gap Band, Riley moved from performing with the band Guy to producing for Brown, Michael Jackson, and his own group, Blackstreet, material that was more directly sexual than that by L.A. and Babyface.

production team, the Bomb Squad, and introduced New York City listeners to the West Coast sound, known by this point as gangsta rap. In 1992 N.W.A. producer and sometime rapper Dr. Dre released the California rap scene's most influential and definitive record, *The Chronic*; its marriage of languid beats and murderous gangsta mentality resulted in phenomenal sales. Most significantly, it launched Death Row Records and the career of Snoop Doggy Dogg.

As early as 1988, other important artists from California began making an impression. Like Oakland's Too $hort, Ice-T relied on his self-styled image as a pimp to propel sales; though his lyrics were well-respected, his single "Cop Killer" (1992), like gangsta rap in general, raised controversy. N.W.A.'s influence could be heard in groups like Compton's Most Wanted, DJ Quik, Above the Law, and countless other gangsta groups, but by the early 1990s groups had surfaced whose approach was the antithesis of N.W.A.'s violence and misogyny. The jazzily virtuosic improvisers Freestyle Fellowship and the Pharcyde, of Los Angeles, and Souls of Mischief, of Oakland, owed more to De La Soul and A Tribe Called Quest than to gangs. Nevertheless, by the mid-1990s Death Row Records and Bad Boy Records were engaged in a "coastal battle." Life imitated art imitating life; the violence that had been confined to songs began to spill over into reality, culminating in the tragic murders of the Notorious B.I.G.

DEATH ROW RECORDS AND INTERSCOPE RECORDS

Among the individuals responsible for the flourishing of hip-hop in Los Angeles in the 1990s was a white man, Jimmy Iovine, a former engineer on recordings by Bruce Springsteen and the new head of Interscope Records. Although Interscope had a stable of successful alternative rock acts—including Nine Inch Nails and Bush—its greatest impact came from its alliance with Death Row Records. Founded by Marion ("Suge") Knight, Death Row rapidly became the home of gangsta rap. Essentially, it was an outlet for the talents of Dr. Dre. The attention drawn to gansta rap's violent lyrics tended to mask the unschooled but innovative nature of the music, shaped by producer Dr. Dre's distinctive slurred, lazy studio sound.

Among the Death Row releases to top the pop charts were Doggystyle (1993) by Snoop Doggy Dogg (Calvin Broadus), who emerged from a cameo role on Dre's own work, and the gritty All Eyez on Me (1996) by Tupac Shakur (2Pac). As the decade progressed, Death Row became increasingly enmeshed in legal proceedings—both financial and criminal—that were reflective of its gangsta rhetoric. Snoop was found innocent of a murder charge, then left the label. Shakur died in Las Vegas as a result of gunshot wounds—a victim of the rivalry between East Coast and West Coast rappers that exploded into murder. Knight was sentenced to nine years for assault, and Interscope severed all connections with Death Row.

(Christopher Wallace), a rapper from New York City, and Tupac Shakur (2pac), a California rapper.

By the late 1990s hip-hop was artistically dominated by the Wu-Tang Clan, from New York City's Staten Island, whose combination of street credibility, neo-Islamic mysticism, and kung fu lore made them one of the most complex groups in the history of rap; by Diddy (known by a variety of names, including Sean "Puffy" Combs and Puff Daddy), performer, producer, and president of Bad Boy Records, who was responsible for a series of innovative music videos; and by the Fugees, who mixed pop music hooks with politics and launched the solo careers of Wyclef Jean and Lauryn Hill.

Although long believed to be popular primarily with urban African American males, hip-hop became the best-selling genre of popular music in the United States in the late 1990s (at least partly by feeding the appetite of some white suburbanites for vicarious thrills). Its impact was global, with formidable audiences and artist pools in cities such as Paris, Tokyo, Sydney, Cape Town, London, and Bristol, Eng. (where the spin-off trip-hop originated). It also generated huge sales of products in the fashion, liquor, electronics, and automobile industries that were popularized by hip-hop artists on cable television stations such as MTV and The Box and in hip-hop-oriented magazines such as *The Source* and *Vibe*. A canny blend of entrepreneurship and aesthetics, hip-hop was the wellspring of several staple techniques of modern pop music, including digital drumming and sampling (which introduced rap listeners to the music of a previous generation of performers, including Chic, Parliament-Funkadelic, and James Brown, while at the same time creating copyright controversies).

HIP-HOP IN THE 21ST CENTURY

As the century turned, the music industry entered into a crisis, brought on by the advent of digital downloading. Hip-hop suffered as severely as or worse than other genres, with sales tumbling throughout the decade. Simultaneously, though, it solidified its standing as the dominant influence on global youth culture. Even the massively popular "boy bands," such as the Backstreet Boys and *NSYNC, drew heavily on hip-hop sounds and styles, and rhythm and blues and even gospel had adapted so fully to the newer approach that stars such as Mary J. Blige, R. Kelly, and Kirk Franklin straddled both worlds.

In the early 2000s, hip-hop's creative centre moved to the American South. Following the success of the increasingly experimental OutKast and the stable of New Orleans–based artists that emerged from two record companies—Cash Money and No Limit Records (which was both founded and anchored by Master P)—the chant-based party anthems of such rappers as Juvenile, 8Ball & MJG, and Three

6 Mafia brought the sounds of the "Dirty South" to the mainstream.

Dr. Dre remained a crucial figure; his New York City–born protégé, 50 Cent, achieved multiplatinum status with 2003's *Get Rich or Die Tryin'*, and Eminem became perhaps the world's biggest pop star when *8 Mile* (2002), the loosely autobiographical film in which he starred, enjoyed huge popular and critical success (his "Lose Yourself" won the Academy Award for best song). However, Dr. Dre remained mostly silent for the remainder of the decade, working on technology for a new brand of headphones but never releasing an album after 1999. Eminem, whose outlaw status was challenged by his Hollywood success, seemed adrift, and the Los Angeles style exemplified by Dr. Dre in the 1990s lost much of its power.

Dr. Dre's legacy, though, was visible in the extent to which hip-hop had become a producers' medium. In the 21st century the music—born from the sonic creations of the deejay—saw its greatest innovations in the work of such studio wizards as Timbaland, Swizz Beatz, and the Neptunes. The focus on producers as both a creative and a commercial force was concurrent with a widespread sense that the verbal dexterity and poetry of hip-hop was waning. The genre had truly become pop music, with all of the resultant pressures of accessibility, and the intricacy and subversive nature of earlier MCs had largely been pushed to the "alternative"/"underground" scene spearheaded by rappers such as Mos Def and Doom. The dissatisfaction with the state of mainstream hip-hop was sufficiently

OUTKAST

Formed in 1992, rap duo OutKast put Atlanta on the hip-hop map in the 1990s and redefined the G-Funk (a variation of gangsta rap) and Dirty South (often profane form of hip-hop that emerged in the U.S. South) music styles with their strong melodies, intricate lyrics, and positive messages.

André Lauren Benjamin and Antwan André Patton joined forces at a performing arts high school in Atlanta. Discovering their mutual admiration for hip-hop and the funk musicians that became their stylistic touchstones (Parliament-Funkadelic, Sly and the Family Stone, and Prince), they formed a rap group, 2 Shades Deep. Recording in a basement studio under the guidance of the Organized Noize production team (hitmakers for Xscape and TLC), Benjamin and Patton, now known respectively as Dré and Big Boi and collectively as OutKast, had a breakthrough hit single with "Player's Ball" in 1993.

In 1994 OutKast released their first album, Southernplayalisticadillacmuzik. A critical and commercial success, it highlighted the duo's originality and penchant for catchy hooks. ATLiens (1996), their follow-up, featured the hit "Elevators (Me and You)" and sold 1.5 million copies. OutKast's third effort, the double-platinum Aquemini (1998), employed more

Outkast's Big Boi and André 3000. Lucy Nicholson/AFP/Getty Images

live instruments and earned a Grammy nomination for the single "Rosa Parks." As OutKast deepened the sophistication of its frequently life-affirming lyrics and broadened its musical eclecticism, it never lost its unique sense of humour. The group's image also became a signature, especially the increasingly flamboyant wardrobe of Dré (renamed André 3000), and their theatricality and stylish music videos became OutKast hallmarks.

Backed by the hit single "B.O.B." ("Bombs over Baghdad"), OutKast's fourth studio album, Stankonia (2000), was a huge crossover success. It earned Grammys for best rap album and best performance by a rap duo/group for the heartfelt "Ms. Jackson," and it placed at or near the top of most critics' yearly "best of" lists. In 2003 the duo released the double album Speakerboxxx/The Love Below, which highlighted the solo abilities of both artists as they each took the lead on one disc. In the process OutKast both renewed its mastery of "old school" rap, largely on the Big Boi-dominated Speakerboxxx, and continued its assault on the boundaries of hip-hop, primarily on The Love Below, on which André 3000 sang as much as he rapped and included funk stylings. The album topped the charts and won three Grammy Awards in 2004: album of the year, best rap album, and best urban/alternative performance for the boisterous "Hey Ya!" In 2006 André 3000 and Big Boi starred in the musical Idlewild and recorded the sound track.

common that in 2006 Nas released an album titled *Hip Hop Is Dead.*

Still, major stars continued to emerge. Many of the biggest figures continued to rise from the South, including Atlanta's T.I. and Lil Wayne from New Orleans. Hip-hop celebrity now often came hand-in-hand with multimedia success, such as a burgeoning film career for Ludacris. The genre continued to be assimilated deeper into nonmusical culture, with some of the genre's early stars—LL Cool J, Ice Cube, Queen Latifah, Ice-T—established as familiar faces in movies and television. Snoop Dogg headlined rock festivals alongside Bruce Springsteen. Perhaps no one represented the cultural triumph of hip-hop better than Jay-Z. As his career progressed, he went from performing artist to label president, head of a clothing line, club owner, and market consultant—along the way breaking Elvis Presley's record for most number one albums on the *Billboard* magazine charts by a solo artist. Candidate Barack Obama made references to Jay-Z during the 2008 presidential campaign, and on the rapper's 2009 album *The Blueprint 3*, he claimed to be a "small part of the reason" for Obama's victory.

Kanye West, one of Jay-Z's producers, emerged as one of the most fascinating and polarizing characters in hip-hop, following the success of his 2004 debut album *The College Dropout*. Musically experimental and fashion-forward, West represented many of hip-hop's greatest possibilities with his penetrating, deeply personal lyrics. However, his endless self-promotion and often arrogant aura also demonstrated some of the elements that now tried the patience of many listeners.

Regardless of hip-hop's own internal struggles, the music's global impact constantly continued to expand. No single artist may have better personified hip-hop in the 21st century than M.I.A. Born in London, raised in her family's native Sri Lanka, trained as a graphic designer, M.I.A. writes politically radical lyrics which are set to musical tracks that draw from wildly diverse sources from around the world. Not only was her album *Kala* named the best album of 2007 by *Rolling Stone*, but M.I.A. was also listed as one of *Time* magazine's "100 Most Influential People"—illustrating the reach and power of a music born decades earlier on litter-strewn playgrounds.

HOUSE

Born in the 1980s in Chicago clubs that catered to gay, predominantly black and Latino patrons, house fused the symphonic sweep and soul diva vocals of 1970s disco with the cold futurism of synthesizer-driven Eurodisco. Invented by deejay-producers such as Frankie Knuckles and Marshall Jefferson, house reached Europe by 1986, with tracks on Chicago labels Trax and DJ International penetrating the British pop charts. In 1988 the subgenre called acid house catalyzed a British youth culture explosion, when

THE WAREHOUSE

While go-go was the rage in Washington, D.C., and hip-hop was ascendant in New York City, gay Chicago was laying the foundation for the most lastingly influential of early 1980s African American dance musics, house. The name came from a club, the Warehouse, where deejay Frankie Knuckles eschewed the contemporary gay dance music style, the ultrafast Hi-NRG. Instead, he made new music by mixing together snatches of other material—gloomily anxious Joy Division tracks, synthesizer-driven Eurodisco, snatches of psychedelia, and old soul hits.

House mixes rapidly made their way to vinyl, notably on Trax and Rocky Jones's DJ International label, which, respectively, produced the first big local hit, Farley Funk's "Love Can't Turn Around" (1986), and the first international house hit, Steve ("Silk") Hurley's "Jack Your Body." The house sound was, in the words of DJ Chip E, "a lot of bottom, real heavy kick drum, snappy snare, bright hi-hat, and a real driving bassline to keep the groove."

dancers discovered that the music's psychedelic bass lines acted synergistically with the illegal drug ecstasy (MDMA, or 3,4-methylenedioxymethamphetamine, a hallucinogen and stimulant).

By 1990 the British scene had divided. Following the bacchanalian spirit of acid house, some preferred manic music designed for large one-time-only raves (all-night parties in warehouses or fields). Others favoured the more "mature," club-oriented style of soulful house called garage (named after New York City's Paradise Garage club). Following early homegrown efforts by the likes of A Guy Called Gerald, Britain also started producing its own mutations of the Chicago sound. Pioneered by Leftfield, another subgenre called progressive house excised the style's gay-disco roots and explored production

techniques that gave the music a hypnotic quality. Bombastic introductions and anthemlike choruses characterized the subgenres labeled handbag and epic house. NU-NRG (a gay, hard-core style) and tech-house (which took an abstract minimalist approach) were other significant subgenres that emerged.

Despite these European versions, house cognoscenti still looked to America's lead—the lush arrangements of auteur-producers such as Masters at Work, Armand Van Helden, and Deep Dish, the stripped-down severity and disco cut-ups of newer Chicago labels such as Relief and Cajual. On both sides of the Atlantic, the continuing proliferation of subgenres testified to house music's adaptability, appeal, and seemingly inexhaustible creativity.

CHAPTER 7

SPORTS

In many respects the best way to understand the social, economic, and symbolic significance of sports in African American history is through the examination of the stories of the individual athletes who have broken racial barriers and records. But before delving into any accounts of individual trial and triumph it is useful to gain a perspective on the environment in which they occurred. The historical overviews of African American participation in baseball, boxing, basketball, and football that follow in this section are intended to supply a context for and deeper understanding of the accomplishments of black athletes in those sports.

BASEBALL

Major league baseball's colour barrier had already been shattered, when Chuck Berry, in 1956, first sang about a game being won by a home run hit by a "brown-eyed handsome man" (his poetic euphemism for an African American). The significance of the line with which Berry sets the scene—"Two, three, the count with nobody on"—is still debated. Because today the balls and strike count is generally cited in that order, some accuse Berry of not understanding the game, noting that the batter could not still be hitting if three strikes had already been recorded. Others argue that earlier in the history of the game, the count had been cited in the reverse order, strikes then balls. It seems more likely, though, that

Berry, one of popular music's most adept lyricists, meant to imply that the batter, like black people in general in American society in the 1950s, already had three strikes against him and still managed to hit the ball out of the park. Baseball images have often been used as symbolic shorthand in American historiography and art, and Berry's reference to the game here reinforces the meaningful place the accomplishments of black baseball players hold in African American history.

SEGREGATION

During baseball's infancy, a colour barrier was put up by the first formal organization of baseball clubs, the National Association of Base Ball Players, which decreed in 1867 that clubs "which may be composed of one or more coloured persons" should not be permitted to compete with its teams of gentlemen amateurs. When the first professional league was formed four years later, it had no written rule barring black players, but it was tacitly understood that they were not welcome.

The colour line was not consistently enforced, though, during the early years of professionalism. At least 60 black players performed in the minor leagues during the late 19th century—mostly in all-black clubs. In 1884 two African Americans played in a recognized major league, the American Association. They were Moses Fleetwood ("Fleet") Walker, a catcher for the Association's Toledo,

Ohio, team, and his brother Welday, an outfielder who appeared in six games for Toledo.

The number of black players in professional leagues peaked in 1887 when Fleet Walker, second baseman Bud Fowler, pitcher George Stovey, pitcher Robert Higgins, and Frank Grant, a second baseman who was probably the best black player of the 19th century, were on rosters of clubs in the International League, one rung below the majors. At least 15 other black players were in lesser professional leagues. Although they suffered harassment and discrimination off the field, they were grudgingly accepted by most of their teammates and opponents.

A League of Colored Base Ball Clubs, organized in 1887 in cities of the Northeast and border states, was recognized as a legitimate minor league under organized baseball's National Agreement and raised hopes of sending black players to big league teams. The league's first games, however, attracted small crowds, and it collapsed after only one week. While no rule in organized baseball ever stated that black players were banned, a so-called "gentlemen's agreement" to exclude blacks eventually prevailed.

There were other disturbing signs of exclusion for black players in 1887. The Syracuse (N.Y.) Stars of the International League suffered a mutiny when pitcher Douglas ("Dug") Crothers refused to sit for a team portrait with his black teammate Robert Higgins. In Newark, N.J., black pitcher Stovey was kept out of an exhibition game with the major league Chicago White Stockings at the insistence of Cap Anson, Chicago's manager and one of the most famous players of baseball's early days. And the St. Louis Browns, American Association champions, refused to play an exhibition game against the all-black Cuban Giants. The night before the scheduled game, eight members of the Browns handed a message to the team's owner that read: "[We] do not agree to play against Negroes tomorrow. We will cheerfully play against white people at any time."

In midseason that year the International League's board of directors told its secretary to approve no more contracts for black players, although it did not oust the league's five blacks. The Ohio State League also wrestled inconclusively with the colour question. It was becoming clear that the colour bar was gradually being raised. Black players were in the minor leagues for the next few years, but their numbers declined steadily. The last black players in the recognized minor leagues during the 19th century were the Acme Colored Giants, who represented Celoron, N.Y., in the Iron and Oil Leagues in 1898.

As the 20th century dawned, separation of the races was becoming the rule, especially in the South, reinforced by the U.S. Supreme Court's *Plessy* v. *Ferguson* decision. In the South, state laws and local ordinances not only placed limits on the use of public facilities by African Americans but forbade athletic competition between blacks and whites. In the North, African Americans were not usually segregated by law, but local custom dictated second-class citizenship for them.

Nevertheless, the idea of black players in the major and minor leagues was not yet unthinkable. In 1901 John J. McGraw, manager of the Baltimore Orioles in the new American League, tried to sign a black second baseman named Charlie Grant by saying that he was a Native American named Tokohama, a member of the Cherokee tribe. The effort failed when rivals correctly identified Grant instead as a member of the Chicago Columbia Giants, a black team. Five years later there was an aborted attempt to bring African American William Clarence Matthews, Harvard University's shortstop from 1902 to 1905, into the National League.

Increasingly, black players who wanted to play professionally had to join all-black teams. (Several dark-skinned players in the big leagues were widely assumed to be black, although they claimed to be white Latin Americans. No admitted black men played in the white leagues at the time.) Ninety percent of the country's African American citizens lived in the South, but migration to Northern states was increasing. With the growing base of potential fans in the North, top-quality black teams appeared in the Northeast and Midwest. Among them were the Genuine Cuban Giants and Cuban X Giants of New York City (both made up of African

Americans despite their names), the Cuban Stars and Havana Stars (both with real Cubans), the Lincoln Giants of New York City, the Philadelphia Giants, the Bacharach Giants of Atlantic City (N.J.), the Homestead (Pa.) Grays, the Hilldale Club of Philadelphia, and the Norfolk (Va.) Red Stockings. In the Midwest the leaders were the Chicago American Giants, the Columbia Giants, Leland Giants, and Union Giants of Chicago, the Kansas City (Mo.) Monarchs, and the Indianapolis ABCs. Especially noteworthy was the All Nations team, composed of African Americans, whites, a Japanese, a Hawaiian, an American Indian, and several Latin Americans. On its roster at various times before World War I were two of the greatest black pitchers, John Donaldson and Jose Mendez.

These teams vied for the mythical "colored championship of the world" and also played white semipro and college teams. Salaries were modest. Journeymen players earned $40 to $75 a month, while a star might command more than $100. Some Chicago teams played in the city's semipro league on weekends, occasionally competing against big leaguers from the Cubs and White Sox who played under assumed names. During the week they played white clubs in nearby towns.

Major league teams often played black teams during spring training trips to Cuba and sometimes had postseason games against black clubs in the United States. In 1909, for example, the Chicago Cubs won three close games in a series with the Leland Giants. In 1915, eastern black teams won four of eight games against big league teams, including a five-hit shutout of the National League champion Philadelphia Phillies by Smokey Joe Williams of the Lincoln Giants. In the late 1920s Commissioner Kenesaw Mountain Landis forbade big league clubs from competing in toto in the off-season. Partisans of black baseball believed it was because black teams often beat the major leaguers.

In the Midwest a few teams barnstormed all season long. The Kansas City (Ks.) Giants, for example, were on the road all summer, traveling mostly by railroad. Their opponents were white semipro teams throughout the Midwestern states and southern Canada. Although a black face was a novelty in the small towns, the players reported that by and large they had little trouble finding food and lodging in the rural areas.

EARLY NEGRO LEAGUES

There were two attempts to establish leagues for black teams in the early years of the 20th century. The first was in 1906 when the International League of Independent Base Ball Clubs was formed in the Philadelphia area. It had two white teams and four black. The championship game pitted two black teams against each other and attracted 10,000 fans to the stadium of the Philadelphia (now Oakland) Athletics. (This was the first time black clubs performed in a major league park, though later most of the top black clubs played in stadiums of major league or top minor league teams.) The league folded after its first season.

Four years later there was an attempt to start a black major league with teams in Chicago; Louisville, Ky.; New Orleans; Mobile, Ala.; St. Louis, Mo.; Columbus, Ohio; Kansas City, Mo.; and Kansas City, Kan. The league died aborning without sanctioning a game.

The first viable black league was formed in 1920 under the leadership of Rube Foster, manager of the Chicago American Giants. Foster had been Negro baseball's best pitcher in the early years of the 20th century and then its best-known manager and promoter. His barnstorming American Giants were known all over the country through their winter tours to California and Florida and traveled big-league style in private railroad cars.

THE NATIONAL NEGRO LEAGUE AND THE EASTERN COLORED LEAGUE

Foster was a visionary who dreamed that the champion of his black major league would play the best of the white league clubs in an interracial world series. His original plan called for a black major league in the Midwest with teams in Chicago; Indianapolis; Detroit; Cincinnati, Ohio; St. Louis; and Kansas City, Mo. It also called for another league in the East with clubs in New York City; Philadelphia; Baltimore, Md.; Washington, D.C.; Pittsburgh; and

Cleveland. Only one eastern owner showed up for the organizational meeting in Kansas City in February 1920, so the eastern league did not materialize.

Nevertheless, the Negro National League (NNL) was established during the two-day meeting. Its teams were Foster's Chicago American Giants, the Indianapolis ABCs, Chicago Giants, Kansas City (Mo.) Monarchs, Detroit Stars, St. Louis Giants, Dayton (Ohio) Marcos, and the Cuban Stars, who had no home city. A few weeks later the Negro Southern League was organized with clubs in the large cities of the South; however, it was regarded as a minor circuit during its on-again, off-again life over the next 30 years.

In December 1923 another black major league with six teams was established in eastern cities. Officially named the Mutual Association of Eastern Colored Baseball Clubs, it was known more familiarly as the Eastern Colored League (ECL). Members were the Brooklyn (N.Y.) Royal Giants, Bacharach Giants of Atlantic City, N.J., Baltimore Black Sox, Hilldale Club of Philadelphia, and the Cuban Stars (no relation to the Cuban Stars of the NNL) and Lincoln Giants of New York City.

All these early leagues were financially shaky. They also had difficulty making up a schedule because few of the clubs owned ballparks or had contracts giving them exclusive use. Many were tenants of teams in the major and minor leagues and were obligated to use the parks when the owners were playing out of town and to vacate them when their hosts returned.

Another debilitating factor was that sometimes a league team would refuse to play a scheduled game if a nonleague opponent promised a bigger payday. Umpiring of league games was sometimes erratic because umpires were hired by the home team. Another handicap was the wide disparity in the quality of the teams; two or three clubs would dominate and earn far more money than their weaker brethren.

From 1924 through 1927, the NNL and ECL champions met in a Negro World Series. The NNL's Chicago American Giants won two championships and the Kansas City Monarchs won one, as did the Hilldale Club, representing the ECL. The ECL succumbed to financial weakness in the spring of 1928. The NNL, bereft of the management acumen and foresight of Foster, who was hospitalized for mental illness in 1926, stumbled on until 1931 before disbanding as the Great Depression deepened and left most fans with empty pockets. Two of its solvent franchises, Chicago and Indianapolis, joined the Negro Southern League for 1932. That year another black circuit, called the East-West League, was started for eastern teams by Cumberland W. Posey, veteran manager of the Homestead Grays, a ball club based in Pittsburgh. The new league barely made it off the ground. By early June its Detroit team had dropped out, the schedule was curtailed, and salaries were slashed. The league did not last the summer.

THE NEGRO LEAGUES GAIN PROMINENCE

The following year the NNL was reborn. Its moving spirit was another Pittsburgher, W.A. (Gus) Greenlee, a numbers-game owner and tavern operator who had entered baseball in 1931 as organizer of the Pittsburgh Crawfords. The new NNL had teams in both the East and the Midwest but became an eastern league in 1937 when the Negro American League (NAL) was formed with teams in Chicago, Kansas City (Mo.), Cincinnati, Detroit, Memphis (Tenn.), St. Louis, Indianapolis (Ind.), and Birmingham (Ala.).

Although the new leagues had fairly frequent franchise shifts, they were somewhat more stable than the circuits of the 1920s. During World War II, which brought prosperity to most blacks as well as whites, Negro baseball became a $2 million-a-year business, probably the most lucrative black-dominated enterprise in the United States at that time. Salaries for journeymen players, which had been about $150 a month during the 1920s, soared to $400 or more during the war. Stars could earn $1,000 a month. Satchel Paige, the most famous player, pitcher, and showman of the Negro leagues, earned $30,000 to $40,000 a year through special deals calling for him to pitch one to three innings for scores of independent teams, both black and white, each season.

To earn such wages, black players competed in up to 150 games a season— half to two-thirds of them against black as

Baseball player Satchel Paige in New York Black Yankees pinstripes, 1941. George Strock/
Time & Life Pictures/Getty Images

well as white nonleague teams. Many of their opponents were local teams within easy reach of their home cities, but others were small-town teams far out on the barnstorming trail. Most teams traveled by bus, ranging from the best that era could offer to aging rattletraps that were prone to break down. In the winter, black stars went to Mexico, Cuba, and other Latin American nations where baseball was popular.

The Negro World Series was resumed in 1942 between champions of the Negro National and Negro American leagues and continued until the NNL disbanded in 1948. Among the most noted Negro league teams was the Homestead Grays, based in both Pittsburgh and Washington, D.C., which won nine pennants during 1937–45 and included the great hitters Josh Gibson (catcher), James ("Cool Papa") Bell (outfielder), and Buck Leonard (first baseman). In the mid-1930s another legendary team, the Pittsburgh Crawfords, included five future Baseball Hall of Fame members: Gibson, Bell, Paige, manager Oscar Charleston, and clutch-hitting third baseman William Julius ("Judy") Johnson.

The World Series, however, was far overshadowed by the East-West All-Star Game, pitting the best players of the NNL against those of the NAL, from 1933 to 1950. It annually attracted as many as 50,000 spectators to Comiskey Park in Chicago and became the biggest social event as well as the chief sports attraction for African Americans. Only heavyweight boxing matches featuring the black champion Joe Louis held the attention of more African Americans.

INTEGRATION

Baseball's colour line was rarely discussed by influential white sportswriters until the early 1930s, but the black weekly press, particularly sports columnists Wendell Smith of the *Pittsburgh Courier* and Sam Lacy of the *Baltimore Afro-American*, kept up a steady drumbeat against the colour line during the late 1930s and World War II. The American Communist Party also urged an end to the colour line, although Smith denigrated the communists' efforts as more hurtful than helpful. The minor furor in the press over the continued exclusion of blacks from Organized Baseball led to sham tryouts of black players by the Chicago White Sox and Boston Red Sox and expressions of interest in African Americans by other major league clubs.

But the times were changing. The triumphs of Louis during the decade and of sprinter Jesse Owens at the 1936 Berlin Olympics, the improving living standards and educational attainments of African Americans, the social and economic changes brought by Pres. Franklin D. Roosevelt's New Deal programs in the 1930s—all of these helped to alter the attitudes of most Americans toward race. Several major league teams either discussed or attempted the racial integration of professional baseball in the 1940s. The interest in integration in the 1940s was sparked by several factors—the increasing economic and political influence of urban blacks, the success of black ballplayers in exhibition games with major leaguers, and especially the participation of African Americans in World War II. The hypocrisy of fighting fascism abroad while tolerating segregation at home was difficult to ignore. During the war, protest signs outside Yankee Stadium read, "If we are able to stop bullets, why not balls?" A major obstacle to integration was removed in 1944 with the death of Commissioner Landis. Though he had made several public declarations that there was no colour barrier in baseball, during his tenure Landis prevented any attempts at signing black players. (He blocked, for example, Bill Veeck's purchase of the Philadelphia Phillies in 1943 after learning that Veeck planned to stock his team with Negro league All-Stars.) On the other hand, Landis's successor, Happy Chandler, was openly supportive of bringing integration to the sport.

In 1947 Jackie Robinson became the first black player in the modern major leagues. His arrival was the result of careful planning by Brooklyn Dodgers President Branch Rickey, a one-time big-league catcher and manager, who began researching the idea of signing a black player and scouting for the right

Jackie Robinson. Hulton Archive/Getty Images

individual when he joined the Dodgers in 1942. In a meeting with Robinson in 1945, Rickey badgered the player for several hours about the abuse and hostility he would receive from players and fans and warned him that he must not retaliate. Robinson agreed and spent the 1946 season with the Dodgers minor league franchise in Montreal in preparation for playing in the big leagues. His first season with Brooklyn was marred by all the hostility that Rickey had predicted (even from a handful of teammates), but it also was marked by Robinson's determined play, which eventually won over fans and opponents, as well as helping the Dodgers win the National League pennant and earning him the Rookie of the Year award. Robinson, who was named Most Valuable Player in the National League after his third year, was soon followed into the major leagues by Larry Doby, a fleet hard-hitting infielder from the black Newark (N.J.) Eagles, and in 1948 by Paige. Both played for the American League Cleveland Indians, who won the World Series in 1948. Several other African Americans joined minor

ERNIE BANKS

Ernie Banks, an 11-time All-Star who starred for the Chicago Cubs from 1953 to 1971, is representative of a generation of African American major league players who began their careers in the Negro leagues. Banks excelled in football, basketball, track and field, and baseball at his Dallas high school. At age 17 he joined a barnstorming Negro league team at a salary rate of $15 per game. In 1950 Cool Papa Bell signed him to the Kansas City Monarchs. Soon after, Banks spent two years in the U.S. Army, after which he returned to the Monarchs. His stay there was short-lived, however, as the recently integrated major leagues were eager to take advantage of the wealth of talent in the Negro leagues.

Signed by the Chicago Cubs in 1953, Banks soon established himself as one of the league's leading power hitters. In addition to his potent bat, he proved to be a skilled defensive player, setting a single-season mark for fielding percentage for a shortstop in 1959. After injuries limited his mobility, Banks moved to first base in 1962.

Banks was named the National League's (NL) Most Valuable Player for two consecutive seasons (1958–59). He hit more than 40 home runs in five different seasons, leading the NL in that category in 1958 and 1960. He also led the league in 1958–59 in runs batted in. Banks was known for his enthusiasm and love of the game, his trademark cry of "let's play two!" reflecting the pure enjoyment he took in baseball. When he retired in 1971, he was the holder of most of the Chicago Cubs' offensive records and had earned the nickname "Mr. Cub" among the team's fans. In his career Banks totaled 512 home runs and 1,636 runs batted in. He was elected into the National Baseball Hall of Fame in 1977; he was only the eighth player to be elected in his first year of eligibility.

league teams, beginning a trend of growing acceptance of blacks in baseball.

The Negro leagues, however, suffered as a result of these developments. Black fans fixed their attention on Robinson, Doby, and the other black players in Organized Baseball and increasingly ignored the black leagues. The talent pool was also shrinking as young stars such as Willie Mays (Birmingham Black Barons) and Hank Aaron (Indianapolis Clowns) and old stars such as Satchel Paige left to play in the major leagues. A few teams tried the integration route by signing a handful of white players, and during the 1950s two teams, the Indianapolis Clowns and Kansas City Monarchs, had female players as gate attractions. The first female player signed was second baseman Toni Stone, who reportedly earned $12,000 a year, well above the pay of true stars.

The NNL died of financial malnutrition in 1948. The NAL lasted until 1960 before disbanding. A few teams continued barnstorming, most notably the Indianapolis Clowns, who mixed comedy and baseball in equal measure. The Clowns were the lineal descendants of the Ethiopian Clowns of the 1940s, who had outraged many fans by wearing grass skirts and painting their bodies in a cartoonish version of cannibals. But the latter-day Clowns played serious baseball, as evidenced by the fact that major league home run king Aaron made his professional debut with them in 1952. The Clowns continued barnstorming until 1973 (with a few whites on the roster) before giving up and ending the saga of the Negro leagues.

The impact of black players on the field was significant. They brought over from the Negro leagues an aggressive style of play that combined power hitting with daring on the base paths. Black players soon established themselves as major league stars. In the 1950s and '60s players such as Mays and Aaron (who surpassed Babe Ruth's all-time career home run record) and pitcher Bob Gibson posted statistics that ranked them among the best ever to play the game. Later Reggie Jackson, Ozzie Smith, and Barry Bonds (who broke both Aaron's record for career home runs and the single season home run record) were definitive players of their respective eras. In 1962 Robinson became the first black player inducted into baseball's Hall of Fame. In the 1970s, membership in the Hall was opened to the bygone stars of the Negro leagues.

By the 1970s, acceptance of black players was commonplace. However, inclusion of minorities in coaching and administrative positions was virtually nonexistent. In 1961 Gene Baker became the first African American to manage a minor league team, and in the mid-1960s there were only two African American coaches in the major leagues. In 1975 the Cleveland Indians made Frank Robinson the first black field manager in major league history. However, opportunities for minorities in managerial positions were rare, and their representation in leadership positions remains an issue.

BOXING

By the early 20th century, boxing had become a path to riches and social acceptance for various ethnic and racial groups. It was at this time that professional boxing became centred in the United States, with its expanding economy and successive waves of immigrants. Famine had driven thousands of Irish to seek refuge in the United States, and by 1915 the Irish had become a major force in professional boxing. German, Scandinavian, and central European fighters also emerged, as did outstanding Jewish and Italian fighters.

African Americans also turned to boxing to "fight their way to the top," and foreign-born black boxers such as Peter Jackson, Sam Langford, and George Dixon went to the United States to capitalize on the opportunities offered by boxing. Of African American boxers, Joe Gans won the world lightweight championship in 1902, and Jack Johnson became the first black heavyweight champion in 1908. Before and after Jack Johnson won his title, prejudice against black boxers was great. Gans was frequently forced by promoters to lose to or underperform against less-talented white fighters. Other black fighters found it difficult or impossible to contend for championships, as white boxers refused to face them. For instance, John L. Sullivan refused to accept the challenges of any black, and Sullivan's successor, Jim Corbett, refused to fight the black Australian Peter Jackson, although

Jackson had fought Corbett to a 63-round draw before Corbett became champion. Jack Dempsey continued the tradition by refusing to meet the African American Harry Wills. During Jack Johnson's reign as champion, he was hounded so relentlessly that he was forced to leave the United States.

Blacks nevertheless continued to pursue fistic careers, particularly during the Great Depression. In 1936 African American fighter Joe Louis was matched against German Max Schmeling in a bout that was invested with both racial and political symbolism. Louis lost to Schmeling in a 12th-round knockout. In 1937 Louis captured the world heavyweight title from James Braddock, but stated he would not call himself a champion until he had beaten Schmeling in a rematch. The fight occurred on June 22, 1938, and was seen on both sides of the Atlantic as a confrontation between the United States and Nazi Germany; the American press made much of the contest between an African American and an athlete seen as a representative of Aryan culture. Both Adolph Hitler and Franklin D. Roosevelt had personal meetings with their respective country's pugilist. Louis's sensational 1st-round victory over Schmeling in the rematch was a pivotal moment for African American athletes, as Louis in victory quickly became a symbol of the triumph of world democracy for Americans of all races.

Other African Americans followed Louis, with Sugar Ray Robinson, Archie

Moore, Ezzard Charles, Henry Armstrong, Ike Williams, Sandy Saddler, Emile Griffith, Bob Foster, Jersey Joe Walcott, Floyd Patterson, Sonny Liston, Muhammad Ali, Joe Frazier, and George Foreman winning world championships in various weight divisions. By the last quarter of the 20th century, African Americans were a dominant force in professional boxing, producing stars such as Sugar Ray Leonard, Marvelous Marvin Hagler, Thomas Hearns, Aaron Pryor, Larry Holmes, Michael Spinks, Mike Tyson, Evander Holyfield, Riddick Bowe, Pernell Whitaker, Shane Mosley, Roy Jones, Jr., and Floyd Mayweather, Jr.

FLOYD MAYWEATHER, JR.

Floyd Mayweather, Jr., was a boxer whose combination of speed, power, and technical prowess made him one of the best pound-for-pound fighters of his generation. Mayweather earned the nickname "Pretty Boy" during his amateur career because of his unmarked face. He won the national Golden Gloves in 1993, 1994, and 1996 but ended his amateur career on a sour note at the 1996 Olympic Games in Atlanta, where he lost a controversial decision to Serafim Todorov of Bulgaria in the semifinals and had to settle for a bronze medal in the featherweight division. Mayweather turned pro on Oct. 11, 1996, scoring a second-round knockout of American Roberto Apodaca. Despite a bitter feud between his two trainers—his father, former boxer Floyd Mayweather, Sr., and his uncle Roger Mayweather, a former holder of the World Boxing Council (WBC) super featherweight (junior lightweight) and super lightweight (junior welterweight) titles—Mayweather flourished, winning the WBC junior lightweight title on Oct. 3, 1998, in his 18th bout by stopping veteran American titleholder Genaro Hernandez in the eighth round. Mayweather also won Ring magazine's Fighter of the Year award in 1998.

Mayweather moved up in weight four times, capturing Ring magazine and WBC lightweight titles in 2001, the WBC super lightweight title in 2005, and Ring magazine and WBC welterweight titles in 2006. At the beginning of 2007, he was already widely considered the best pound-for-pound fighter in the world, remaining undefeated in 38 professional bouts (24 by knockout). However, it was not until he defeated fellow American Oscar De La Hoya for the WBC super welterweight (junior middleweight) title that Mayweather gained mainstream recognition. More than the fight itself, it was the four-part documentary 24/7, which was broadcast on HBO cable television during the buildup to the fight, that boosted Mayweather's profile. He emerged as a riveting character with an ego as large as his talent and a proclivity for being alternatively obnoxious and charming. Mayweather's fight against De La Hoya was an enormous financial success, smashing existing pay-per-view and live-gate records; some 2.4 million households purchased the fight, generating approximately $134.4 million in pay-per-view revenue, and a crowd of 16,700 spectators at the MGM Grand in Las Vegas created a live gate of $19 million.

Later in the year, in a bid to enhance his crossover appeal, Mayweather appeared as a contestant on ABC television's Dancing with the Stars. *He returned to the ring in December 2007 and scored a 10th-round knockout against Britain's previously undefeated Ricky Hatton in Las Vegas. The bout attracted another capacity crowd and, together with his victory over De La Hoya, earned Mayweather Ring magazine's Fighter of the Year award for that year.*

In June 2008, just months before a scheduled rematch with De La Hoya, Mayweather announced his retirement from boxing. While most observers assumed that the "retirement" would be temporary, some 18 months passed between Mayweather's fight with Hatton and his return to the ring in September 2009 against Juan Manuel Márquez, a natural lightweight and crowd favourite who moved up two divisions to accept the bout. Although Márquez showed great fortitude, the judges awarded Mayweather a unanimous decision after 12 rounds. Much excitement and more than a little gamesmanship attended the buildup to Mayweather's next scheduled fight, against Filipino sensation Manny Pacquiao, whom Mayweather's father accused of using performance-enhancing drugs, leading to prolonged wrangling over the nature of the blood testing that would precede the fight.

BASKETBALL

One of the more memorable bits featured on Bill Cosby's album *Inside the Mind of Bill Cosby* (1972) is the comedian's fanciful and funny explanation of the origins of basketball. In Cosby's version, the game's creator, YMCA physical-education instructor James Naismith, is joined in a barn in Springfield, Mass., by Willie, an African American janitor, who helps him develop basketball's rules. Naismith challenges Willie to defend the trash can at which Naismith has been shooting at with a ball. When Willie does so by hitting him with a broom, Naismith calls the first foul in the history of basketball.

In truth, all-black and all-white teams met in exhibition games beginning in the 1920s and by the late 1930s even competed in "world" championship tournaments; however, blacks and whites would not play on the same teams until the 1950s. Early in the era of segregated play, the New York Rens (short for Renaissance) were generally regarded as black basketball's finest team, but it was another team, the Harlem Globetrotters, that left a more recognizable mark on the history of the game.

The team was organized in Chicago in 1926 as the all-black Savoy Big Five. Sports promoter Abe Saperstein acquired the team soon after and owned it until his death in 1966. In January 1927 the team debuted in Hinckley, Ill., under the name New York Globetrotters. The name was changed in 1930 to Harlem Globetrotters to capitalize on Harlem's cultural cachet. The barnstorming team amassed an impressive record over the next decade and in 1939 participated in the first professional basketball championship, losing to the Harlem Rens in the final game. The next year the Globetrotters won the tournament.

It was about this time that they first experimented with adding comedy to their games. Inman Jackson was the first to assume the role of "clown prince" on the team. As the National Basketball Association became racially integrated in the 1950s, the opportunities for competitive games on the barnstorming circuit dried up. As a result, the team made comedic entertainment its central focus. Some outstanding Globetrotters were Reece "Goose" Tatum, Marques Haynes, Clarence Wilson, "Meadowlark" Lemon, and Herb "Geese" Ausbie. Wilt Chamberlain, regarded as one of basketball's greatest big men, also played briefly for the Globetrotters before beginning his illustrious career in the National Basketball Association (NBA). Lynette Woodard was the first woman to play for the team, which continues to travel the world with its signature mix of skill and showmanship.

In the spring of 1950 Earl Lloyd, who played collegiate basketball at West Virginia State College, became the second black player to be drafted by an NBA team; Chuck Cooper had been chosen by the Boston Celtics a few picks before Lloyd's selection by the Washington Capitols. Nate ("Sweetwater") Clifton, however, was the first African American to sign an NBA contract, joining the New York Knicks that summer. The schedule resulted in Lloyd being the first black player to take the court in an NBA game, on Oct. 31, 1950. He scored six points in that first game. Over the next

Meadowlark Lemon of the Harlem Globetrotters, May 1968. Express Newspapers/Hulton Archive/ Getty Images

years, more African Americans began joining NBA teams.

The history of professional basketball changed in 1956 when Boston Celtics coach Red Auerbach traded established star "Easy" Ed Macauley to the St. Louis

Hawks for the rights to draft Bill Russell, an African American who had led the University of San Francisco to two consecutive National Collegiate Athletic Association (NCAA) championships (1954–55 and 1955–56). With the 6-foot, 10-inch (208 centimetres) Russell turning shot-blocking into an art form, Boston dominated the NBA for more than a decade, winning 11 championships in the centre's storied 13-year career, the final years of which were spent as the Celtics player-coach. During this period the Celtics also became the first team in the NBA to start an all-black lineup. Russell's stellar African American teammates included Tom "Satch" Sanders, Sam Jones, and K.C. Jones (who would also later coach the Celtics). Russell's battles with fellow pivotman Chamberlain (especially during Chamberlain's tenure with the Philadelphia 76ers and Los Angeles Lakers, the lineup of the last of which also featured All-Stars Jerry West and Elgin Baylor) were constant highlights of NBA play during the 1960s.

An outspoken civil rights activist, Russell was not shy about addressing the racism he encountered in Boston, which acquired a controversial reputation as

ELGIN BAYLOR

Regarded as one of basketball's greatest forwards, Elgin Baylor played with a graceful style that enabled him to score and rebound with seeming ease. Baylor, 6 feet 5 inches (196 cm) tall, was an All-American (1958) at Seattle University, where he played from 1955 to 1958, guiding the team to the National Collegiate Athletic Association (NCAA) championship tournament finals in 1958. He signed with the National Basketball Association (NBA) Lakers (Minneapolis, Minn., and, later, Los Angeles) in 1958 and was named Rookie of the Year in 1959. During his 14-year career he averaged 27.4 points per game, with a 38.2 average in the 1961–62 season—a feat made even more impressive by the fact that, as a U.S. Army reservist, Baylor played only on weekends and did not practice with the Lakers that season. His 71 points in a 1960 game was an NBA record until it was broken by Wilt Chamberlain's 100 (1962). Baylor set the single-game scoring record for the NBA Finals when he tallied 61 points against the Boston Celtics in game five of the 1962 finals. Though he played with some of the finest players in Laker franchise history, including Wilt Chamberlain, Jerry West, and Gail Goodrich, Baylor never won an NBA championship. He was named to the All-NBA first team 10 times, and he retired as the NBA's third-leading all-time rebounder with a career total of 11,463. Baylor was elected to the Naismith Memorial Basketball Hall of Fame in 1976 and was named one of the NBA's 50 greatest players of all time in 1996.

After his playing career ended, Baylor coached the New Orleans Jazz (1974–79). In 1986 he was named vice president of basketball operations for the Los Angeles Clippers. Despite being named Executive of the Year in 2006, his tenure managing the Clippers was marked by mostly losing seasons and clashes with team ownership, and he resigned from his position in 2008.

a city where racism was seldom thinly veiled, largely as a result of the hostile reaction to school busing by some white Bostonians. That reputation was reinforced for some during the 1980s when the Celtics fielded a predominantly white line-up at a time when the NBA had come to be dominated by black players. As a result, during the NBA's halcyon decade of the 1980s the frequent contests for the league's championship between the Celtics, led by white superstar Larry Bird, and the Lakers, led by African African superstar Magic Johnson, had a strong racial subtext.

In the 1960s, '70s, and '80s, there was an explosion of talented African American players in the collegiate and professional game, which had come to include the rival American Basketball Association, where high-flying Julius Erving, better known as "Dr. J," first practiced his on-court acrobatics. From this period alone came a myriad of African Americans who in 1996 would be named by the NBA as the leagues's 50 greatest players. Among them were Russell, Chamberlain, Baylor, Johnson, Sam Jones, Moses Malone, Earl "the Pearl" Monroe, Robert Parish, Willis Reed, Oscar Robertson, Walt Frazier, George Gervin, Hal Greer, Nate Archibald, Elvin Hayes, Nate Thurmond, Wes Unseld, Lenny Wilkens, and James Worthy.

Another player on that list, towering Kareem Abdul-Jabbar, one of the NBA's most unstoppable scoring machines, had also enjoyed a remarkable career (as Lew Alcindor) at the University of California at Los Angeles, which experienced a long period as college basketball's dominant power with a mixture of black and white stars. The college game's first outstanding integrated team was Loyola University of Chicago, which won the 1963 NCAA championship with a starting line-up that featured four black players. In 1966 Texas Western University (now the University of Texas at El Paso) would be the first university to win the championship with an all-black starting team. At the head of the list of teams that represented black excellence in basketball in subsequent decades was Georgetown University, coached by John Thompson, a member of the pantheon of great black college coaches that also includes John McLendon (pioneer of the fast break), Nolan Richardson, Tubby Smith, and John Chaney.

In the late 1980s and 1990s, basketball belonged to Michael Jordan. Widely considered the greatest player in the history of basketball, Jordan, whose soaring play earned him the nickname "Air," led the Chicago Bulls to six NBA championships. His popularity not only transcended race but national borders, and he was the focus of a marketing effort unlike any seen before for an athlete. Other great African American players whose accomplishments were obscured somewhat by Jordan's shadow were his Bulls teammate Scottie Pippen, Charles Barkley, Clyde Drexler, Hakeem Olajuwon, Karl Malone, Shaquille O'Neal, Patrick Ewing, David Robinson, Gary Patton, Reggie Miller, Dominique Wilkins, and Isiah Thomas.

ALLEN IVERSON

Athletic success and controversy came to Allen Iverson at an early age. At Bethel High School, he led the school's gridiron football and basketball teams to state championships his junior year. At age 17 he was jailed after being accused of starting a racially charged brawl in a bowling alley, but his conviction was later overturned because of lack of evidence. He was offered a scholarship to Georgetown University in Washington, D.C., where in two years he averaged 23 points per game and won two Big East Conference Defensive Player of the Year awards before making the decision to leave school to play professionally. Iverson was chosen first overall in the 1996 National Basketball Association (NBA) draft by the Philadelphia 76ers.

Although he was one of the smallest players in the league, standing 6 feet (183 cm) tall and weighing 165 pounds (75 kilograms), Iverson made a big splash immediately, leading his team with a scoring average of 23.5 points per game and winning Rookie of the Year honours. His quickness and his signature crossover dribble often left even the best defenders helpless. Off the court his baggy clothing, flashy jewelry, and braided hair were not part of the image the NBA wanted to promote. During his early years in the league, he clashed frequently with coaches and team officials, was portrayed by the media as a selfish, disruptive player, and had several run-ins with the law. Yet he developed a huge following of young fans who identified with his rebellious image.

Despite the controversies that followed him, Iverson proved his talent on the court, taking the league scoring title in 1998–99 and winning the scoring title, the steals title, and Most Valuable Player honours in 2000–01 while guiding the 76ers to the NBA Finals. In the middle of the 2006–07 season he was traded to the Denver Nuggets, where he was teamed with young superstar Carmelo Anthony. Iverson was an extremely proficient scorer, and in 2007 he became the sixth fastest player in NBA history to score 20,000 career points. Denver, however, failed to advance beyond the first round of the play-offs, and Iverson expressed a desire to play for a contender. Three games into the 2008–09 season, he was traded to the Detroit Pistons, but the Pistons finished the season with a losing record and were swept in the first round of the play-offs, leading Iverson and the team to part ways. He signed with the Memphis Grizzlies in September 2009, but, unhappy with his role on the team, he left the Grizzlies after playing only three games, and his contract was terminated soon thereafter. Iverson then announced his retirement from professional basketball, but he instead returned for a second stint with the 76ers after signing with the team in December 2009. The return of the still-popular Iverson led to an upswing in home attendance for the 76ers that proved to be short-lived. He left the team in February 2010 to spend time with his ailing daughter, and the next month the 76ers announced that he would not return for the remainder of the 2009–10 season.

The 21st century has produced another class of extraordinary African American basketball players, at the head of which most certainly are LeBron James, Kobe Bryant, Carmelo Anthony, Kevin Garnett, Dwayne Wade, Dwight Howard, Tim Duncan, Tracy McGrady, Jason Kidd, Ray Allen, and Allen Iverson. Iverson, who is known for both explosive play on the court and controversy away from the game, is also significant as the first great athlete to be strongly identified with the hip-hop movement.

FOOTBALL

Through the end of World War II, very few African American athletes had an opportunity to play mainstream football at any level. A separate and decidedly unequal black football world first emerged in the 1890s as part of the larger expansion of college football. The first documented game between all-black colleges was played in 1892 in North Carolina between Biddle University and Livingston College. The first black college conferences, the Colored Intercollegiate Athletic Association and the Southern Intercollegiate Athletic Conference, were formed in 1912, followed by the Southwestern Athletic Conference in 1920 and the Midwestern Athletic Association in 1926. Black college football was woefully underfunded, but it had its own All-Americans (stars such as "Jazz" Byrd, Ben Stevenson, "Tarzan" Kendall, and "Big Train" Moody), its great rivalries (Howard-Lincoln, Tuskegee-Atlanta, Morgan-Hampton, Wiley-Prairie View), its own pageantry, and even its own scandals. All of this took place outside the consciousness of the mainstream football public but was thoroughly covered by a thriving black press.

Mainstream football, however, was not altogether segregated. William Henry Lewis and William Tecumseh Sherman Jackson were black teammates for Amherst College in 1889, and Lewis made Walter Camp's All-America team in 1892 after he had moved to Harvard to play football while attending law school (he later became an assistant U.S. attorney general). A handful of black players were always part of big-time college football, and some—including Lewis, Fritz Pollard at Brown, Paul Robeson at Rutgers, and Duke Slater at Iowa—were among the early game's greatest stars. Yet, until 1939, when UCLA fielded a team that included Jackie Robinson, Kenny Washington, and two other black teammates, no college had more than one or two black players, and most continued to have none.

The routine indignities facing the black pioneers on predominantly white teams and campuses became compounded when intersectional games were scheduled between segregated Southern schools and marginally integrated Northern ones. Typically, the Northern school agreed to "bench" its one or two black players so as not to offend Southern sensibilities. Such incidents occasionally aroused local protest from progressive student groups and were thoroughly covered in the black press, but they went largely unreported in the mainstream media. By the late 1930s the typical arrangement was to hold out the black players for games played in the segregated South but to allow them to play at home, an accommodation that continued into the 1950s. The first integrated college football game in the South

FRITZ POLLARD

Fritz Pollard was the first African American selected to a backfield position on Walter Camp's All-America team (1916) and the first African American head coach in the National Football League (NFL), with the Akron Pros in 1921. Although he was only 5 feet 7 inches (170 cm) tall and weighed a mere 150 pounds (68 kg), Pollard won the grudging acceptance of his teammates at Brown University in Rhode Island in 1915, leading the team to a victory over Yale and an invitation to the Tournament of Roses game in Pasadena, Calif. Pollard had a subpar game in a 14–0 defeat to Washington State, but he became the first African American to play in the Rose Bowl game. In 1916 Pollard's outstanding play led Brown to a season of eight victories and one defeat, including wins over both Yale and Harvard.

After service in World War I, Pollard became head football coach at Lincoln University (Pennsylvania) and began playing professional football for Akron in the informal Ohio League in 1919. The following year Pollard was the star player for the Akron Pros, who won the first National Football League (NFL) championship. Pollard continued to play and coach in the NFL until 1926. In 1923, while playing for the Hammond Pros, he became the first African American quarterback in the league. Pollard also facilitated integration in the NFL by recruiting other African American players such as Paul Robeson, Jay Mayo Williams, and John Shelbourne and by organizing the first interracial all-star game featuring NFL players in 1922.

After he was let go by Akron (which had changed its name to the Indians) in 1926, Pollard continued to promote integration in professional football as a coach of the barnstorming Chicago Black Hawks (1928–32) and the New York Brown Bombers (1935–37). In 1954 Pollard became the second African American selected to the College Football Hall of Fame. He was posthumously inducted into the Pro Football Hall of Fame in 2005.

took place in 1947 between Virginia and Harvard, whose Chester Pierce was permitted to play. Many Northern schools solved the problem simply by not scheduling teams from the South, and bowl games likewise avoided racial incidents by matching up only Southern teams. The Cotton Bowl was integrated, without incident, in 1948, the Orange Bowl in 1955. The Sugar Bowl was integrated by the University of Pittsburgh's Bobby Grier in 1956, only after Georgia's segregationist governor, Marvin Griffin, backed down from threats to keep Georgia Tech from playing. The integration of Southern college teams progressed gradually over the postwar years. The Big 6 conference was integrated in 1947 and the Missouri Valley Conference in 1950; but the Atlantic Coast Conference did not begin integrating until 1963, the Southwest Conference until 1966, and the Southeastern Conference until 1967.

The NFL had been integrated at the beginning, with Fritz Pollard among the league's first stars and some 13 African

Syracuse University running back Ernie Davis (44) in a 1960 game. Rich Clarkson/Sports Illustrated/Getty Images

American players hired between 1920 and 1933. Between 1934 and 1945, however, a "gentleman's agreement," apparently at the instigation of George Preston Marshall, owner of the Boston (later Washington) Redskins, kept the NFL all-white. The reintegration of professional football began in 1946—in the NFL, where the Rams risked losing their lease on the Los Angeles Coliseum if they did not sign Kenny Washington (the Rams signed Woody Strode as well, to give Washington a black roommate); and in the rival All-America Football Conference, where coach Paul Brown immediately signed Bill Willis and Marion Motley for his Cleveland Browns—and it was completed in 1962, when Marshall signed Bobby Mitchell to play for the Redskins. The first generation of black NFL stars came almost exclusively from the mainstream football world, but in the 1960s NFL scouts discovered the black colleges, Eddie Robinson's Grambling Tigers in particular. This golden era for black college football was short-lived, however,

BOB HAYES

"Bullet" Bob Hayes was a track-and-field phenom who also put his blazing speed to use as a wide receiver. Hayes began running as a boy with his brother Ernest, who was training to be a boxer. At Matthew W. Gilbert High School in Jacksonville, Fla., Hayes played running back on the football team and sprinted, as he also did at Florida Agricultural and Mechanical University (Tallahassee) in 1960–64. He set a world record (9.1 seconds) for the 100-yard (914 metre) dash in 1963. At the 1964 Olympic Games in Tokyo, he won the gold medal for the 100-metre (109 yard) dash and tied the world record (10.0 seconds). He also won a gold medal as the anchor of the 4 × 100-metre (109 yard) relay team. The relay victory was a world-record performance (39.0 seconds) highlighted by Hayes, who was trailing by 4 metres (4.4 yards) when he received the baton and won the race by 3 metres (3.3 yards), covering his leg in an estimated 8.6 seconds.

After retiring from sprinting, Hayes played professional football as wide receiver for the Dallas Cowboys for 10 seasons, beginning in 1965. He helped the Cowboys win the Super Bowl in 1972. At the time of his retirement from football in 1976, he held team records for career touchdowns (71), average yards per reception (20.0), and average yards per kick return (11.1), among others. In 2009 Hayes was elected to the Pro Football Hall of Fame.

as integration ended the black colleges' monopoly on local African American athletic talent.

Once integration had begun in earnest in football, the African American presence in both the college and professional games expanded exponentially. Many of football's most exciting and most revered players were black. The first African American to win the Heisman Trophy was Syracuse University running back Ernie Davis, in 1961. Since then the award, for collegiate football's best player, has routinely been presented to black players, including Archie Griffith (a two-time winner), Herschel Walker, Bo Jackson, Desmond Howard, and Reggie Bush, to name but a few. Like its collegiate counterpart, the Professional Football Hall of Fame is full of African American inductees. Any attempt at identifying pro football's greatest African American players is bound to leave out many who are worthy of inclusion, but a short list would necessarily begin with running backs Jim Brown, Gayle Sayers, Walter Payton, Emmitt Smith, Barry Sanders, and O. J. Simpson; receivers Jerry Rice, Paul Warfield, Bob Hayes, John Mackey, and Randy Moss; linemen Jim Parker and Art Shell; and defensive players Reggie White, Lawrence Taylor, and Willie Lanier.

Even after African Americans constituted large portions of the rosters of both college and professional teams, the glamour position of quarterback seemed to be reserved for white

Tony Dungy, then head coach of the Indianapolis Colts, pictured in Dec. 28, 2008. Dungy would announce his retirement the following month. The Colts' Feb. 4, 2007 win over the Chicago Bears in Super Bowl XLI made Dungy the first black coach to win an NFL championship. Jamie Squire/Getty Images

players, but this, too, would change. Among the first African Americans to distinguish himself as a a quarterback was Doug Williams, who was named the Most Valuable Player in Super Bowl XXII in 1988, in which he led the Washington Redskins to a 42–10 victory over the Denver Broncos. Other African Americans who have excelled at the position include Warren Moon, Randall Cunningham, Donovan McNabb, and Steve McNair. Notwithstanding Fritz Pollard's ascendance as a head coach early in the history of the game or Eddie Robinson's success at a traditionally black school (Grambling University), where he became college football's first coach to win 400 games, it took football a long time to provide head coaching opportunities for African Americans. But this situation also changed, though less often (at least proportionately), in collegiate football than in the pro game, where both teams in the 2006 Super Bowl, the Chicago Bears and the Indianapolis Colts, were coached by African Americans—Lovie Smith and Tony Dungy, respectively.

EPILOGUE

"A change is gonna come," wrote, sang, and hoped Sam Cooke in the mid-1960s in the soul style that was built upon the foundation of gospel music, just as the civil rights movement that reached its apex in the 1960s was founded on the bedrock of abolitionist activism. In the second half of the 20th century, many great changes did indeed come for African Americans. The march for social justice and equality was long and hard; often nonviolent protest was met with violence of the worst kind. The homes and churches of African Americans were bombed, inspirational leaders were assassinated, riots erupted, and inner cities burned. But "separate but equal" was finally thrown into history's dustbin by the U.S. Supreme Court, buses and schools were integrated, colour lines were broken in sports, sweeping civil rights and voting acts were passed, and the rich bounty of African American art and culture became fully and finally American culture. In the early 21st century inequities remained, many of them class-based, but Sam Cooke's hope had become Barack Obama's hope, and with Obama's inauguration as the 44th president of the United States, change certainly had come.

1942–59: THE BIRTH OF THE CIVIL RIGHTS MOVEMENT

1942: Charles Richard Drew, developer and director of blood plasma programs during World War II, resigns as the armed forces begin to accept the blood of blacks but resolve to racially segregate the supply.

1942: The interracial Congress of Racial Equality (CORE) is founded in Chicago as the Committee of Racial Equality. Its direct-action tactics achieve national prominence during the Freedom Rides of 1961.

c. 1942: Bebop is born out of the musical experiments of jazz musicians in Harlem, including saxophonist Charlie Parker, trumpeter Dizzy Gillespie, and pianist Thelonious Monk.

1943: Dancer Bill "Bojangles" Robinson appears with singer Lena Horne in the wartime all-black musical film *Stormy Weather*.

1945: *Ebony* magazine is founded by John H. Johnson of Chicago. Modeled after *Life* but intended for the black middle class, the magazine is an instant success.

1945: Adam Clayton Powell, Jr., pastor of the Abyssinian Baptist Church in Harlem, is elected to the U.S. House of Representatives as a Democrat from Harlem, serving 11 successive terms.

Stormy Weather *movie poster.* GAB Archive/ Redferns/Getty Images

c. 1946: Saxophonist Charlie Parker, though plagued by drug abuse, produces many of the finest recordings of his career, including "Now's the Time," "Koko," "Yardbird Suite," and "Ornithology."

1947: Jackie Robinson joins the Brooklyn Dodgers, becoming the first African American baseball player in the major leagues.

1947: Historian John Hope Franklin gains international attention with the publication of *From Slavery to Freedom*, an enduring survey of African American history.

1948: Satchel Paige, legendary baseball pitcher of the Negro leagues, finally enters the majors after the "gentlemen's agreement" prohibiting the signing of black players is relaxed.

1949: *Billboard* magazine's label of "race records" for its black music chart is officially changed to the designation "rhythm and blues," a term coined two years earlier by Jerry Wexler, a white reporter at the magazine and later a legendary record producer.

1949: Ralph Bunche is awarded the Nobel Peace Prize for his work as United Nations mediator in the Arab-Israeli dispute in Palestine.

Ralph Bunche in London, Eng., 1952. Derek Berwin/Hulton Archive/Getty Images

1950: Gwendolyn Brooks is awarded the Pulitzer Prize for poetry for *Annie Allen* (1949), becoming the first African American writer to win the award.

1950: After refusing to disavow his membership in the Communist Party, Paul Robeson—singer, actor, and activist—has his passport withdrawn by the U.S. State Department.

1952: Ralph Ellison publishes his masterpiece, *Invisible Man*, which receives the National Book Award in 1953.

1954: On May 17 the U.S. Supreme Court rules unanimously in *Brown* v. *Board of Education of Topeka* that racial segregation in public schools violates the Fourteenth Amendment to the Constitution.

1954: In the World Series against the Cleveland Indians, New York Giants outfielder Willie Mays makes "the catch." His extraordinary over-the-shoulder catch remains one of the most talked-about plays in baseball history.

1955: Lynchings continue in the South with the brutal slaying of a 14-year-old Chicago youth, Emmett Till, in Money, Miss. *Jet* magazine publishes a picture of the mutilated corpse.

1955: Rosa Parks, secretary of the Montgomery, Ala., chapter of the NAACP, refuses to surrender her seat when ordered to do so by a local bus driver, leading to the Montgomery bus boycott of 1955–56.

1955: Opera diva Leontyne Price is triumphant in the title role of the National

Broadcasting Company's *Tosca*, making her the first African American to sing opera for television.

1955: Singer, songwriter, and guitarist Chuck Berry travels from St. Louis, Mo., to Chicago, where he records "Maybellene," an immediate sensation among teenagers. The hit helps shape the evolution of rock and roll.

1956: Clifford Brown, the most influential trumpeter of his generation, dies at age 25 in a car accident. Noted for his lyricism and grace of technique, Brown is a principal figure in the hard-bop idiom.

1956: Arthur Mitchell, future director of the Dance Theatre of Harlem, becomes the only black dancer in the New York City Ballet. George Balanchine creates several roles especially for him.

1956: Tennis player Althea Gibson becomes the first African American to win a major title—the Wimbledon doubles—as well as the French singles and doubles and Italian singles.

1957: The Southern Christian Leadership Conference is established by the Rev. Martin Luther King, Jr., and others to coordinate and assist local organizations working for the full equality of African Americans.

1957: Pres. Dwight D. Eisenhower orders federal troops into Little Rock, Ark., after unsuccessfully trying to persuade Governor Orval Faubus to give up efforts to block desegregation at Central High School.

1957: Fullback Jim Brown begins his professional football career with the Cleveland Browns. He leads the National Football League in rushing for eight of his nine seasons.

1958: Boxer Sugar Ray Robinson, considered by many to be the greatest fighter in history, wins back the middleweight title for the last time by defeating Carmen Basilio in a savage fight.

Sugar Ray Robinson at his last Madison Square Garden appearance, 1965. Library of Congress Prints and Photographs Division

Dancer and choreographer Alvin Ailey, surrounded by other dancers, c. 1965. Hulton Archive/Getty Images

1958: Alvin Ailey founds the Alvin Ailey American Dance Theater. Composed primarily of African Americans, the dance company tours extensively both in the United States and abroad.

1958: Mahalia Jackson, known as the "Queen of Gospel Song," joins Duke Ellington in his gospel interlude *Black, Brown, and Beige* at the 1958 Newport Jazz Festival.

1959: Trumpeter Miles Davis records *Kind of Blue*, often considered his masterwork, with composer-arranger-pianist Bill Evans and tenor saxophonist John Coltrane.

1959: Singer Ray Charles records "What'd I Say," which becomes his first million-seller and exemplifies the emergence of soul music, combining rhythm and blues with gospel.

1959: *Raisin in the Sun*, by Lorraine Hansberry, becomes the first drama by a black woman to be produced on Broadway. The 1961 film version features Sidney Poitier and receives a special award at Cannes.

1959: Motown Record Corporation is founded in Detroit by Berry Gordy, Jr. The "Motown sound" dominates black popular music through the 1960s and attracts a huge white crossover audience as well, becoming the "Sound of Young America."

1959: Baseball player Ernie Banks, regarded as one of the finest power hitters in the history of the game, is named the National League's Most Valuable Player for a second consecutive season.

1959: Pioneer free jazz musician Ornette Coleman and his quartet play for the first time at New York's Five Spot Café. The historic performance receives a highly polarized reaction from the audience.

1960–69: BLACK POWER

1960: Jim Stewart and Estelle Axton, a white brother and sister, found Stax Records of Memphis, Tenn., which comes to define the Southern soul music sound identified with artists such as Sam and Dave, Booker T. and the MG's, and Otis Redding.

1960: The sit-in movement is launched in Greensboro, N.C., when black college students insist on service at a local segregated lunch counter.

1960: Inspired by the sit-in movement, jazz drummer Max Roach composes and records the historic *Freedom Now Suite* with lyricist Oscar Brown, Jr., and Roach's wife, vocalist Abbey Lincoln.

1961: Testing desegregation practices in the South, the Freedom Rides, sponsored by CORE, encounter overwhelming violence, particularly in Alabama, leading to federal intervention.

1961: Whitney Young is appointed executive director of the National Urban League. He builds a reputation for his behind-the-scenes work to bridge the gap between white political and business leaders and poor blacks.

1962: Basketball player Wilt Chamberlain becomes the first player to score more than 4,000 points in regular-season National Basketball Association games.

1962: The U.S. Supreme Court rules that the University of Mississippi must admit its first African American student, James Meredith.

1962: *The New Yorker* magazine publishes a long article by author James Baldwin on aspects of the civil-rights struggle. The article becomes a best-seller in book form as *The Fire Next Time.*

1963: In Birmingham, Ala., Police Commissioner Eugene "Bull" Connor uses water hoses and dogs against civil rights protesters, many of whom are children, increasing pressure on Pres. John F. Kennedy to act.

1963: Medgar Evers, Mississippi field secretary for the NAACP, is shot and killed in an ambush in front of his home, following a historic broadcast on the subject of civil rights by Pres. John F. Kennedy.

1963: The Rev. Martin Luther King, Jr., writes "Letter from a Birmingham Jail" to eight clergymen who attacked his role in Birmingham. Widely reprinted, it soon becomes a classic of protest literature.

1963: Sidney Poitier wins the Academy Award as best actor for his

Wilt Chamberlain, 1965. Focus On Sport/ Getty Images

performance in *Lilies of the Field*. In 1967 he would star in two films concerning race relations, *Guess Who's Coming to Dinner* and *In the Heat of the Night*.

1963: The civil rights movement reaches a dramatic climax with a massive march on Washington, D.C., organized chiefly by Bayard Rustin. Among the themes of the march "for jobs and freedom" is a demand for passage of the Civil Rights Act. In Washington an interracial audience of more than 200,000 hears Martin Luther King, Jr., deliver his famous "I Have a Dream" speech.

Martin Luther King, Jr., waves to the crowd on the Washington, D.C. Mall, Aug. 28, 1963. AFP/Getty Images

c. 1963: Free jazz, an approach to jazz improvisation that emerged during the late 1950s, gains momentum and influence among a wide variety of jazz artists led by Ornette Coleman, Eric Dolphy, Sun Ra, and others.

1964: Malcolm X leaves the Nation of Islam, announcing the formation of his own religious organization. He makes the pilgrimage to Mecca, modifying his views on black separatism upon his return.

1964: LeRoi Jones's play *Dutchman* appears off-Broadway and wins critical acclaim. The play exposes the suppressed anger and hostility of American blacks toward the dominant white culture.

1964: The bodies of three murdered civil rights workers—two white, one black—are found in Philadelphia, Miss.

1964: Pres. Lyndon Baines Johnson signs the Civil Rights Act into law, giving federal law enforcement agencies the power to prevent racial discrimination in employment, voting, and the use of public facilities.

1964: The Rev. Martin Luther King, Jr., is awarded the Nobel Prize for Peace in Oslo, Nor.

1964: Bob Gibson, pitcher for the St. Louis Cardinals, begins an unprecedented streak of seven straight World Series wins by taking Game Five and, on two days' rest, Game Seven.

1964: Jazz saxophonist John Coltrane records his masterpiece, *A Love Supreme*.

1964: The Twenty-fourth Amendment ends the poll tax in federal elections.

1965: The Voting Rights Act is passed following the Selma-to-Montgomery March, which garnered the nation's attention when marchers were beaten mercilessly by state troopers at the Edmund Pettus Bridge.

1965: The Watts area of Los Angeles explodes into violence following the arrest of a young male motorist charged with reckless driving. At the riot's end, 34 are dead, 1,032 injured, and 3,952 arrested.

1966: The Black Panther Party for Self-Defense is founded in Oakland, Calif., by Huey Newton and Bobby Seale, with the original purpose of protecting residents from acts of police brutality.

1966: Charting a new course for the civil rights movement, Stokely Carmichael, chairman of the Southern Christian Leadership Conference, uses the phrase "black power" at a rally during the James Meredith March in Mississippi.

1966: Bill Russell, one of the greatest defensive centres in the history of basketball, becomes the first black coach of a major professional sports team (the Boston Celtics) in the United States.

1966: Edward Brooke of Massachusetts becomes the first African American to be popularly elected to the U.S. Senate.

1966: The African American holiday of Kwanzaa, patterned after various African harvest festivals, is created by Maulana Karenga, a black-studies professor at California State University at Long Beach.

1967: After being denied his seat in the Georgia state legislature (although duly elected) for opposing U.S. involvement in the Vietnam War, civil rights activist Julian Bond is finally sworn in on January 9.

1967: Singer Aretha Franklin, the "Queen of Soul," releases a series of hits including "I Never Loved a Man," "Baby, I Love You," and "Respect," the last of which becomes something of an anthem for the civil rights movement.

1967: Heavyweight champion Muhammad Ali refuses to submit to induction into the armed forces. Convicted of violating the Selective Service Act, Ali is barred from the ring and stripped of his title.

1967: Blues and rock guitarist Jimi Hendrix makes his spectacular debut at the Monterey International Pop Festival, following the successful release of his first album, *Are You Experienced?*

1967: Huey P. Newton, cofounder of the Black Panther Party, is convicted on a charge of manslaughter in the death of an Oakland policeman, leading to the rapid expansion of the party nationwide.

1967: Thurgood Marshall, who as a lawyer argued *Brown* v. *Board of Education of Topeka*, becomes the first African American U.S. Supreme Court justice.

1967: Carl Stokes (Cleveland) and Richard Hatcher (Gary, Ind.) are elected the first African American mayors of major U.S. cities.

1968: Eldridge Cleaver, the Black Panther Party's minister of information, publishes the autobiographical *Soul on Ice.*

1968: On April 4 the Rev. Martin Luther King, Jr., is assassinated in Memphis, Tenn. Over the next week riots break out in some 125 cities around the country. Ralph Abernathy succeeds him as president of the Southern Christian Leadership Conference, carrying out the SCLC's Poor People's Campaign.

1968: Bob Beamon sets the world record in the long jump at the 1968 Olympic Games in Mexico City, surpassing the previous mark by 21 inches (53 cm).

1968: After winning the gold medal, sprinter Tommie Smith and team-mate John Carlos give a black-power salute during the awards ceremony, leading to their suspension by the U.S. Olympic Committee.

1968: Actor James Earl Jones wins acclaim and a Tony Award for his portrayal of legendary boxer Jack Johnson in Howard Sackler's play *The Great White Hope* and later stars in the film version (1970).

1968: Amiri Baraka (formerly LeRoi Jones) and Larry Neal publish *Black Fire: An Anthology of Afro-American Writing* in the spirit of the black aesthetic movement, which seeks to create a populist art form to promote black nationalism.

1968: Shirley Chisholm becomes the first black American woman to be elected to the U.S. Congress, defeating civil-rights leader James Farmer.

Shirley Chisholm in a Brooklyn, N.Y., voting booth, Nov. 5, 1968. New York Daily News/ Getty Images

1969: Black Panther Party cofounder Bobby Seale is ordered bound and gagged by the judge after Seale protests that he was being denied his constitutional right to counsel during his trial for conspiracy to incite rioting at the Democratic National Convention in Chicago the previous year.

1970–90: MAYORS, CONGRESSMEN, AND ASTRONAUTS

1970: Baseball player Curt Flood, with the backing of the Major League Baseball Players Association, unsuccessfully challenges the reserve clause but begins its eventual demise.

1971: Author Ernest J. Gaines publishes *The Autobiography of Miss Jane Pittman,* a fictional remembrance by an elderly black woman of the years between Reconstruction and the civil rights movement.

1971: Angela Davis is arraigned on charges of murder, kidnapping, and conspiracy for her alleged participation in a violent attempted escape from the Hall of Justice in Marin county, Calif., in 1970.

1971: In *Swann* v. *Charlotte-Mecklenburg Board of Education* the Supreme Court upholds the constitutionality of court-ordered plans to achieve desegregation of schools, affirming the busing of schoolchildren in Charlotte, N.C.

1972: Writer Ishmael Reed publishes *Mumbo Jumbo.* Its irreverent tone successfully revives the tradition of the black satiric novel.

1972: Shirley Chisholm, a member of the House of Representatives from New York, is the first African American woman to make a serious bid for the U.S. presidency.

1973: Gladys Knight and the Pips produce the million-selling album *Imagination,* winning two Grammy Awards.

1974: Baseball player Hank Aaron hits his 715th home run, breaking Babe Ruth's record, which had stood since 1935.

1974: Actress Cicely Tyson is lauded for her role as the 110-year-old title character of the television drama *The Autobiography of Miss Jane Pittman,* which was adapted from the Ernest J. Gaines novel.

1974: In the storied "Rumble in the Jungle," boxer George Foreman, previously undefeated in professional bouts, falls to Muhammad Ali in eight rounds at Kinshasa, Zaire (now Democratic Republic of the Congo).

1975: Playwright Ntozake Shange receives considerable acclaim for her theatre piece *For Colored Girls Who Have Considered Suicide/When the Rainbow Is Enuf.*

1975: Tennis player Arthur Ashe wins the singles title at Wimbledon, becoming

Tennis player Arthur Ashe hoists the Wimbledon singles championship trophy, July 1975. David Ashdown/Hulton Archive/ Getty Images

the first African American man to win the prestigious championship.

1975: Elijah Muhammad, leader of the Nation of Islam, dies. After his son renames the organization and integrates it into orthodox Islam, Minister Louis Farrakhan reclaims and rebuilds the Nation of Islam.

1975: Frank Robinson becomes the first African American manager of a Major League Baseball team, the Cleveland Indians.

1976: Barbara Jordan, congressional representative from Texas, delivers the keynote address at the Democratic National Convention, confirming her reputation as one of the most eloquent public speakers of her era.

1976: Congressman Andrew Young of Georgia becomes the first African American U.S. ambassador to the United Nations.

1977: Alex Haley's *Roots: The Saga of an American Family* (1976) is adapted for television, becoming one of the most popular shows in the history of American television.

1977: Benjamin L. Hooks becomes the executive director of the NAACP, succeeding Roy Wilkins. Stressing the need for affirmative action and increased minority voter registration, Hooks serves until 1993.

1978: In the Bakke decision, the U.S. Supreme Court rules against fixed racial quotas but upholds the use of race as a factor in making decisions on admissions for professional schools.

1978: Sociologist William Julius Wilson publishes *The Declining Significance of Race*, which maintains that class divisions and global economic changes, more than racism, created a large black underclass.

1979: Lou Brock of the St. Louis Cardinals steals his 935th base, becoming Major League Baseball's all-time career stolen-base leader.

1979: *United Steelworkers of America v. Weber* permits an affirmative action program to privilege African Americans if the program is intended to remedy past discrimination.

1981: Civil-rights leader Andrew Young is elected mayor of Atlanta, an office he holds through 1989.

1982: Playwright Charles Fuller wins the Pulitzer Prize for drama for *A Soldier's Play,* which examines conflict among black soldiers on a Southern army base during World War II.

1982: Singer Michael Jackson creates a sensation with the album *Thriller,* which becomes one of the most popular albums of all time, selling more than 40 million copies.

1983: Writer Alice Walker receives the Pulitzer Prize for *The Color Purple.*

1983: Harold Washington wins the Democratic nomination by upsetting incumbent Mayor Jane Byrne and Richard M. Daley and is elected the first African American mayor of Chicago.

1983: Civil-rights leader Jesse Jackson announces his intention to run for the Democratic presidential nomination,

Astronaut Guion S. Bluford, Jr., exercising on a treadmill aboard the U.S. space shuttle Challenger *in Earth orbit, 1983.* NASA

becoming the first African American man to make a serious bid for the presidency.

1983: Guion Bluford, Jr., becomes the first African American in space as a member of the crew of the space shuttle *Challenger.*

1984: *The Cosby Show,* starring comedian Bill Cosby, becomes one of the most popular situation comedies in television history and is praised for its broad cross-cultural appeal and avoidance of racial stereotypes.

1986: Playwright August Wilson receives the Pulitzer Prize for *Fences,* winning it again for *The Piano Lesson* in 1990. Both are from his cycle of plays chronicling the black American experience.

1986: Established by legislation in 1983, Martin Luther King, Jr., Day is first celebrated as a U.S. national holiday.

1987: Basketball forward Julius Erving, noted for his balletic leaps toward the basket and climactic slam dunks, retires after becoming the third professional player to score a career total of 30,000 points.

1988: Runner Florence Griffith Joyner captures three gold medals and a silver in the Seoul Olympics.

1989: Modern dancer Judith Jamison becomes the artistic director of the Alvin Ailey American Dance Theater, following Ailey's death.

1989: David Dinkins becomes the first African American to be elected mayor of New York City.

1990: John Edgar Wideman becomes the first author to twice receive the prestigious PEN/Faulkner Award for Fiction, for his novels *Sent for You Yesterday* (1983) and *Philadelphia Fire* (1990).

1990: Author Walter Mosley publishes his first novel, *Devil in a Blue Dress,* which introduces the enduring character of "Easy" Rawlins, an unwilling amateur detective from the Watts section of Los Angeles in 1948.

1990: Jazz drummer Art Blakey dies. Since founding the Jazz Messengers in 1954, he is responsible for nurturing generations of young jazz musicians, including Clifford Brown, Jackie McLean, and Lee Morgan.

1991–PRESENT: THE SPIRIT OF THE MILLENNIUM

1991: The Senate votes 52–48 to confirm the nomination of Justice Clarence Thomas to the Supreme Court following charges of sexual harassment by former aide Anita Hill during confirmation hearings.

1991: With much fanfare, Henry Louis Gates, Jr., is appointed W.E.B. Du Bois professor of humanities at Harvard University, where he proceeds to build the university's Department of Afro-American Studies.

1992: Riots break out in Los Angeles, sparked by the acquittal of four white police officers caught on videotape beating Rodney King, a black motorist. The riots cause at least 55 deaths and $1 billion in damage.

1992: Author Terry McMillan publishes *Waiting to Exhale*, which follows four middle-class women, each of whom is looking for the love of a worthy man. The book's wild popularity leads to a film adaptation.

1992: Mae Jemison becomes the first African American woman astronaut, spending more than a week orbiting Earth in the space shuttle *Endeavour*.

1992: Carol Moseley Braun becomes the first African American woman elected to the U.S. Senate, representing the state of Illinois.

1993: Poet Maya Angelou, author of the autobiographical work *I Know Why the Caged Bird Sings* (1970), composes and delivers a poem for the inauguration of President Bill Clinton.

1993: Cornel West, progressive postmodern philosopher, finds a mainstream audience with the publication of his text *Race Matters*, which closely examines the black community around the time of the 1992 Los Angeles riots.

1993: Poet Rita Dove, author of the Pulitzer Prize-winning *Thomas and Beulah*, is chosen as poet laureate of the United States.

1993: Writer Toni Morrison, winner of the Pulitzer Prize for fiction for *Beloved*, receives the Nobel Prize for Literature.

1993: Joycelyn Elders becomes the first African American woman to serve as the U.S. surgeon general.

1994: With his defeat of Michael Moore, 26, in Las Vegas, George Foreman at 45 becomes the world's oldest heavyweight boxing champion.

1995: In one of the most celebrated criminal trials in American history, former football running back O.J. Simpson is acquitted of the murders of his ex-wife Nicole Brown Simpson and her friend Ronald Goldman.

1995: Minister Louis Farrakhan, leader of the Nation of Islam, rises to the height of his influence as the most prominent organizer of the "Million Man March" of African American men in Washington, D.C.

1996: At the Olympic Games in Atlanta, sprinter Michael Johnson becomes the first man to win gold medals in the 200 metres (219 yards) and the 400 metres (437 yards), setting a

200-metre (219 yard) world record of 19.32 seconds.

1996: The subject of Ebonics (or Black English vernacular) is debated throughout the United States.

1997: Tiger Woods becomes the first African American golfer to win the Masters Tournament.

1997: Many African American women join the Million Woman March in Philadelphia.

1998: Michael Jordan, often considered the greatest all-around player in the history of basketball, leads the Chicago Bulls to their sixth championship.

1998: The "Little Rock Nine"—nine black students who were prevented from attending a formerly all-white public school and whose case became

Rosa Parks is presented the Congressional Medal of Honor by U.S. Vice Pres. Al Gore, Nov. 28, 1999. Jeff Kowalsky/AFP/Getty Images

a test of power between federal and state governments—are awarded the Congressional Gold Medal.

1999: Rosa Parks is awarded the Congressional Gold Medal.

1999: The mistaken shooting and killing of an African immigrant, Amadou Diallo, by New York City policemen causes a national outcry.

2000: Tennis player Venus Williams becomes the first African American woman since Althea Gibson (1958) to win the singles championship at Wimbledon. Later in the year Williams becomes the first African American woman to win a gold medal in singles and doubles tennis at the same Olympic Games.

2000: In response to widespread protest and a boycott by the NAACP, the South Carolina Senate passes a bill to remove the Confederate flag from the statehouse.

2001: General Colin Powell becomes the first African American to serve as U.S. secretary of state. He was also the first African American chairman of the Joint Chiefs of Staff (1989–93).

2001: Condoleezza Rice is named national security adviser, becoming the first woman and second African American to hold this position. Concurrently, Roderick Paige is named secretary of education and is the first African American to hold this position.

2001: Bishop Wilton Gregory becomes the first African American to be elected president of the U.S. Conference of Catholic Bishops.

Condoleezza Rice. U.S. Department of State

2002: Athlete Vonetta Flowers wins a gold medal in the women's bobsled event, becoming the first African American to win at the Winter Olympics.

2002: Suzan-Lori Parks, with her play *Topdog/Underdog,* becomes the first African American woman to win the Pulitzer Prize for drama.

2002: Halle Berry becomes the first African American woman to win the Academy Award for best actress.

2003: The U.S. Supreme Court issues a ruling on affirmative action in education, which upholds the use of race in collegiate admissions policies.

2003: 1st Lt. Vernice Armour becomes the first African American female combat pilot in the U.S. Marine Corps and U.S. military history.

2004: Barack Obama becomes the third African American to be elected to the U.S. Senate after Reconstruction.

2005: Condoleezza Rice succeeds Colin Powell as U.S. secretary of state, becoming the first African American woman to hold the post.

2005: Floodwater from Hurricane Katrina breeches New Orleans's levee system and inundates the city, wreaking havoc on the tens of thousands of people who have not evacuated.

2006: Warren Moon becomes the first African American quarterback inducted into the Pro Football Hall of Fame.

2006: Deval Patrick wins election as Massachusetts's first black governor.

2007: Outfielder Barry Bonds breaks the major league career home run record by hitting his 756th home run.

2007: The eloquent silhouettes of artist Kara Walker are the focus of a major traveling exhibit, "Kara Walker: My Complement, My Enemy, My Oppressor, My Love," organized by the Walker Art Center in Minneapolis, Minn.

2008: Barack Obama is elected president of the United States, becoming the first African American to win that office.

2008: Tony Dungy becomes the first African American head coach to win a Super Bowl when his Indianapolis Colts defeat the Chicago Bears.

2009: While preparing for a series of high-profile concerts he hoped would spark a comeback, Michael Jackson dies suddenly of cardiac arrest.

2009: Eric Holder becomes the first African American to serve as U.S. attorney general.

Appendix: Primary Sources

Below are four telling primary source documents that offer insight into some of the pivotal events of African American history since World War II. The first is the text of the landmark Supreme Court ruling *Brown* v. *Board of Education of Topeka*. The last three are speeches by Barack Obama: the first delivered when he was a candidate for a seat in the U.S. Senate, the second when he was campaigning for the presidency, and the third delivered as he assumed the highest office of the U.S. government.

EARL WARREN: *BROWN ET AL. V. BOARD OF EDUCATION OF TOPEKA ET AL.*

The trigger event of the civil rights movement of the 1950s and 1960s may be said to have occurred on May 17, 1954, when the Supreme Court handed down its decision in *Brown* v. *Board of Education of Topeka*. The decision, written by Chief Justice Earl Warren for a unanimous Court, directly reversed the famous ruling in *Plessy* v. *Ferguson* (1896). In the earlier case the Court had upheld a Louisiana law requiring separate railroad facilities, on the grounds that if equality of accommodations existed African Americans had no recourse under the equal protection of the laws clause of the Fourteenth Amendment. The 1954 ruling held, on the contrary, that even if educational opportunities for African Americans were equal

to those for whites, African Americans were nevertheless deprived under the same clause of the same amendment.

United States Reports [Supreme Court], Vol. 347, pp. 483ff.

These cases come to us from the states of Kansas, South Carolina, Virginia, and Delaware. They are premised on different facts and different local conditions, but a common legal question justifies their consideration together in this consolidated opinion.[1]

In each of the cases, minors of the Negro race, through their legal representatives, seek the aid of the courts in obtaining admission to the public schools of their community on a non-segregated basis. In each instance, they had been denied admission to schools attended by white children under laws requiring or permitting segregation according to race. This segregation was alleged to deprive the plaintiffs of the equal protection of the laws under the Fourteenth Amendment. In each of the cases other than the Delaware case, a three-judge federal District Court denied relief to the plaintiffs on the so-called "separate but equal" doctrine announced by this Court in *Plessy* v. *Ferguson*, 163 U.S. 537. Under that doctrine, equality of treatment is accorded when the races are provided substantially equal facilities, even though these facilities be separate. In the Delaware case, the Supreme Court of Delaware adhered to that doctrine, but ordered that the plaintiffs be admitted to the white schools because of their superiority to the Negro schools.

The plaintiffs contend that segregated public schools are not "equal" and cannot be made "equal," and that hence they are deprived of the equal protection of the laws. Because of the obvious importance of the question presented, the Court took jurisdiction.[2] Argument was heard in the 1952 Term, and reargument was heard this Term on certain questions propounded by the Court.[3]

Reargument was largely devoted to the circumstances surrounding the adoption of the Fourteenth Amendment in 1868. It covered exhaustively consideration of the amendment in Congress, ratification by the states, then-existing practices in racial segregation, and the views of proponents and opponents of the amendment. This discussion and our own investigation convince us that, although these sources cast some light, it is not enough to resolve the problem with which we are faced. At best, they are inconclusive. The most avid proponents of the postwar amendments undoubtedly intended them to remove all legal distinctions among "all persons born or naturalized in the United States." Their opponents, just as certainly, were antagonistic to both the letter and the spirit of the amendments and wished them to have the most limited effect. What others in Congress and the state legislatures had in mind cannot be determined with any degree of certainty.

An additional reason for the inconclusive nature of the amendment's history, with respect to segregated schools, is the status of public education at that time.[4] In the South, the movement toward free common schools, supported by general taxation, had not yet taken hold. Education of white children was largely in the hands of private groups. Education of Negroes was almost nonexistent, and practically all of the race were illiterate. In fact, any education of Negroes was forbidden by law in some states. Today, in contrast, many Negroes have achieved outstanding success in the arts and sciences as well as in the business and professional world. It is true that public-school education at the time of the amendment had advanced further in the North, but the effect of the amendment on Northern states was generally ignored in the congressional debates.

Even in the North, the conditions of public education did not approximate those existing today. The curriculum was usually rudimentary; ungraded schools were common in rural areas; the school term was but three months a year in many states; and compulsory school attendance was virtually unknown. As a consequence, it is not surprising that there should be so little in the history of the Fourteenth Amendment relating to its intended effect on public education.

In the first cases in this Court construing the Fourteenth Amendment, decided shortly after its adoption, the Court interpreted it as proscribing all state-imposed discriminations against the Negro race.[5] The doctrine of "separate but equal" did not make its appearance in this Court until 1896 in the case of *Plessy v. Ferguson, supra,* involving not education but transportation.[6] American courts have since labored with the doctrine for over half a century.

In this Court there have been six cases involving the "separate but equal" doctrine in the field of public education.[7] In *Cumming* v. *County Board of Education,* 175 U. S. 528, and *Gong Lum* v. *Rice,* 275 U. S. 78, the validity of the doctrine itself was not challenged.[8] In more recent cases, all on the graduate-school level, inequality was found in that specific benefits enjoyed by white students were denied to Negro students of the same educational qualifications. *Missouri ex rel. Gaines* v. *Canada,* 305 U. S. 337; *Sipuel* v. *Oklahoma,* 332 U. S. 631; *Sweatt* v. *Painter,* 339 U. S. 629; *McLaurin* v. *Oklahoma State Regents,* 339 U. S. 637. In none of these cases was it necessary to reexamine the doctrine to grant relief to the Negro plaintiff. And in *Sweatt* v. *Painter, supra,* the Court expressly reserved decision on the question whether *Plessy* v. *Ferguson* should be held inapplicable to public education.

In the instant cases, that question is directly presented. Here, unlike *Sweatt* v. *Painter,* there are findings below that the Negro and white schools involved have been equalized, or are being equalized, with respect to buildings, curricula, qualifications and salaries of teachers, and other "tangible" factors.[9] Our decision, therefore, cannot turn on merely a comparison of these tangible factors in

the Negro and white schools involved in each of the cases. We must look instead to the effect of segregation itself on public education.

In approaching this problem, we cannot turn the clock back to 1868 when the amendment was adopted, or even to 1896 when *Plessy* v. *Ferguson* was written. We must consider public education in the light of its full development and its present place in American life throughout the nation. Only in this way can it be determined if segregation in public schools deprives these plaintiffs of the equal protection of the laws.

Today, education is perhaps the most important function of state and local governments. Compulsory school-attendance laws and the great expenditures for education both demonstrate our recognition of the importance of education to our democratic society. It is required in the performance of our most basic public responsibilities, even service in the armed forces. It is the very foundation of good citizenship. Today it is a principal instrument in awakening the child to cultural values, in preparing him for later professional training, and in helping him to adjust normally to his environment. In these days, it is doubtful that any child may reasonably be expected to succeed in life if he is denied the opportunity of an education. Such an opportunity, where the state has undertaken to provide it, is a right which must be made available to all on equal terms.

We come then to the question presented: Does segregation of children in public schools solely on the basis of race, even though the physical facilities and other "tangible" factors may be equal, deprive the children of the minority group of equal educational opportunities? We believe that it does.

In *Sweatt* v. *Painter, supra,* in finding that a segregated law school for Negroes could not provide them equal educational opportunities, this Court relied in large part on "those qualities which are incapable of objective measurement but which make for greatness in a law school." In *McLaurin* v. *Oklahoma State Regents, supra,* the Court, in requiring that a Negro admitted to a white graduate school be treated like all other students, again resorted to intangible considerations: ". . . his ability to study, to engage in discussions and exchange views with other students, and, in general, to learn his profession." Such considerations apply with added force to children in grade and high schools. To separate them from others of similar age and qualifications solely because of their race generates a feeling of inferiority as to their status in the community that may affect their hearts and minds in a way unlikely ever to be undone. The effect of this separation on their educational opportunities was well stated by a finding in the Kansas case by a court which nevertheless felt compelled to rule against the Negro plaintiffs:

> *Segregation of white and colored children in public schools has a detrimental effect upon the colored children. The impact is greater when it has the sanction of the law; for the policy of separating the races is usually interpreted as denoting the inferiority of the Negro group. A sense of inferiority affects the motivation of a child to learn. Segregation with the sanction of law, therefore, has a tendency to [retard] the educational and mental development of Negro children and to deprive them of some of the benefits they would receive in a racial[ly] integrated school system.*[10]

Whatever may have been the extent of psychological knowledge at the time of *Plessy* v. *Ferguson,* this finding is amply supported by modern authority.[11] Any language in *Plessy* v. *Ferguson* contrary to this finding is rejected.

We conclude that in the field of public education the doctrine of "separate but equal" has no place. Separate educational facilities are inherently unequal. Therefore, we hold that the plaintiffs and others similarly situated for whom the actions have been brought are, by reason of the segregation complained of, deprived of the equal protection of the laws guaranteed by the Fourteenth Amendment. This disposition makes unnecessary any discussion whether such segregation also violates the due process clause of the Fourteenth Amendment.[12]

Because these are class actions, because of the wide applicability of this decision, and because of the great variety of local conditions, the formulation of decrees in these cases presents problems of considerable complexity. On reargument, the consideration of appropriate relief was necessarily subordinated to the primary question—the constitutionality of segregation in public education. We have now announced that such segregation is a denial of the equal protection of the laws. In order that we may have the full assistance of the parties in formulating decrees, the cases will be restored to the docket, and the parties are requested to present further argument on Questions 4 and 5 previously propounded by the Court for the reargument this Term.[13] The attorney general of the United States is again invited to participate. The attorneys general of the states requiring or permitting segregation in public education will also be permitted to appear as *amici curiae* upon request to do so by Sept. 15, 1954, and submission of briefs by Oct. 1, 1954.[14]

Footnotes

1   In the Kansas case, Brown v. Board of Education, *the plaintiffs are Negro children of elementary-school age residing in Topeka. They brought this action in the United States District Court for the District of Kansas to enjoin enforcement of a Kansas statute which permits, but does not require, cities of more than 15,000 population to maintain separate school facilities for Negro and white students. Kan. Gen. Stat. Sec. 72–1724 (1949). Pursuant to that authority, the Topeka Board of Education elected to establish segregated elementary schools. Other public schools in the community, however, are operated on a nonsegregated basis. The three-judge District Court, convened under 28 U.S.C. Sec. 2281 and 2284, found that segregation in public education has a detrimental effect upon Negro children, but denied relief on the ground that*

the Negro and white schools were substantially equal with respect to buildings, transportation, curricula, and educational qualifications of teachers. 98 F. Supp. 797. The case is here on direct appeal under 28 U.S.C. Sec. 1253. In the South Carolina case, Briggs v. Elliott, *the plaintiffs are Negro children of both elementary and high-school age residing in Clarendon County. They brought this action in the United States District Court for the Eastern District of South Carolina to enjoin enforcement of provisions in the state constitution and statutory code which require the segregation of Negroes and whites in public schools. S.C. Const., Art. XI, Sec. 7; S.C. Code Sec. 5377 (1942). The three-judge District Court, convened under 28 U.S.C. Sec. 2281 and 2284, denied the requested relief. The court found that the Negro schools were inferior to the white schools and ordered the defendants to begin immediately to equalize the facilities. But the court sustained the validity of the contested provisions and denied the plaintiffs admission to the white schools during the equalization program. 98 F. Supp. 529. This Court vacated the District Court's judgment and remanded the case for the purpose of obtaining the court's views on a report filed by the defendants concerning the progress made in the equalization program. 342 U.S. 350. On remand, the District Court found that substantial equality had been achieved except for buildings and that the defendants were proceeding to rectify this inequality as well. 103 F. Supp. 920. The case is again here on direct appeal under 28 U.S.C. Sec. 1253. In the Virginia case,* Davis v. County School Board, *the plaintiffs are Negro children of high-school age residing in Prince Edward County. They brought this action in the United States District Court for the Eastern District of Virginia to enjoin enforcement of provisions in the state constitution and statutory code which require the segregation of Negroes and whites in public schools. Va. Const., Sec. 140; Va. Code Sec. 22–221 (1950). The three-judge District Court, convened under 28 U.S.C. Sec. 2281 and 2284, denied the requested relief. The court found the Negro school inferior in physical plant, curricula, and transportation, and ordered the defendants forthwith to provide substantially* equal curricula and transportation and to "proceed with all reasonable diligence and dispatch to remove" the inequality in physical plant. But, as in the South Carolina case, the court sustained the validity of the contested provisions and denied the plaintiffs admission to the white schools during the equalization program. 103 F. Supp. 337. The case is here on direct appeal under 28 U.S.C. Sec. 1253. In the Delaware case, Gebhart v. Belton, the plaintiffs are Negro children of both elementary and high-school age residing in New Castle County. They brought this action in the Delaware Court of Chancery to enjoin enforcement of provisions in the state constitution and statutory code which require the segregation of Negroes and whites in public schools. Del. Const., Art. X, Sec. 2; Del. Rev. Code Sec. 2631 (1935). The chancellor gave judgment for the plaintiffs and ordered their immediate admission to schools previously attended only by white children on the ground that the Negro schools were inferior with respect to teacher training, pupil-teacher ratio, extracurricular activities, physical plant, and time and distance involved in travel. 87 A. 2d 862. The chancellor also found that segregation itself results in an inferior education for Negro children (see note 10, infra), but did not rest his decision on that ground. Id., at 865. The chancellor's decree was affirmed by the Supreme Court of Delaware, which intimated, however, that the defendants might be able to obtain a modification of the decree after equalization of the Negro and white schools had been accomplished. 91 A. 2nd 137, 152. The defendants, contending only that the Delaware courts had erred in ordering the immediate admission of the Negro plaintiffs to the white schools, applied to this Court for certiorari. The writ was granted, 344 U.S. 891. The plaintiffs, who were successful below, did not submit a crosspetition.

2   344 U.S. 1, 141, 891.

3   345 U.S. 972. The attorney general of the United States participated both Terms as amicus curiae.

4   For a general study of the development of public education prior to the amendment, see Butts and Cremin, A History of Education in American Culture (1953), Pts. I, II; Cubberley, Public Education in the United States (1934

ed.), cc. II–XII. School practices current at the time of the adoption of the Fourteenth Amendment are described in Butts and Cremin, supra, at 269–275; Cubberley, supra, at 288–339, 408–431; Knight, Public Education in the South (1922), cc. VIII, IX. See also H. Ex. Doc. No. 315, 41st Cong., 2nd Sess. (1871). Although the demand for free public schools followed substantially the same pattern in both the North and the South, the development in the South did not begin to gain momentum until about 1850, some twenty years after that in the North. The reasons for the somewhat slower development in the South (e.g., the rural character of the South and the different regional attitudes toward state assistance) are well explained in Cubberley, supra, at 408–423. In the country as a whole, but particularly in the South, the war virtually stopped all progress in public education. Id., at 427–428. The low status of Negro education in all sections of the country, both before and immediately after the war, is described in Beale, A History of Freedom of Teaching in American Schools (1941), 112–132, 175–195. Compulsory school-attendance laws were not generally adopted until after the ratification of the Fourteenth Amendment, and it was not until 1918 that such laws were in force in all the states. Cubberley, supra, at 563–565.

5   Slaughter-House Cases, 16 Wall. 36, 67–72 (1873); Strauder v. West Virginia, 100 U. S. 303, 307–308 (1880): "It ordains that no state shall deprive any person of life, liberty, or property, without due process of law, or deny to any person within its jurisdiction the equal protection of the laws. What is this but declaring that the law in the states shall be the same for the black as for the white; that all persons, whether colored or white, shall stand equal before the laws of the states, and, in regard to the colored race, for whose protection the amendment was primarily designed, that no discrimination shall be made against them by law because of their color? The words of the amendment, it is true, are prohibitory, but they contain a necessary implication of a positive immunity, or right, most valuable to the colored race—the right to exemption from unfriendly legislation against them distinctively as colored—exemption from

legal discriminations, implying inferiority in civil society, lessening the security of their enjoyment of the rights which others enjoy, and discriminations which are steps toward reducing them to the condition of a subject race." See also Virginia v. Rives, 100 U.S. 313, 318 (1880); Ex parte Virginia, 100 U.S. 339, 344-345 (1880).

6   The doctrine apparently originated in Roberts v. City of Boston, 59 Mass. 198, 206 (1850), upholding school segregation against attack as being violative of a state constitutional guarantee of equality. Segregation in Boston public schools was eliminated in 1855. Mass. Acts 1855, c. 256. But elsewhere in the North, segregation in public education has persisted in some communities until recent years. It is apparent that such segregation has long been a nationwide problem, not merely one of sectional concern.

7   See also Berea College v. Kentucky, 211 U.S. 45 (1908).

8   In the Cumming case, Negro taxpayers sought an injunction requiring the defendant school board to discontinue the operation of a high school for white children until the board resumed operation of a high school for Negro children. Similarly, in the Gong Lum case, the plaintiff, a child of Chinese descent, contended only that state authorities had misapplied the doctrine by classifying him with Negro children and requiring him to attend a Negro school.

9   In the Kansas case, the court below found substantial equality as to all such factors. 98 F. Supp. 797, 798. In the South Carolina case, the court below found that the defendants were proceeding "promptly and in good faith to comply with the court's decree." 103 F. Supp. 920, 921. In the Virginia case, the court below noted that the equalization program was already "afoot and progressing" (103 F. Supp. 337, 341); since then, we have been advised, in the Virginia attorney general's brief on reargument, that the program has now been completed. In the Delaware case, the court below similarly noted that the state's equalization program was well under way. 91 A. 2d 137, 149.

10 A similar finding was made in the Delaware case: "I conclude from the testimony that, in our Delaware society, state-imposed segregation in education itself results in the Negro children, as a class, receiving educational opportunities which are substantially inferior to those available to white children otherwise similarly situated." 87 A. 2d 862, 865.

11 K. B. Clark, Effect of Prejudice and Discrimination on Personality Development (Midcentury White House Conference on Children and Youth, 1950); Witmer and Kotinsky, Personality in the Making (1952), c. VI; Deutscher and Chein, "The Psychological Effects of Enforced Segregation: A Survey of Social Science Opinion," 26 J. Psychol. 259 (1948); Chein, "What are the Psychological Effects of Segregation Under Conditions of Equal Facilities?" 3 Int. J. Opinion and Attitude Res. 229 (1949); Brameld, Educational Costs, in Discrimination and National Welfare (MacIver, ed., 1949), 44-48; Frazier, The Negro in the United States (1949), 674-681. And see generally Myrdal, An American Dilemma (1944).

12 See Bolling v. Sharpe, post, p. 497, concerning the due process clause of the Fifth Amendment.

13 "4. Assuming it is decided that segregation in public schools violates the Fourteenth Amendment "(a) would a decree necessarily follow providing that, within the limits set by normal geographic school districting, Negro children should forthwith be admitted to schools of their choice, or "(b) may this Court, in the exercise of its equity powers, permit an effective gradual adjustment to be brought about from existing segregated systems to a system not based on color distinctions? "5. On the assumption on which questions 4 (a) and (b) are based, and assuming further that this Court will exercise its equity powers to the end described in question 4 (b), "(a) should this Court formulate detailed decrees in these cases; "(b) if so, what specific issues should the decrees reach; "(c) should this Court appoint a special master to hear evidence with a view to recommending specific terms for such decrees; "(d) should this Court remand to the courts of first instance with directions to frame decrees in these cases, and if so what general directions should the decrees of this Court include and what procedures should the courts of first instance follow in arriving at the specific terms of more detailed decrees?"

14 See Rule 42, Revised Rules of this Court (effective July 1, 1954).

BARACK OBAMA: KEYNOTE ADDRESS AT THE 2004 DEMOCRATIC NATIONAL CONVENTION

By the time of the 2004 election campaign, political pundits routinely divided the United States into red and blue states, whose colour not only indicated which political party was locally dominant but also signified the supposed prevalence of a set of social and cultural values. According to the received wisdom, the Republican red states—generally located in the South, West, and lower Midwest— were conservative, God-fearing, pro-life, opposed to big government and same-sex marriage, small-town and suburban, and enamored of NASCAR. The Democratic blue states—found mostly on the coasts, in the Northeast, and in the Upper Midwest—were liberal, secular, politically correct, pro-choice, urban, and connoisseurs of wine, cheese, and latte. Though the symbolic palette dated only to the 2000 election and reversed the colors theretofore generally used to represent the Democratic and Republican parties, it was firmly established when Sen. John F. Kerry of Massachusetts, a decorated Vietnam War veteran who later prominently opposed the war, was chosen by the Democrats to face Republican incumbent George W. Bush in one of the most partisan and polarizing presidential elections in recent American history. The keynote address at the Democratic Convention in Boston was delivered by Barack Obama, who was about to become only the third African American since Reconstruction to be elected to the U.S. Senate. Obama became an instant national figure with his eloquent address, in which he debunked the country's artificial red-blue division and offered "the audacity of hope," a phrase that would become the title of the book he published shortly before becoming a candidate for the 2008 presidential election.

Source: *Keynote address delivered from the 2004 Democratic National Convention*, Boston, Mass., July 24, 2004.

On behalf of the great state of Illinois, crossroads of a nation, Land of Lincoln, let me express my deepest gratitude for the privilege of addressing this convention. Tonight is a particular honor for me because, let's face it, my presence on this stage is pretty unlikely. My father was a foreign student, born and raised in a small village in Kenya. He grew up herding goats, went to school in a tin-roof shack. His father, my grandfather, was a cook, a domestic servant to the British.

But my grandfather had larger dreams for his son. Through hard work and perseverance my father got a scholarship to study in a magical place, America, that shone as a beacon of freedom and opportunity to so many who had come before. While studying here, my father met my mother. She was born in a town on the other side of the world, in Kansas. Her father worked on oil rigs and farms through most of the Depression. The day after Pearl Harbor he signed up for duty; joined Patton's army, marched across Europe. Back home, my grandmother raised their baby and went to work on a bomber assembly line. After the war, they studied on the G.I. Bill, bought a house through FHA, and later moved west in search of opportunity.

And they, too, had big dreams for their daughter. A common dream, born of two continents. My parents shared not only an improbable love, they shared an abiding faith in the possibilities of this nation. They would give me an African name, Barack, or "blessed," believing that in a tolerant America your name is no barrier to success. They imagined me going to the best schools in the land, even though they weren't rich, because in a generous America you don't have to be rich to achieve your potential. They're both passed away now. Yet, I know that, on this night, they look down on me with great pride.

I stand here today, grateful for the diversity of my heritage, aware that my parents' dreams live on in my two precious daughters. I stand here knowing that my story is part of the larger American story, that I owe a debt to all of those who came before me, and that, in no other country on earth, is my story even possible. Tonight, we gather to affirm the greatness of our nation—not because of the height of our skyscrapers, or the power of our military, or the size of our economy. Our pride is based on a very simple premise, summed up in a declaration made over two hundred years ago, "We hold these truths to be self-evident, that all men are created equal. That they are endowed by their Creator with certain inalienable rights. That among these are life, liberty and the pursuit of happiness."

That is the true genius of America, a faith in the simple dreams of its people, an insistence on small miracles. That we can tuck in our children at night and know that they are fed and clothed and safe from harm. That we can say what we think, write what we think, without hearing a sudden knock on the door. That we can have an idea and start our own business without paying a bribe or hiring somebody's son. That we can participate in the political process without fear of retribution, and that our votes will be counted—at least, most of the time.

This year, in this election we are called to reaffirm our values and commitments, to hold them against a hard reality and see how we're measuring up to the legacy of our forbearers, and the promise of future generations. And fellow Americans—Democrats, Republicans, Independents—I say to you tonight: We have more work to do. More work to do for the workers I met in Galesburg, Illinois, who are losing their union jobs at the Maytag plant that's moving to Mexico, and now are having to compete with their own children for jobs that pay seven bucks an hour. More to do for the father that I met who was losing his job and choking back the tears, wondering how he would pay $4,500 dollars a month for the drugs his son needs without the health benefits that he counted on. More to do for the young woman in East St. Louis, and thousands more like her, who has the grades, has the drive, has the will, but doesn't have the money to go to college.

Don't get me wrong. The people I meet in small towns and big cities, in diners and office parks, they don't expect government to solve all their problems. They know they have to work hard to get ahead, and they want to. Go into the collar counties around Chicago, and people will tell you they don't want their tax money wasted by a welfare agency or by the Pentagon. Go into any inner city neighborhood, and folks will tell you that government alone can't teach our kids to learn. They know that parents have to parent, that children can't achieve unless we raise their expectations and turn off the television sets and eradicate the slander that says a black youth with a book is acting white. No, people don't expect government to solve all their problems. But they sense, deep in their bones, that with just a slight change in priorities, we can make sure that every child in America has a decent shot at life, and that the doors of opportunity remain open to all. They know we can do better. And they want that choice.

In this election, we offer that choice. Our party has chosen a man to lead us who embodies the best this country has to offer. And that man is John Kerry. John Kerry understands the ideals of community, faith, and sacrifice because they've

defined his life. From his heroic service to Vietnam, to his years as a prosecutor and lieutenant governor, through two decades in the United States Senate, he has devoted himself to this country. Again and again, we've seen him make tough choices when easier ones were available. His values and his record affirm what is best in us.

John Kerry believes in an America where hard work is rewarded. So instead of offering tax breaks to companies shipping jobs overseas, he'll offer them to companies creating jobs here at home. John Kerry believes in an America where all Americans can afford the same health coverage our politicians in Washington have for themselves. John Kerry believes in energy independence, so we aren't held hostage to the profits of oil companies, or the sabotage of foreign oil fields. John Kerry believes in the constitutional freedoms that have made our country the envy of the world, and he will never sacrifice our basic liberties nor use faith as a wedge to divide us. And John Kerry believes that in a dangerous world war must be an option sometimes, but it should never be the first option.

A while back, I met a young man named Shamus in a VFW Hall in East Moline, Illinois. He was a good-looking kid, six two or six three, clear eyed, with an easy smile. He told me he'd joined the Marines and was heading to Iraq the following week. As I listened to him explain why he'd enlisted, his absolute faith in our country and its leaders, his devotion to duty and service, I thought this young man was all that any of us might ever hope for in a child. But then I asked myself: Are we serving Shamus as well as he is serving us? I thought of the more than 900 service men and women, sons and daughters, husbands and wives, friends and neighbors, who won't be returning to their own hometowns. I thought of the families I had met who were struggling to get by without a loved one's full income, or whose loved ones had returned with a limb missing or nerves shattered, but still lacked long-term health benefits because they were reservists. When we send our young men and women into harm's way, we have a solemn obligation not to fudge the numbers or shade the truth about why they're going, to care for their families while they're gone, to tend to the soldiers upon their return, and to never ever go to war without enough troops to win the war, secure the peace, and earn the respect of the world.

Now let me be clear. We have real enemies in the world. These enemies must be found. They must be pursued and they must be defeated. John Kerry knows this. And just as Lieutenant Kerry did not hesitate to risk his life to protect the men who served with him in Vietnam, President Kerry will not hesitate one moment to use our military might to keep America safe and secure. John Kerry believes in America. And he knows that it's not enough for just some of us to prosper. For alongside our famous individualism, there's another ingredient in the American saga.

A belief that we're all connected as one people. If there is a child on the south side of Chicago who can't read, that matters to me, even if it's not my child. If there is a senior citizen somewhere who can't pay for her prescription and has to choose between medicine and the rent, that makes my life poorer, even if it's not my grandmother. If there's an Arab American family being rounded up without benefit of an attorney or due process, that threatens my civil liberties. It's that fundamental belief—I am my brother's keeper. I am my sister's keeper—that makes this country work. It's what allows us to pursue our individual dreams and yet still come together as one American family. E pluribus unum: "Out of many, one."

Yet even as we speak, there are those who are preparing to divide us, the spin masters, the negative ad peddlers who embrace the politics of anything goes. Well, I say to them tonight, there is not a liberal America and a conservative America—there is the United States of America. There is not a black America and a white America and Latino America and Asian America; there's the United States of America. The pundits like to slice-and-dice our country into Red States and Blue States; Red States for Republicans, Blue States for Democrats. But I've got news for them, too. We worship an awesome God in the Blue States, and we don't like federal agents poking around in our libraries in the Red States. We coach Little League in the Blue States and have gay friends in the Red States. There are patriots who opposed the war in Iraq and there are patriots who supported it. We are one people, all of us pledging allegiance to the stars and stripes, all of us defending the United States of America.

In the end, that's what this election is about. Do we participate in a politics of cynicism or do we participate in a politics of hope? John Kerry calls on us to hope. John Edwards calls on us to hope. I'm not talking about blind optimism here— the almost willful ignorance that thinks unemployment will go away if we just don't talk about it, or the health care crisis will solve itself if we just ignore it. No, I'm talking about something more substantial. It's the hope of slaves sitting around a fire singing freedom songs; the hope of immigrants setting out for distant shores; the hope of a young naval lieutenant bravely patrolling the Mekong Delta; the hope of a millworker's son who dares to defy the odds; the hope of a skinny kid with a funny name who believes that America has a place for him, too. The audacity of hope!

In the end, that is God's greatest gift to us, the bedrock of this nation: the belief in things not seen, the belief that there are better days ahead. I believe that we can give our middle class relief and provide working families with a road to opportunity. I believe we can provide jobs to the jobless, homes to the homeless, and reclaim young people in

cities across America from violence and despair. I believe that as we stand on the crossroads of history, we can make the right choices, and meet the challenges that face us. America!

Tonight, if you feel the same energy I do, the same urgency I do, the same passion I do, the same hopefulness I do— if we do what we must do, then I have no doubt that all across the country, from Florida to Oregon, from Washington to Maine, the people will rise up in November, and John Kerry will be sworn in as President, and John Edwards will be sworn in as Vice President, and this country will reclaim its promise, and out of this long political darkness a brighter day will come. Thank you and God bless you.

BARACK OBAMA: A MORE PERFECT UNION (2008)

In March 2008, in the midst of his campaign for the U.S. presidency, Barack Obama came under fire for his association with Jeremiah Wright, the fiery minister of Obama's church, Trinity United Church of Christ, on the South Side of Chicago. As particularly inflammatory segments of Wright's sermons appeared on YouTube and sound bites were broadcast on many radio stations, Obama denounced his pastor's statements. When that strategy proved ineffective, Obama delivered the following speech on race in America, which was at least in part an effort to contextualize Wright's remarks. In a series of appearances in April, Wright himself effectively rejected Obama's efforts to ease anxieties about him, and the then-senator was forced to give up his church membership. Nevertheless, Obama's discourse on race proved a remarkably nuanced and thoughtful essay on a topic that has divided the United States from the time of the country's settlement.

"We the people, in order to form a more perfect union."

Two hundred and twenty-one years ago, in a hall that still stands across the street, a group of men gathered and, with these simple words, launched America's improbable experiment in democracy. Farmers and scholars; statesmen and patriots who had traveled across an ocean to escape tyranny and persecution finally made real their declaration of independence at a Philadelphia convention that lasted through the spring of 1787.

The document they produced was eventually signed but ultimately unfinished. It was stained by this nation's original sin of slavery, a question that divided the colonies and brought the convention to a stalemate until the founders chose to allow the slave trade to continue for at least twenty more years, and to leave any final resolution to future generations.

Of course, the answer to the slavery question was already embedded within our Constitution—a Constitution that had at its very core the ideal of equal citizenship under the law; a Constitution that promised its people liberty, and justice, and a union that could be and should be perfected over time.

And yet words on a parchment would not be enough to deliver slaves from bondage, or provide men and women of every color and creed their full rights and obligations as citizens of the United States. What would be needed were Americans in successive generations who were willing to do their part—through protests and struggle, on the streets and in the courts, through a civil war and civil disobedience and always at great risk—to narrow that gap between the promise of our ideals and the reality of their time.

This was one of the tasks we set forth at the beginning of this campaign—to continue the long march of those who came before us, a march for a more just, more equal, more free, more caring and more prosperous America. I chose to run for the presidency at this moment in history because I believe deeply that we cannot solve the challenges of our time unless we solve them together—unless we perfect our union by understanding that we may have different stories, but we hold common hopes; that we may not look the same and we may not have come from the same place, but we all want to move in the same direction—towards a better future for our children and our grandchildren.

This belief comes from my unyielding faith in the decency and generosity of the American people. But it also comes from my own American story.

I am the son of a black man from Kenya and a white woman from Kansas.

I was raised with the help of a white grandfather who survived a Depression to serve in Patton's army during World War II and a white grandmother who worked on a bomber assembly line at Fort Leavenworth while he was overseas. I've gone to some of the best schools in America and lived in one of the world's poorest nations. I am married to a black American who carries within her the blood of slaves and slaveowners—an inheritance we pass on to our two precious daughters. I have brothers, sisters, nieces, nephews, uncles and cousins, of every race and every hue, scattered across three continents, and for as long as I live, I will never forget that in no other country on Earth is my story even possible.

It's a story that hasn't made me the most conventional candidate. But it is a story that has seared into my genetic makeup the idea that this nation is more than the sum of its parts—that out of many, we are truly one.

Throughout the first year of this campaign, against all predictions to the contrary, we saw how hungry the American people were for this message of unity. Despite the temptation to view my candidacy through a purely racial lens, we won commanding victories in states with some of the whitest populations in the country. In South Carolina, where the Confederate flag still flies, we built a powerful coalition of African Americans and white Americans.

This is not to say that race has not been an issue in the campaign. At various stages in the campaign, some commentators have deemed me either "too black" or "not black enough." We saw racial tensions bubble to the surface during the week before the South Carolina primary. The press has scoured every exit poll for the latest evidence of racial polarization, not just in terms of white and black, but black and brown as well.

And yet, it has only been in the last couple of weeks that the discussion of race in this campaign has taken a particularly divisive turn.

On one end of the spectrum, we've heard the implication that my candidacy is somehow an exercise in affirmative action; that it's based solely on the desire of wide-eyed liberals to purchase racial reconciliation on the cheap. On the other end, we've heard my former pastor, Reverend Jeremiah Wright, use incendiary language to express views that have the potential not only to widen the racial divide, but views that denigrate both the greatness and the goodness of our nation; that rightly offend white and black alike.

I have already condemned, in unequivocal terms, the statements of Reverend Wright that have caused such controversy. For some, nagging questions remain. Did I know him to be an occasionally fierce critic of American domestic and foreign policy? Of course. Did I ever hear him make remarks that could be considered controversial while I sat in church? Yes. Did I strongly disagree with many of his political views? Absolutely—just as I'm sure many of you have heard remarks from your pastors, priests, or rabbis with which you strongly disagreed.

But the remarks that have caused this recent firestorm weren't simply controversial. They weren't simply a religious leader's effort to speak out against perceived injustice. Instead, they expressed a profoundly distorted view of this country—a view that sees white racism as endemic, and that elevates what is wrong with America above all that we know is right with America; a view that sees the conflicts in the Middle East as rooted primarily in the actions of stalwart allies like Israel, instead of emanating from the perverse and hateful ideologies of radical Islam.

As such, Reverend Wright's comments were not only wrong but divisive, divisive at a time when we need unity; racially charged at a time when we need to come together to solve a set of monumental problems—two wars, a terrorist threat, a falling economy, a chronic health care crisis and potentially devastating climate change; problems that are neither black or white or Latino or Asian, but rather problems that confront us all.

Given my background, my politics, and my professed values and ideals, there will no doubt be those for whom my statements of condemnation are not enough. Why associate myself with Reverend Wright in the first place, they may ask? Why not join another church? And I confess that if all that I knew of Reverend Wright were the snippets of those sermons that have run in an endless loop on the television and YouTube, or if Trinity United Church of Christ conformed to the caricatures being peddled by some commentators, there is no doubt that I would react in much the same way.

But the truth is, that isn't all that I know of the man. The man I met more than twenty years ago is a man who helped introduce me to my Christian faith, a man who spoke to me about our obligations to love one another; to care for the sick and lift up the poor. He is a man who served his country as a U.S. Marine; who has studied and lectured at some of the finest universities and seminaries in the country, and who for over thirty years led a church that serves the community by doing God's work here on Earth—by housing the homeless, ministering to the needy, providing day care services and scholarships and prison ministries, and reaching out to those suffering from HIV/AIDS.

In my first book, *Dreams From My Father*, I described the experience of my first service at Trinity:

"People began to shout, to rise from their seats and clap and cry out, a forceful wind carrying the reverend's voice up into the rafters…. And in that single note—hope!—I heard something else; at the foot of that cross, inside the thousands of churches across the city, I imagined the stories of ordinary black people merging with the stories of David and Goliath, Moses and Pharaoh, the Christians in the lion's den, Ezekiel's field of dry bones. Those stories—of survival, and freedom, and hope—became our story, my story; the blood that had spilled was our blood, the tears our tears; until this black church, on this bright day, seemed once more a vessel carrying the story of a people into future generations and into a larger world. Our trials and triumphs became at once unique and universal, black and more than black; in chronicling our journey, the stories and songs gave us a means to reclaim memories that we didn't need to feel shame about . . . memories that all people might study and cherish—and with which we could start to rebuild."

That has been my experience at Trinity. Like other predominantly black churches across the country, Trinity embodies the black community in its entirety—the doctor and the welfare mom, the model student and the former gang-banger. Like other black churches, Trinity's services are full of raucous laughter and sometimes bawdy humor. They are full of dancing, clapping, screaming and shouting that may seem jarring to the untrained ear. The church contains in full the kindness and cruelty, the fierce intelligence and the shocking ignorance, the struggles and successes, the love and yes, the bitterness and bias that make up the black experience in America.

And this helps explain, perhaps, my relationship with Reverend Wright. As imperfect as he may be, he has been like family to me. He strengthened my faith, officiated my wedding, and baptized my children. Not once in my conversations with him have I heard him talk about any ethnic group in derogatory terms, or treat whites with whom he interacted with anything but courtesy and respect. He contains within him the contradictions—the good and the bad—of the community that he has served diligently for so many years.

I can no more disown him than I can disown the black community. I can no more disown him than I can my white grandmother—a woman who helped raise me, a woman who sacrificed again and again for me, a woman who loves me as much as she loves anything in this world, but a woman who once confessed her fear of black men who passed by her on the street, and who on more than one occasion has uttered racial or ethnic stereotypes that made me cringe.

These people are a part of me. And they are a part of America, this country that I love.

Some will see this as an attempt to justify or excuse comments that are simply inexcusable. I can assure you it is not. I suppose the politically safe thing would be to move on from this episode and just hope that it fades into the woodwork. We can dismiss Reverend Wright as a crank or a demagogue, just as some have dismissed Geraldine Ferraro, in the aftermath of her recent statements, as harboring some deep-seated racial bias.

But race is an issue that I believe this nation cannot afford to ignore right now. We would be making the same mistake that Reverend Wright made in his offending sermons about America—to simplify and stereotype and amplify the negative to the point that it distorts reality.

The fact is that the comments that have been made and the issues that have surfaced over the last few weeks reflect the complexities of race in this country that we've never really worked through—a part of our union that we have yet to perfect. And if we walk away now, if we simply retreat into our respective corners, we will never be able to come together and solve challenges like health care, or education, or the need to find good jobs for every American.

Understanding this reality requires a reminder of how we arrived at this point. As William Faulkner once wrote, "The past isn't dead and buried. In fact, it isn't even past." We do not need to recite here the history of racial injustice in this country. But we do need to remind ourselves that so many of the disparities that exist in the African American community today can be directly traced to inequalities passed on from an earlier generation that suffered under the brutal legacy of slavery and Jim Crow.

Segregated schools were, and are, inferior schools; we still haven't fixed them, fifty years after Brown v. Board of Education, and the inferior education they provided, then and now, helps explain the pervasive achievement gap between today's black and white students.

Legalized discrimination—where blacks were prevented, often through violence, from owning property, or loans were not granted to African American business owners, or black homeowners could not access F[ederal] H[ousing] A[dministration] mortgages, or blacks were excluded from unions, or the police force, or fire departments—meant that black families could not amass any meaningful wealth to bequeath to future generations. That history helps explain the wealth and income gap between black and white, and the concentrated pockets of poverty that persist in so many of today's urban and rural communities.

A lack of economic opportunity among black men, and the shame and frustration that came from not being able to provide for one's family, contributed to the erosion of black families—a problem that welfare policies for many years may have worsened. And the lack of basic services in so many urban black neighborhoods—parks for kids to play in, police walking the beat, regular garbage pick-up and building code enforcement—all helped create a cycle of violence, blight and neglect that continue to haunt us.

This is the reality in which Reverend Wright and other African Americans of his generation grew up. They came of age in the late fifties and early sixties, a time when segregation was still the law of the land and opportunity was systematically constricted. What's remarkable is not how many failed in the face of discrimination, but rather how many men and women overcame the odds; how many were able to make a way out of no way for those like me who would come after them.

But for all those who scratched and clawed their way to get a piece of the American Dream, there were many who didn't make it—those who were ultimately defeated, in one way or another, by discrimination. That legacy of defeat was passed on to future generations—those young men and increasingly young women who we see standing on street corners or languishing in our prisons, without hope or prospects for the future. Even for those blacks who did make it, questions of race, and racism, continue to define their worldview in fundamental ways. For the men and women of Reverend Wright's generation, the memories of humiliation and doubt and fear have not gone away; nor has the anger and the bitterness of those years. That anger may not get expressed in public, in front of white co-workers or white friends. But it does find voice in the barbershop or around the kitchen table. At times, that anger is exploited by politicians, to gin up votes along racial lines, or to make up for a politician's own failings.

And occasionally it finds voice in the church on Sunday morning, in the pulpit and in the pews. The fact that so many people are surprised to hear that anger in some of Reverend Wright's sermons simply reminds us of the old truism that the most segregated hour in American life occurs on Sunday morning. That anger is not always productive; indeed, all too often it distracts attention from solving real problems; it keeps us from squarely facing our own complicity in our condition, and prevents the African American community from forging the alliances it needs to bring about real change. But the anger is real; it is powerful; and to simply wish it away, to condemn it without understanding its roots, only serves to widen the chasm of misunderstanding that exists between the races.

In fact, a similar anger exists within segments of the white community. Most working- and middle-class white Americans don't feel that they have been particularly privileged by their race. Their experience is the immigrant experience—as far as they're concerned, no one's handed them anything, they've built it from scratch. They've worked hard all their lives, many times only to see their jobs shipped overseas or their pension dumped after a lifetime of labor. They are anxious about their futures, and feel their dreams slipping away; in an era of stagnant wages and global competition, opportunity comes to be seen as a zero-sum game, in which your dreams come at my expense. So when they are told to bus their children to a school across town; when they hear that an African American is getting an advantage in landing a good job or a spot in a good college because of an injustice that they themselves never committed; when they're told that their fears about crime in urban neighborhoods are somehow prejudiced, resentment builds over time.

Like the anger within the black community, these resentments aren't always expressed in polite company. But they have helped shape the political landscape for at least a generation. Anger over welfare and affirmative action helped forge the Reagan Coalition. Politicians routinely exploited fears of crime for their own electoral ends. Talk-show hosts and conservative commentators built entire careers unmasking bogus claims of racism while dismissing legitimate discussions of racial injustice and inequality as mere political correctness or reverse racism.

Just as black anger often proved counterproductive, so have these white resentments distracted attention from the real culprits of the middle class squeeze—a corporate culture rife with inside dealing, questionable accounting practices, and short-term greed; a Washington dominated by lobbyists and special interests; economic policies that favor the few over the many. And yet, to wish away the resentments of white Americans, to label them as misguided or even racist, without recognizing they are grounded in legitimate concerns—this too widens the racial divide, and blocks the path to understanding.

This is where we are right now. It's a racial stalemate we've been stuck in for years. Contrary to the claims of some of my critics, black and white, I have never been so naïve as to believe that we can get beyond our racial divisions in a single election cycle, or with a single candidacy—particularly a candidacy as imperfect as my own.

But I have asserted a firm conviction—a conviction rooted in my faith in God and my faith in the American people—that working together we can move beyond some of our old racial wounds, and that in fact we have no choice if we are to continue on the path of a more perfect union.

For the African American community, that path means embracing the burdens of our past without becoming victims of our past. It means continuing to insist on a full measure of justice in every aspect of American life. But it also means binding our particular grievances—for better health care, and better schools, and better jobs—to the larger aspirations of all Americans—the white woman struggling to break the glass ceiling, the white man who's been laid off, the immigrant trying to feed his family. And it means taking full responsibility for own lives—by demanding more from our fathers, and spending more time with our children, and reading to them, and teaching them that while they may face challenges and discrimination in their own lives, they must never succumb to despair or cynicism; they must always believe that they can write their own destiny.

Ironically, this quintessentially American—and yes, conservative—notion of self-help found frequent expression in Reverend Wright's sermons. But what my former pastor too often failed to understand is that embarking on a program of self-help also requires a belief that society can change.

The profound mistake of Reverend Wright's sermons is not that he spoke about racism in our society. It's that he spoke as if our society was static; as if no progress has been made; as if this country—a country that has made it possible for one of his own members to run for the highest office in the land and build a coalition of white and black; Latino and Asian, rich and poor, young and old—is still irrevocably bound to a tragic past. But what we know—what we have seen—is that America can change. That is the true genius of this nation. What we have already achieved gives us hope—the audacity to hope—for what we can and must achieve tomorrow.

In the white community, the path to a more perfect union means acknowledging that what ails the African American community does not just exist in the minds of black people; that the legacy of discrimination—and current incidents of discrimination, while less overt than in the past—are real and must be addressed. Not just with words, but with deeds—by investing in our schools and our communities; by enforcing our civil rights laws and ensuring fairness in our criminal justice system; by providing this generation with ladders of opportunity that were unavailable for previous generations. It requires all Americans to realize that your dreams do not have to come at the expense of my dreams; that investing in the health, welfare, and education of black and brown and white children will ultimately help all of America prosper.

In the end, then, what is called for is nothing more, and nothing less, than what all the world's great religions demand—that we do unto others as we would have them do unto us. Let us be our brother's keeper, Scripture tells us. Let us be our sister's keeper. Let us find that common stake we all have in one another, and let our politics reflect that spirit as well.

For we have a choice in this country. We can accept a politics that breeds division, and conflict, and cynicism. We can tackle race only as spectacle—as we did in the O.J. trial—or in the wake of tragedy, as we did in the aftermath of Katrina—or as fodder for the nightly news. We can play Reverend Wright's sermons on every channel, every day and talk about them from now until the election, and make the only question in this campaign whether or not the American people think that I somehow believe or sympathize with his most offensive words. We can pounce on some gaffe by a Hillary supporter as evidence that she's playing the race card, or we can speculate on whether white men will all flock to John McCain in the general election regardless of his policies.

We can do that.

But if we do, I can tell you that in the next election, we'll be talking about some other distraction. And then another one. And then another one. And nothing will change.

That is one option. Or, at this moment, in this election, we can come together and say, "Not this time." This time we want to talk about the crumbling schools that are stealing the future of black children and white children and Asian children and Hispanic children and Native American children. This time we want to reject the cynicism that tells us that these kids can't learn; that those kids who don't look like us are somebody else's problem. The children of America are not those kids, they are our kids, and we will not let them fall behind in a 21st century economy. Not this time.

This time we want to talk about how the lines in the Emergency Room are filled with whites and blacks and Hispanics who do not have health care; who don't have the power on their own to overcome the special interests in Washington, but who can take them on if we do it together.

This time we want to talk about the shuttered mills that once provided a decent life for men and women of every race, and the homes for sale that once belonged to Americans from every religion, every region, every walk of life. This time we want to talk about the fact that the real problem is not that someone who doesn't look like you might take your job; it's that the corporation you work for will ship it overseas for nothing more than a profit.

This time we want to talk about the men and women of every color and creed who serve together, and fight together, and bleed together under the same proud flag. We want to talk about how to bring them home from a war that never should've been authorized and never should've been

waged, and we want to talk about how we'll show our patriotism by caring for them, and their families, and giving them the benefits they have earned.

I would not be running for President if I didn't believe with all my heart that this is what the vast majority of Americans want for this country. This union may never be perfect, but generation after generation has shown that it can always be perfected. And today, whenever I find myself feeling doubtful or cynical about this possibility, what gives me the most hope is the next generation—the young people whose attitudes and beliefs and openness to change have already made history in this election.

There is one story in particular that I'd like to leave you with today—a story I told when I had the great honor of speaking on Dr. King's birthday at his home church, Ebenezer Baptist, in Atlanta.

There is a young, twenty-three year old white woman named Ashley Baia who organized for our campaign in Florence, S.C. She had been working to organize a mostly African American community since the beginning of this campaign, and one day she was at a roundtable discussion where everyone went around telling their story and why they were there.

And Ashley said that when she was nine years old, her mother got cancer. And because she had to miss days of work, she was let go and lost her health care. They had to file for bankruptcy, and that's when Ashley decided that she had to do something to help her mom.

She knew that food was one of their most expensive costs, and so Ashley convinced her mother that what she really liked and really wanted to eat more than anything else was mustard and relish sandwiches. Because that was the cheapest way to eat.

She did this for a year until her mom got better, and she told everyone at the roundtable that the reason she joined our campaign was so that she could help the millions of other children in the country who want and need to help their parents too.

Now Ashley might have made a different choice. Perhaps somebody told her along the way that the source of her mother's problems were blacks who were on welfare and too lazy to work, or Hispanics who were coming into the country illegally. But she didn't. She sought out allies in her fight against injustice.

Anyway, Ashley finishes her story and then goes around the room and asks everyone else why they're supporting the campaign. They all have different stories and reasons. Many bring up a specific issue. And finally they come to this elderly black man who's been sitting there quietly the entire time. And Ashley asks him why he's there. And he does not bring up a specific issue. He does not say health care or the economy. He does not say education or the war. He does not say that he was there because of Barack Obama. He simply says to everyone in the room, "I am here because of Ashley."

"I'm here because of Ashley." By itself, that single moment of recognition between that young white girl and that old black man is not enough. It is not enough to give health care to the sick, or jobs to the jobless, or education to our children.

But it is where we start. It is where our union grows stronger. And as so many generations have come to realize over the course of the two-hundred and twenty-one years since a band of patriots signed that document in Philadelphia, that is where the perfection begins.

BARACK OBAMA: INAUGURAL ADDRESS

On Jan. 20, 2009, a frigid morning in Washington, D.C., and across much of the country, Barack Obama, became the 44th president of the United States. He was only the second man to swear his oath of office on the Bible used by Abraham Lincoln for that purpose. The *Washington Post* estimated that 1.8 million people filled the National Mall to witness this emotion-filled event—the vast majority by means of strategically placed large-screen televisions—and countless others filled living rooms and other meeting places throughout the country and, indeed, the world. The event's general air of celebration was tempered with sober evaluation of the nation's enormous hurdles and hard work ahead.

My fellow citizens:

I stand here today humbled by the task before us, grateful for the trust you have bestowed, mindful of the sacrifices borne by our ancestors. I thank President Bush for his service to our nation, as well as [for] the generosity and cooperation he has shown throughout this transition.

Forty-four Americans have now taken the presidential oath. The words have been spoken during rising tides of prosperity and the still waters of peace. Yet, every so often the oath is taken amidst gathering clouds and raging storms. At these moments, America has carried on not simply because of the skill or vision of those in high office, but because we the people have remained faithful to the ideals of our forebears, and true to our founding documents.

So it has been. So it must be with this generation of Americans.

That we are in the midst of crisis is now well understood. Our nation is at war, against a far-reaching network of violence and hatred. Our economy is badly weakened, a consequence of greed and irresponsibility on the part of some, but also our collective failure to make hard choices and prepare the nation for a new age. Homes have been lost; jobs shed; businesses shuttered. Our health care is too costly; our schools fail too many; and each day brings further evidence that the ways we use energy strengthen our adversaries and threaten our planet.

These are the indicators of crisis, subject to data and statistics. Less measurable but no less profound is a sapping of confidence across our land— a nagging fear that America's decline is inevitable, that the next generation must lower its sights.

Today I say to you that the challenges we face are real. They are serious and they are many. They will not be met easily or in a short span of time. But know this, America—they will be met.

On this day, we gather because we have chosen hope over fear, unity of purpose over conflict and discord.

On this day, we come to proclaim an end to the petty grievances and false promises, the recriminations and worn-out dogmas, that for far too long have strangled our politics.

We remain a young nation, but in the words of Scripture, the time has come to set aside childish things. The time has come to reaffirm our enduring spirit; to choose our better history; to carry forward that precious gift, that noble idea, passed on from generation to generation: the God-given promise that all are equal, all are free, and all deserve a chance to pursue their full measure of happiness.

In reaffirming the greatness of our nation, we understand that greatness is never a given. It must be earned. Our journey has never been one of shortcuts or settling for less. It has not been the path for the fainthearted—for those who prefer leisure over work, or seek only the pleasures of riches and fame. Rather, it has been the risk takers, the doers, the makers of things—some celebrated but more often men and women obscure in their labor, who have carried us up the long, rugged path towards prosperity and freedom.

For us, they packed up their few worldly possessions and traveled across oceans in search of a new life.

For us, they toiled in sweatshops and settled the West; endured the lash of the whip and plowed the hard earth.

For us, they fought and died, in places like Concord and Gettysburg; Normandy and Khe Sanh.

Time and again these men and women struggled and sacrificed and worked till their hands were raw so that we might live a better life. They saw America as bigger than the sum of our individual ambitions; greater than all the differences of birth or wealth or faction.

This is the journey we continue today. We remain the most prosperous, powerful nation on Earth. Our workers are no less productive than when this crisis began. Our minds are no less inventive, our goods and services no less needed than they were last week or last month or last year. Our capacity remains undiminished. But our time of standing pat, of protecting narrow interests and putting off unpleasant decisions—that time has surely passed. Starting today, we must pick ourselves up, dust ourselves off, and begin again the work of remaking America.

For everywhere we look, there is work to be done. The state of our economy calls for action, bold and swift, and we will act—not only to create new jobs, but to lay a new foundation for growth. We will build the roads and bridges, the electric grids and digital lines that feed our commerce and bind us together. We will restore science to its rightful place, and wield technology's wonders to raise health care's quality and lower its cost. We will harness the sun and the winds and the soil to fuel our cars and run our factories. And we will transform our schools and colleges and universities to meet the demands of a new age. All this we can do. All this we will do.

Now, there are some who question the scale of our ambitions—who suggest that our system cannot tolerate too many big plans. Their memories are short. For they have forgotten what this country has already done; what free men and women can achieve when imagination is joined to common purpose, and necessity to courage.

What the cynics fail to understand is that the ground has shifted beneath them—that the stale political arguments that have consumed us for so long no longer apply. The question we ask today is not whether our government is too big or too small, but whether it works—whether it helps families find jobs at a decent wage, care they can afford, a retirement that is dignified. Where the answer is yes, we intend to move forward. Where the answer is no, programs will end. And those of us who manage the public's dollars will be held to account—to spend wisely, reform bad habits, and do our business in the light of day—because only then can we restore the vital trust between a people and their government.

Nor is the question before us whether the market is a force for good or ill. Its power to generate wealth and expand freedom is unmatched, but this crisis has reminded us that without a watchful eye, the market can spin out of control. The nation cannot prosper long when it favors only the prosperous. The success of our economy has always depended not just on the size of our gross domestic product, but on the reach of our prosperity; on the ability to extend opportunity to every willing heart—not out of charity, but because it is the surest route to our common good.

As for our common defense, we reject as false the choice between our safety and our ideals. Our Founding Fathers, faced with perils we can scarcely imagine, drafted a charter to assure the rule of law and the rights of man, a charter expanded by the blood of generations. Those ideals still light the world, and we will not give them up for expedience's sake. And so to all the other peoples and governments who are watching today, from the grandest capitals to the small village where my father was born: know that America is a friend of each nation and every man, woman, and child who seeks a future of peace and dignity, and we are ready to lead once more.

Recall that earlier generations faced down fascism and communism not just with missiles and tanks, but with the [sic] sturdy alliances and enduring convictions. They understood that our power alone cannot protect us, nor does it entitle us to do as we please. Instead, they knew that our power grows through its prudent use; our security emanates from the justness of our cause, the force

of our example, the tempering qualities of humility and restraint.

We are the keepers of this legacy. Guided by these principles once more, we can meet those new threats that demand even greater effort—even greater cooperation and understanding between nations. We will begin to responsibly leave Iraq to its people, and forge a hard-earned peace in Afghanistan. With old friends and former foes, we'll work tirelessly to lessen the nuclear threat, and roll back the specter of a warming planet. We will not apologize for our way of life, nor will we waver in its defense, and for those who seek to advance their aims by inducing terror and slaughtering innocents, we say to you now that our spirit is stronger and cannot be broken; you cannot outlast us, and we will defeat you.

For we know that our patchwork heritage is a strength, not a weakness. We are a nation of Christians and Muslims, Jews and Hindus—and nonbelievers. We are shaped by every language and culture, drawn from every end of this Earth; and because we have tasted the bitter swill of civil war and segregation, and emerged from that dark chapter stronger and more united, we cannot help but believe that the old hatreds shall someday pass; that the lines of tribe shall soon dissolve; that as the world grows smaller, our common humanity shall reveal itself; and that America must play its role in ushering in a new era of peace.

To the Muslim world, we seek a new way forward, based on mutual interest and mutual respect. To those leaders around the globe who seek to sow conflict, or blame their society's ills on the West—know that your people will judge you on what you can build, not what you destroy. To those who cling to power through corruption and deceit and the silencing of dissent, know that you are on the wrong side of history; but that we will extend a hand if you are willing to unclench your fist.

To the people of poor nations, we pledge to work alongside you to make your farms flourish and let clean waters flow; to nourish starved bodies and feed hungry minds. And to those nations like ours that enjoy relative plenty, we say we can no longer afford indifference to the suffering outside our borders; nor can we consume the world's resources without regard to effect. For the world has changed, and we must change with it.

As we consider the road that unfolds before us, we remember with humble gratitude those brave Americans who, at this very hour, patrol far-off deserts and distant mountains. They have something to tell us, just as the fallen heroes who lie in Arlington whisper through the ages. We honor them not only because they are guardians of our liberty, but because they embody the spirit of service; a willingness to find meaning in something greater than themselves. And yet, at this moment—a moment that will define a generation—it is precisely this spirit that must inhabit us all.

For as much as government can do and must do, it is ultimately the faith and determination of the American people upon which this nation relies. It is the kindness to take in a stranger when the levees break, the selflessness of workers who would rather cut their hours than see a friend lose their job which sees us through our darkest hours. It is the firefighter's courage to storm a stairway filled with smoke, but also a parent's willingness to nurture a child, that finally decides our fate.

Our challenges may be new. The instruments with which we meet them may be new. But those values upon which our success depends—honesty and hard work, courage and fair play, tolerance and curiosity, loyalty and patriotism—these things are old. These things are true. They have been the quiet force of progress throughout our history. What is demanded then is a return to these truths. What is required of us now is a new era of responsibility—a recognition, on the part of every American, that we have duties to ourselves, our nation, and the world, duties that we do not grudgingly accept but rather seize gladly, firm in the knowledge that there is nothing so satisfying to the spirit, so defining of our character, than giving our all to a difficult task.

This is the price and the promise of citizenship.

This is the source of our confidence—the knowledge that God calls on us to shape an uncertain destiny.

This is the meaning of our liberty and our creed—why men and women and children of every race and every faith can join in celebration across this magnificent

Mall, and why a man whose father less than sixty years ago might not have been served in a local restaurant can now stand before you to take a most sacred oath.

So let us mark this day with remembrance, of who we are and how far we have traveled. In the year of America's birth, in the coldest of months, a small band of patriots huddled by dying camp-fires on the shores of an icy river. The capital was abandoned. The enemy was advancing. The snow was stained with blood. At the moment when the outcome of our revolution was most in doubt, the father of our nation ordered these words be read to the people:

"Let it be told to the future world . . . that in the depth of winter, when nothing but hope and virtue could survive . . . that the city and the country, alarmed at one common danger, came forth to meet (it)."

America: in the face of our common dangers, in this winter of our hardship, let us remember these timeless words. With hope and virtue, let us brave once more the icy currents, and endure what storms may come. Let it be said by our children's children that when we were tested we refused to let this journey end, that we did not turn back nor did we falter; and with eyes fixed on the horizon and God's grace upon us, we carried forth that great gift of freedom and delivered it safely to future generations.

Thank you. God bless you. And God bless the United States of America.

GLOSSARY

affidavit A sworn or written statement made under oath.

affirmative action an active effort to improve employment or educational opportunities for members of minority groups and for women.

amalgamate To mix.

apartheid Former policy in South Africa that sanctioned racial segregation and political and economic discrimination against nonwhites.

argot Special language that is particular to a certain group.

bandores A guitarlike stringed instrument.

contrapuntal Characterized by two or more independent melodies sounded together.

copula The link that connects the subject and predicate of a proposition, a linking verb.

dichotomous Divided into two parts.

eclecticism Made of selected pieces, ideas, or styles from different sources.

embouchure The way a musician positions his or her mouth while playing a wind instrument.

epistolary novel A novel told through the medium of letters written by one or more of the characters.

exhortation A forceful argument for something.

extant Still existing; not lost or destroyed.

fodder Feed for domestic animals such as cattle or sheep.

funk A type of urban dance music with strong, syncopated bass lines and drumbeats.

generative Having the ability to make or start something.

griot A traditional West African troubadour-historian.

heterogeneity Made up of unlike elements.

historiography The process of writing about history or written history itself.

honky-tonk A cheap, noisy dance hall or nightclub.

hymnody The singing and writing of hymns, or the hymns themselves.

invective Abusive language.

irascible Temperamental and easily angered.

"Jim Crow" laws Laws that enforced racial segregation in the South following the end of Reconstruction, named for a derogatory epithet for African Americans derived from a 19th century minstrel routine.

melisma In singing, the stretching of syllable over a run of notes.

notorious Infamous.

obbligato A musical part that complements and accompanies the main melody in a song, usually played by one instrument.

odious Something that evokes hatred or disgust.

onomatopoetically Something named in a manner that suggests the sound associated with it.

passacaglia A form of musical variations based on a repeating harmonic pattern.

paterfamilias The male head of a family.

polarized Divided up into opposing groups.

progenitor An ancestor or forefather.

promissory note A promise to pay for something in the future.

pyrotechnics A stunning show of virtuosity.

roman à clef A novel in which real people and events appear in a disguised form.

sea change A marked transformation.

sharecropper A tenant farmer who works the land for an agreed share of the value of the crop minus charges for seeds, tools, living quarters, and food.

scat A jazz singing style using nonsense syllables instead of words.

shellac A resinlike substance secreted by an insect that was the main raw ingredient used to make records.

sorghum A cereal grass bearing a dense grain used for making syrup.

syncopated A kind of offbeat rhythm created by accenting normally weak beats.

stasis A state of stagnation.

sui generis One of a kind, unique.

tympani Orchestral kettledrums. Also spelled timpani.

toasts Vernacular long-form poems recited in specialized street slang.

trenchant Incisive, keen.

vibrato In music, slight and quick variations in pitch that result in a pulsating effect.

BIBLIOGRAPHY

CIVIL RIGHTS MOVEMENT

Taylor Branch, *Parting the Waters: America in the King Years, 1954-63* (1988), *Pillar of Fire: America in the King Years, 1963-65* (1998), and *At Canaan's Edge, America in the King Years, 1965-68* (2006), offer fascinating portraits of Martin Luther King, Jr., and other key figures in the modern civil rights movement. Clayborne Carson, Emma J. Lapsansky-Werner, and Gary B. Nash, *The Struggle for Freedom: A History of African Americans* (2005), considers the civil rights movement and freedom struggle within the larger context of African American history. Clayborne Carson, *In Struggle: SNCC and the Black Awakening of the 1960s*, 2nd ed. (1995), is a comprehensive examination of this important organization. Clayborne Carson, David J. Garrow, Vincent Harding, Darlene Clark Hine, and Toby Kleban Levine (eds.), *The Eyes on the Prize Civil Rights Reader*, rev. ed. (1991); Tim McNeese, *The Civil Rights Movement: Striving for Justice* (2008); and Christopher Waldrep, *African Americans Confront Lynching: Strategies of Resistance from the Civil War to the Civil Rights Era* (2009), are all very useful.

LITERATURE

Studies of major genres and literary traditions in African American literature include Bernard W. Bell, *The Afro-American Novel and Its Tradition* (1987); Barbara T. Christian, *Black Women Novelists: The Development of a Tradition, 1892-1976* (1980); Robert B. Stepto, *From Behind the Veil: A Study of Afro-American Narrative*, 2nd ed. (1991); and Jean Wagner, *Black Poets of the United States: From Paul Laurence Dunbar to Langston Hughes* (1973). Among the major anthologies of African American literature are Henry Louis Gates, Jr., et al. (eds.), *The Norton Anthology of African American Literature* (2003); and Patricia Liggins Hill et al. (eds.), *Call & Response: The Riverside Anthology of the African American Literary Tradition* (1998). W.D. Samuels, *Encyclopedia of African-American Literature* (2007), is comprehensive.

JAZZ

Marshall Winslow Stearns, *The Story of Jazz* (1956, reissued 1976), is ideal for the newcomer to the music; Nat Shapiro and Nat Hentoff (eds.), *Hear Me Talkin' to Ya* (1955, reissued 1992), is a colourful history of jazz in musicians' own words; Leonard Feather, *Inside Jazz* (1997; originally published as *Inside Bebop*, 1949), was the first knowledgeable book about the bebop revolution. Eric Hobsbawm (Francis Newton), *The Jazz Scene*, rev. ed. (1993), presents a highly intelligent, objective view of postwar jazz.

BLUES, RHYTHM AND BLUES, SOUL, GOSPEL, FUNK, AND HIP-HOP

Craig Werner, *A Change Is Gonna Come: Music, Race & the Soul of America* (1999), nominally spans jazz, blues, and gospel but considers much more in its insightful study of music as a reflection of African American history and existence. *Lift Every Voice: The History of African American Music* (2009) is a useful general survey. Works of blues history and criticism include Paul Oliver, *The Story of the Blues* (1969, reissued 1982); and Lawrence Cohn et al., *Nothing but the Blues: The Music and the Musicians* (1993). Charlie Gillett, *Making Tracks: Atlantic Records and the Growth of a Multi-Billion-Dollar Industry* (1974, reissued as *Making Tracks: The Story of Atlantic Records*, 1993), covers the history of Atlantic Records. Peter Guralnik, *Sweet Soul Music: Rhythm and Blues and the Southern Dream of Freedom* (1986, reprinted 1994), gives a comprehensive overview of the soul movement. Nelson George, *Where Did Our Love Go?: The Rise & Fall of the Motown Sound* (1985), is the best history of Motown Records, its triumphs, and its failures. Gerald Early, *One Nation Under a Groove: Motown and American Culture* (1995), provides a concise analysis of Motown within the context of historical trends in post–World War II American culture. Rickey Vincent, *Funk: The Music, the People, and the Rhythm of The One* (1996), presents a comprehensive analysis of funk music and its social context. Alan Light (ed.), *The Vibe History of Hip Hop* (1999), explores the full scope of hip-hop's origins and expansion with contributions from more than 50 writers; Jeff Chang, *Can't Stop, Won't Stop: A History of the Hip-Hop Generation* (2005), examines the sociocultural and musical history of the genre.

SPORTS

D.K. Wiggins (ed.), *Out of the Shadows: A Biographical History of African American Athletes* (2006), is useful in its breadth. Robert Peterson, *Only the Ball Was White* (1970, reprinted 1984), examines the history of African American players and the Negro leagues; David Quentin Voigt, *Baseball, an Illustrated History* (1987), includes consideration of black baseball. Racial aspects of football are documented in Arthur R. Ashe, Jr., *A Hard Road to Glory—Football: The African-American Athlete in Football* (1993); Michael Hurd, *Black College Football, 1892–1992: One Hundred Years of History, Education and Pride*, rev., expanded 2nd ed. (1998); and Charles K. Ross, *Outside the Lines: African Americans and the Integration of the National Football League* (1999). Nelson George, *Elevating the Game: Black Men and Basketball* (1992), is a thought-provoking historical overview of African American involvement in basketball.

INDEX